The Still Hunter

The Classic Guide Book to Stealthy Hunting of Deer – How to Track, Shoot and Maintain Your Equipment and Hunting Rifle

By Theodore Van Dyke

Published by Pantianos Classics

ISBN-13: 978-1987703962

First published in 1882

Contents

Chapter One - Introduction 5

Chapter Two 9

Chapter Three 13

Chapter Four - The Senses of The Game and The Hunter 20

Chapter Five - The Daily Life of Deer and Antelope 26

Chapter Six - Looking for Deer That Are on Foot 30

Chapter Seven - Looking for Deer Lying Low 38

Chapter Eight - The First Sight of Game 44

Chapter Nine - The First Shot at A Deer 51

Chapter Ten - Running Time 58

Chapter Eleven - Hunting on Snow 63

Chapter Twelve - The Surest Way to Track Deer When Very
Wild 69

Chapter Thirteen - Tracking on Bare Ground 74

Chapter Fourteen - Still-Hunting on Open Ground 80

Chapter Fifteen - Deer on Open Ground 85

Chapter Sixteen - A Day in The Table-Lands 90

Chapter Seventeen - Another Kind of Open Ground 98

Chapter Eighteen - The Still-Hunter's Cardinal Virtue 104

Chapter Nineteen - Hunting in The Open and In Timber
Combined 109

Chapter Twenty - Subordinate Principles 114

Chapter Twenty-One - Two Or More Persons Hunting in Company, Hunting on Horseback 118

Chapter Twenty-Two - Special Modes of Hunting, The Cow Bell and Tiring Down Deer 123

Chapter Twenty-Three - Deer in Bands. General Hints, etc..... 126

Chapter Twenty-Four - To Manage A Deer When Hit................ 131

Chapter Twenty-Five - The Rifle on Game at Rest 138

Chapter Twenty-Six - The Rifle on Moving Game........................ 144

Chapter Twenty-Seven - The Rifle on Moving Game (Continued) 151

Chapter Twenty-Eight - Long Range Shooting at Game 158

Chapter Twenty-Nine - The Effect of Recoil Upon Shooting ... 163

Chapter Thirty - The Killing Power of Bullets, Explosive, Expansive, and Other Bullets, Slit Bullets, Buckshot, etc. 167

Chapter Thirty-One - The Hunting-Rifle, and Flight of Balls ... 175

Chapter Thirty-Two - The Sighting of Hunting-Rifles................ 178

Chapter Thirty-Three - The Loading, Care, and Management of Rifles.. 186

Chapter Thirty-Four - Moccasins, Buckskin, Etc. Advice Conclusion... 192

Chapter One - Introduction

STILL-HUNTING, the most scientific of all things pertaining to hunting, has hitherto been almost confined to the backwoodsman or frontiersman, and has been little enjoyed by those born and reared at any distance from facilities for learning practically the ways of the wild woods and plains. Thousands of our best shots with the shot-gun are men born and bred in the city. But of the thousands who enjoy the still-hunt the majority are backwoodsmen. One great reason of this is that the art is one requiring for proficiency more life in the forest than the average city man can spend there. But another great reason has been the almost utter lack of any information or instruction upon the subject. For this, the greatest and most important branch of the whole art of hunting has, I may safely say, been totally neglected by the great body of writers upon field-sports. Most attempts in that line have been like " The Deer-Stalkers" of Frank Forrester a short fancy sketch, not intended to convey any instruction. And where the subject has been touched upon at all in works on hunting, the information given has been so extremely general in its nature and form of expression, and so utterly lacking in qualifications and exceptions quite as essential as the rules themselves, that to a beginner in the woods it is of little more use than the maps in a child's atlas are to a tourist Consequently he who would single-handed and alone outgeneral the bounding beauties of the forest and plain, and with a single ball trip their wily feet, is nearly always compelled to work out his own knowledge of how to do it. And this he must generally do, as I had to do it, by a long series of mortifying failures.

I have spent too many days alone in the depths of the forest primeval and on the mountain's shaggy breast not to know full well that printed precepts are poor substitutes for Nature's wild school of object-teaching. Yet from that same life I have learned another thing quite as true; namely, that while instruction cannot carry one bodily to the desired goal, it can nevertheless clear the road of hundreds of stumps and fallen logs, cut away a vast amount of tangled brush, and bridge many a Serbonian bog.

Not without hesitation have I undertaken to explore this "dark continent" of the world of field-sports. At this day a writer upon almost any other subject has the roads, paths, blaze-marks, and charts of a dozen or more explorers before him. I have nothing to follow; the only work upon deer, that of Judge Caton, thorough and fine as it is, deals only with the anatomy, physiology, and natural history of deer; all those habits which it is essential for the still-hunter to thoroughly understand being as much beyond the scope of his work as the part he has treated of is beyond the scope of this work. The same is the case with the part upon rifles and shooting; nearly everything in print on the subject pertaining only to target-rifles and target-shooting. Besides this dearth of pioneers to clear the road, the habits of large game generally, and of deer especially, vary so much with climate, elevation, and character of country, quality, distribution, and quantity of food, amount and nature of the disturbance to which the game may be subjected, and other causes, that there can be no man who thoroughly understands still-hunting in every part of the United States. Moreover, the deer is so irregular in some of its movements, so difficult to observe closely, and so quick to change many of its habits after a little persecution or change in methods of hunting, that it is not probable that any one person thoroughly understands the animal even in any one State. And I have heard the very best and oldest hunters of my acquaintance say that they were continually learning something new about deer. But there is still enough that is both universal and certain to carry the learner over far the greater part of the difficulties and save him many an aching limb and sinking heart.

To impart this is, however, no easy task for any one. Unfortunately those who best know in practice the rules of hunting are almost necessarily deficient in power to lay out and finish in the details a treatise on a subject so extensive and recondite. The "old hunter" to whom the learner must now resort for his advice knows practically a great deal; but between what he knows and what he can or will tell there is a difference as wide as it is provoking. Even if he were never so well disposed to impart his knowledge, it would require at least fifty long and elaborate lectures of several hours each for him to do so in his language. Moreover, the average "old hunter" or Leatherstocking is full of wrong theories, which he either does not follow in the field or, if he does, he succeeds in spite of them by virtue of his other qualifications. The stock of nonsensical theories held by the old-time country " old hunter" with the old single shot-gun is nothing to the mass of absurdities that a very successful old Leatherstocking can dispense on the subject of deer-hunting, rifles, and rifle-shooting. So that unless constantly by his side in the field a thing to which any good hunter will seriously object the beginner can learn little from him. I have had to work out almost every particle of my information from a mine of stubborn ore. And I flatter myself that I can save to those who will take the pains to study not merely read this work, at least two thirds of the labor, vexation, and disappointment through which I was compelled to flounder; though I started in with keen eyes, tireless feet, unflagging hope, and years of experience in all branches of hunting with the shot-gun, beginning even in childhood.

To be exhaustive without being exhausting is one of the most delicate tasks ever set a didactic writer. To avoid being tedious I have intentionally omitted:

1st. All that part of the natural history and habits of our game which does not bear directly upon the question of how to find and shoot it; such as its birth, nurture, growth, and shedding of horns, all of which may be found in other and better books such as Judge Caton's.

2nd. A large mass of vague and unreliable theories held about hunting and shooting even by successful hunters. We are never so wise as when we know

6

what it is that we do not know. There are many movements of game that it is impossible to reduce to rule, in which the animal seems governed only by the caprice of the passing moment. As there are doctors who will never admit ignorance upon any point, but will explain to you at once, like the physicians in the plays of Moliere, the efficient causes of the most slippery phenomena, so there are hosts of hunters who have ever on their tongue's end an exact explanation of every movement of a deer. Agreeing with Sir William Hamilton that "contented ignorance is better than presumptuous wisdom," I have omitted all such dubious theories.

3rd. Everything that can be safely in trusted to the beginner's common-sense; though I have been cautious about presuming too much upon this.

The art of still-hunting deer carries with it nearly the whole art of still-hunting other large American game. As a good and accomplished lawyer has only a few special points of practice to learn in transplanting himself from State to State, -so the thorough still- hunter will go from deer to antelope, elk, or other game, already equipped with five sixths of the knowledge necessary to hunt them. And this very knowledge will, as it does in the case of the lawyer, enable him to learn the rest in one fourth of the time in which a beginner could do it. Consequently a large portion of this work applies to antelope also without special reference.

It is a common idea that shooting game with a rifle does not call for a very high degree of skill with it, or for very much knowledge of the principles of shooting. That considerable game is killed by very ordinary shooting is true. But it is equally true that as much game is lost by bad shooting as by bad hunting. And it is quite as true that bad shooting is as much due to downright, solid ignorance of the rifle, the principles of projectiles, and the use of the rifle in the field as distinguished from its use at the target, as to nervousness, excitement, want of practice, and all other causes put together. The extent of this ignorance, even among very successful hunters, is amazing; their success being due to their good hunting, energy, and perseverance, and in spite of their poor shooting. I therefore deem a treatise on the hunting-rifle: and its use in the field an indispensable part of any work on still-hunting. And since this information cannot be found to any valuable extent in any other work on shooting that I have seen, I have treated the subject quite fully, omitting however, out of regard for the reader's patience, much that can be trusted to his intelligence and much that may be found in works on the rifle and on target-shooting.

It is to be expected that many hunters, and good ones too, will differ from many of my views. Among even the best and most intelligent sportsmen there is much disagreement on even the simplest points. It is therefore vain for anyone to expect endorsement upon every point from the man who declares that a gun is safest with the hammer resting on the cap; who thinks a slow twist makes a "slow ball," a quick twist a "quick ball," a gain twist a "strong ball;" who sincerely believes that his rifle shoots on a level line for two hundred yards; who talks of putting a ball in the heart of a running deer at three hundred yards as a matter of course, and discourses about knocking a deer down "in his tracks" as he would knock down a cabbage-head with a club. It is also impossible for any writer upon field-sports to avoid occasional mistakes. There are others, doubtless, who would make less than I do. But they do not write. And from the length of time the world has waited for such a book it is fair to presume that they do not intend to write. Therefore take this as the best you can get, and bear lightly on its infirmities.

Some will think I have been too fond of repetition. But there are principles which cannot otherwise be understood in their practical extent. The great trouble is to make one understand in the concrete what he knows well enough in the abstract. Other principles require repetition in their different applications, requiring contemplation under different points of view. Many will think that I have been too fond of analysis, have drawn distinctions too fine, and have been too lavish with refinements and caution. Undoubtedly deer may be killed in large numbers without heeding one half the advice I give. There are still parts of our country where deer are yet so plenty and tame that anyone who can shoot at all can kill some. Often when concentrated by deep snows, fires, or other causes, and enfeebled by starvation, the wildest of deer or antelope may fall easy victims to any one of brute strength and brute heart. Even when deer are scarce, wild, and in full strength the varies block-head may occasionally stumble over one and kill it with a shot-gun. And in almost any place where the ground or brush does not make too much noise beneath the feet, if there are any deer at all, brute endurance in getting over ground enough, assisted by brute perseverance, will bring success.

But from all this we can draw only one conclusion; namely, that the greater the success one has by careless or unscientific methods, the better it would be and the more ease and pleasure he would have in it by doing it scientifically. And to put the beginner on the very best track, I have treated, throughout this work, of deer very wild. This is rendered the more necessary by the fact that in nearly all places the deer of to-day is not the deer of thirty years ago; in many places not even the deer of ten years ago.

Deer become more wary as hunters increase. They change their habits to suit new styles of hunting and fire-arms. And these tendencies have been so transmitted by descent that the average six-months-old fawn of to-day is a far more delicate article to handle than were most of the mighty old bucks on which the Leatherstocking "old hunter" of thirty years ago won his name and fame.

It is quite common to hear still-hunting denounced as "pot-hunting" by the advocates of driving deer with hounds. That the market-hunter is almost always a still-hunter is unfortunately true. It is also a sad truth that the man who murders woodcock in May for Delmonico's epicures possesses a breech-loader. But this hardly makes the use of the breechloader pot-hunting. I have seen it stated that a still-hunter on snow was certain to secure the deer that he once took the track of. All this savors of sour grapes. No man who ever had any experience in still-hunting ever committed such stuff to paper. But to correct at the outset any misapprehension I will say that, with whatever proficiency in still-hunting any mortal ever reaches, with all the advantages of snow, ground, wind, and sun in his favor, many a deer will, in the very climax of triumphant assurance, slip through his fingers like the thread of a beautiful dream.

Chapter Two

Much has been written about the essential qualities of a good deer-hunter, the only effect of which is to deter from attempting it many a man who might easily enjoy still-hunting, or "deer-stalking" as our English cousins call it. To make a good professional hunter who shall kill a large number of deer in a season, and do it on all kinds of ground and in all kinds of weather, does undoubtedly require such physical and other qualities as are mentioned by Stonehenge, Forrester, and others. But on the other hand any man of sufficient savoir faire, strength, and energy to make a respectable bag of quail or woodcock in any of the Eastern States, whether he be bred in the backwoods or in Fifth Avenue, whether a knight of the trigger or only a carpet-knight, can by study and practice make a fair amateur still-hunter; that is, one who can go where deer or antelope are moderately plenty and kill, not great quantities, but enough for good sport and quite as much as any man has any business to kill.

We will leave the equipment for hunting for future consideration; and, supposing you already prepared, let us see where we are to find our game.

To find ground where deer are plenty enough for good sport is still an easy matter even at the present rate of destruction. And there need be no fear that they will soon be too scarce. The days of the market's lofty prerogative are numbered. The American people are fast awaking to the fact that the true question before them is not, Why should not he who kills game have a right to sell it? Why should not he who cannot hunt his own game have a right to buy it? They are fast awaking to see that a far higher question than either of those imperiously demands an immediate answer. That question is, shall we have game for those who are able to hunt it for themselves, who need the health-giving medicine of the woods far more than epicures need their palates tickled, or shall we have game for none? Shall we have game for our own people forever under close restrictions, or shall our woods become a cheerless blank in order that the present generation of epicures in New York and Boston may wax fat for a few years? And when America awakes from sleep she spends little time in yawning and rubbing her eyes.

The deer is still found in nearly every State in the Union, though in many is not now plenty enough for still-hunting unless upon snow. In Canada and the northern tier of States in the Great West, in nearly all the Territories, in most of the Southern and Southwestern States, and on the Pacific coast it is still

9

quite abundant in large tracts of country. But it is quite impossible to lay down any reliable rule for finding where deer are abundant, for there is no other kind of game whose movements and habits are so influenced by locality, climate, season, elevation and shape of ground, quality, quantity, and distribution of food, amount and nature of hunting to which they are exposed, as well as by snow, flies, scarcity of water, timber, brush, etc., as are the movements and habits of deer. Besides all this there is sometimes a caprice about their movements that will overturn all calculations even when based upon the most reliable data. Sometimes deer will shift hundreds of miles on the approach of winter, as they do in Northern Wisconsin and that part of Michigan lying north of it. Yet in other places of apparently the same character they move little or not at all. In places their migrations are very regular, in others so irregular as to appear quite accidental, occurring only at intervals of several years, often without apparent cause. In general they are regular. The snow-belts of mountains they are quite apt to forsake in winter for the warmer or barer foot-hills or valleys below, sometimes going many miles away into the lowland ranges, sometimes lingering around the mountains' feet, sometimes returning early in the spring to the high ranges, sometimes remaining in the low ground for the greater part of the summer. Even when in the high mountains their movements will vary. Sometimes they will keep along the highest ridges on which timber or brush is to be found, descending only at night to the little meadows or valleys below to water and feed; while at other times they will be most numerous half-way down the mountain, and are frequently more plenty, even in summer, in the foot-hills than in the high ground. Sometimes they will be found most plenty in thick brush; and again the thick brush will be almost bare of them and they will be found in the gulches and breaks of comparatively open ground. Sometimes they will be most numerous in the depths of the heaviest timber, sometimes on the edge of it where it breaks into scrub oak, hazel and other brush, sometimes in the long grass of the sloughs on the prairie. Often they will be most plenty in the dense undergrowth of river bottoms, and again in the high bluffy lands along them; sometimes in the heaviest swamps and places abounding in lakes or ponds; sometimes in the valleys and low ravines, and again mainly on the ridges and points. By all this I mean that the greater part of the deer will be in such places, and not that they are exclusively on such ground; for in a country abounding in deer generally more or less will be found on nearly all kinds of ground and at every season, except perhaps on the mountain-tops in case of deep snows in winter. The habits of deer in regard to shifting will often vary very much in the same section of country. In some parts of Southern California fully three fourths of the deer on a certain range will leave it for another range. In other parts the same deer will always be found on the same old circle where you have found them for years, and if killed out there will be few or none to be found there for a year or two. While antelope generally have a far more extensive daily or weekly range than deer, they are less apt to shift from section to section for any cause but snow. Some of the bands yet remaining in

10

San Diego County, Cal., stay on their old range through the severest droughts, clinging to their native plain long after horses and cattle have been starved out upon it, refusing to leave it though there be good feed in other sections not far away. But it must not be inferred that the antelope in all sections retains this love for his native heath. Such may be the case, but a few instances do not prove it. And all through the study of still-hunting you cannot be too careful how you draw conclusions from a few instances, and especially about the migratory movements of deer. The plain truth is that there is no trustworthy rule by which to decide in what section deer or antelope are plenty enough to afford good sport. The only reliance is on:

1. General reputation of a range.
2. Information from those hunting or living upon it.
3. Personal inspection of the range.

When a certain section has the reputation of being a good deer-range, such reputation is not apt to be baseless. But when you reach it you will probably have to decide for yourself whether it will reward you to hunt it. And probably you will have to decide for yourself upon which part the most game is likely to be found; for though few sources of information are more reliable than general reputation of a range few are more unreliable than special information about it. The opinion of persons who are not hunters is bad enough about almost any kind of game, but almost worthless about deer. Some people are always seeing some wonderful thing, while others never see anything beyond their immediate business. One man will declare that "the woods is lined with 'em" because he occasionally sees one or two along the road or near a spring, taking them, of course, every time for different deer, or because he sees a few tracks in his turnip-patch, counting unconsciously a deer to every track, as is usual with most persons not hunters, and with too many that are. Another dogmatically assures you that " deer are mighty scarce" because he does not see some every time he goes smashing through dry leaves and dead sticks with hobnailed stogey boots to look for his cattle in the woods.

The opinion even of good hunters is very unreliable. Unless they are hunting they know little about what part of the range the deer are actually most plenty upon. And if they are hunting, a stranger can scarcely expect them to introduce him to their best preserves. That is a little thicker cream than can be reasonably expected to rise on even the richest milk of human kindness. Yet there are many hunters capable of just such weakness whose hearts open at once towards the genial, gentlemanly stranger who gives himself no airs and makes no pretensions. And right here it is my duty to say that if you are out for only two or three days hunt, if your object be only to kill a deer for the sake of saying you have killed one, and you do not intend to continue still-hunting, the very best thing you can do is to entwine yourself around the heart of such a hunter and, if necessary, pay him a fair price to work you up a good shot. If you cannot do this and have little time or patience to spend, you

11

had better go home and leave deer alone, for the chances are that, that even with all the advice that anyone can give, you will be deeply disappointed.

There is scarcely any kind of ground on which deer may not sometimes be found in considerable numbers, provided it be somewhat broken and contain some cover, brush or trees. The deer loves cover and will have it. He loves browse and will have it, though he will be sometimes miles away from it. He loves ground more or less rough, and will rarely be found away from it unless there are extra inducements elsewhere, in the line of brush, long grass, or other good food and cover. As a rule, he loves water; though he belongs to that class of animals that will drink water if conveniently obtained, but can go without it entirely, even in the hottest summer weather, like the valley quail of Southern California. The deer will, however, often go a long distance for water, and this fact, combined with the fact that he can and often will go without it, makes the water question somewhat unreliable in determining his whereabouts.

A kind of ground that in some parts of the country will never contain a deer may in other sections afford good sport. Yonder wide stretch of plain that looks so bare to the eye, and is so far away from timber or hills that in Minnesota or Wisconsin a hunter would not look at it, may in Southern California, Arizona, or Mexico contain numbers of deer in those gulches, cuts, gullies, and creek bottoms where from a distance the shrubbery looks too thin and sparse for even a jack-rabbit to live in. Yonder mountain, that even through the glass seems only a frowning mass of castle, crag, and boulder, may on inspection yield many a deer stowed away in its little brushy ravines or plateaus. And yonder wavy sea of stony ground, so utterly bare of grass, so bare even of brush except in the ravines, so bare of water that you cannot camp there, may at times afford you good sport. Hence it is about as puzzling to say where deer may not be found as to say where they may be.

There is not so much difficulty about the antelope. There seems, indeed, to be no kind of ground too poor for him to live on and keep, too, in fair condition, though, unlike the deer, he lives mainly on grass in-stead of browse. Though he loves the plains, he has no objection to high rolling hills if they are not too brushy. But he hates brush and timber; and though he will occasionally go into thin brush or into very open timber, he need never be sought where either one is thick or extensive.

No matter how carefully you may hunt, a deer often keeps a little gulch handy into which one jump makes him safe.

As a rule, good deer and antelope hunting must be sought in pretty wild sections; and generally the wilder they are the better. This rule, again, has its exceptions, and they must not be forgotten. Many tracts of howling wilderness and many undisturbed and splendid mountain-sides are almost entirely bare of deer at all times, though all the conditions of good deer-range exist. On the other hand, many a tract that has been settled for years and contains two or three or four settlers cabins to the square mile will often contain deer enough for excellent sport. It is much the same with antelope; many a fine plain having been bare of them within the memory of the oldest Indians, others having a band or two that care nothing for its settlements, except to keep just out of shot, remaining on their old haunts until, one by one, they fade away before the relentless rifle.

Neither the deer nor the antelope can, however, be called an admirer of civilization. Sometimes deer will at once forsake a good-sized valley or timber grove because a settler has moved into it, though this is apt to be the case only when it is isolated from the rest of the range. Antelope, too, will often cease to run up a valley leading from the plain when settlers have moved in, and this even though not hunted. Both of them hate sheep and will generally desert ground over which sheep range. But for cattle and horses they care nothing; in fact, rather seem to enjoy their company at times, provided the herdsmen do not come among them too often. But all such things affect only parts of the range and have little to do in determining its general character.

Chapter Three

Having selected the general range or tract upon which you will hunt, the next point is to determine upon what part of it will be best to hunt. For deer are not distributed generally over the whole even of the best ranges, but are more or less concentrated in particular parts. And this is so even when they are not banded but are living separately. The same is true of antelope even when the does are scattered with their kids and are not banded as they generally are. It is also a provoking fact that you have probably noticed in other branches of hunting, that the very best-looking ground is often bare of game. And deer, above all other things, fail to appreciate your kindness in selecting their abiding-places, and prefer to make their own selections.

For these reasons you will do well to make the exploration of your ground and inspection of signs, etc., the principal object of your first day's hunt. I do not mean that you are to go carelessly or without a keen outlook for game. But before you can hunt to much advantage you must learn what is commonly termed "the lay of the land," and also know upon what parts of it the most deer are ranging. "The lay of the land" is of such importance that it must never be neglected. Every ridge, every pass, every valley, every spot that you are likely ever to travel again should be deeply impressed upon the memory, with its general character - either as a deer's feeding-ground, lying-down ground, lounging-ground, skulking-ground, or ground upon which deer rarely or never stop. The courses of all valleys should be noted so that you will know how the wind is in any one of them at any time, how the sun shines in them, the facilities for traveling in them quietly, and for seeing what is in them without climbing too high on the ridges. The best routes along the ridges should also be noted, with the best point of observation from any of them. In short, study how the ground may be traversed so as best to take advantage of the principles hereafter laid down.

In most ranges the question of food will, at the proper time of year, aid you more than anything else in determining what hunters call the "run of the deer." The deer is a browsing animal. He cares but little for grass in general; though when it is young and tender, or when other kinds of food are scarce or the browse is old and tough, he will eat even grass. And some of the grasses, such as young wheat, oats, barley, eta, deer frequently eat. I have never known a deer to eat what is known as "dry feed," to wit, sundried grass, as antelope and stock do in California. Nor have I ever found "dry feed" in a deer's stomach. They eat the buds, twigs, and leaves of a vast variety of shrubs and trees. And this makes their feeding-ground for a large part of the year too general to be of much aid in determining their favorite haunts. They are fond of turnips, cabbage, beans, grapevines, and garden-stuff generally; but all such food is too accidental to influence their movements much. There is a long list of berries and fruits which they will eat; and individuals sometimes extend their researches beyond this list. I once shot a fat buck that contained half a peck of the worst kind of prickly pears. There are, however, but few fruits or nuts that influence their movements much, and of these the principal are chestnuts, beechnuts, and acorns. Wherever there is abundance of these, in a very short time after they begin to fall the deer will gather in to feed on them, sometimes shifting ground many miles to get convenient access to them. And of all these the most universal is the acorn. Deer are very fond of bush and scrub-oak acorns, which they begin to eat earlier in the season than the tree acorns, not being obliged to await their falling. But ground on which these grow is apt to be too brushy and make too much noise for very successful hunting. The best ground, for the beginner especially, is the ground known as "oak ridges," consisting of small "hog-backs" or higher ridges covered with black oak, red oak, and white oak. These are found throughout all the heavy forests of the Eastern and Western States, and here one has a prospect of interviewing a bear, as he too is fond of acorns. Moreover, if you hunt east of the Missouri you can do little till the leaves have fallen, and by that time, if it is a " acorn season," there will be more or less acorns upon almost any good deer-range. So you had better go first to the "oak ridges."

One of the first points upon which you should satisfy yourself is this question: How much are the deer disturbed by still-hunting? For it is a settled fact, of which you must never lose sight, that a deer's habits and movements will be very much and very quickly influenced by still-hunting.

It is a common idea with hunters that driving deer with hounds drives them away and makes them wilder. This may in some places be true. It may also be generally true if swift hounds be used. But there are places where it is not so, and within my observation deer have little fear of slow dogs. Deer that had been made so wild with still-hunting that it was almost impossible to get even sight of them except under the happiest combination of soft snow, favorable wind, and rolling ground, I have seen play along for half a mile across an open pine-chopping before two curs wallowing and yelping through the snow behind them. They seemed to consider it only fun, stopping every few jumps and looking back at the curs until they got within a few feet of them. About the tamest deer I ever met were some that were habitually chased with hounds and never still-hunted, and one of these I actually approached within five yards with a shot-gun.

But more than any other thing they fear the still-hunter. Right well they learn, and quickly too, that mischief without warning now lurks in every corner of the once peaceful home. And quickly they adapt themselves to this change of affairs. I have seen men that were successful hunters ten and even five years ago, but who had not hunted of late, traverse their old grounds without getting a shot or scarcely seeing a "flag;" seeing plenty of tracks, however, and coming home wondering where the deer all were. I have seen deer that I positively knew had no other disturbance than my own hunting desert entirely the low hills and open cañons in which they were keeping before I began to trouble them, shift a thousand feet higher up, keep in the thick chaparral all day, and double their vigilance when they were out of it. They soon learn to watch more of the time; to lie down where they can see their back track; to go farther back into higher, rougher, and more brushy ground; to lie down longer during the day; to feed, water, and lounge about more at night; and to be on foot less during the day. They also learn to run on hearing a noise without stopping to look back; to keep on running long past the point where you can head them off; to slip away before you get in sight of them; to skulk and hide in thick brush and let you pass them; and a score of other tricks we will notice as we go on.

While I prefer still-hunting to hounding as a far more scientific, wide-awake, and manly sport, as well as more healthful and less monotonous, there is no doubt in my mind which makes deer the wildest and drives them out the quickest. I have not a particle of interest in the question of "still-hunting versus hounding;" for the world is all before me and I shall hunt as I choose, but I want the beginner to under-stand thoroughly the effect of still-hunting on his game, whether my opinion suit him or not.

Keeping well in mind these points, go directly to the oak ridges if it is acorn time; for here you will find the most indications as to the number of deer about, though these indications are the least reliable of all. The less the deer are disturbed the more time they will spend upon these ridges, and generally the larger will be the proportion of deer from the whole range that frequent them to feed. Hence the greater will be the quantity of what is called "sign."

Signs consist of tracks, droppings, beds, pawing or scraping places, places where the brush has been hooked with horns, or the bark of small trees frayed by the rubbing of horns against it, the nipped-off shoots and twigs of brush, etc. Of these the only reliable signs by which to judge of the number of deer about are the tracks, droppings, and beds. All else you need not consider at present. The fraying of bark is only where the buck has rubbed the velvet from his horns. As this is done late in the summer it is of no use to you now.

The hooked brush indicates the commencement of " running-time;" of which here-after. It will, however, give you some idea of the number of bucks about; though one energetic buck will fight a great many bushes in one night. The same is true of pawing and scraping places, except where snow is pawed up to get at acorns.

Having reached the ridges, pass on from ridge to ridge, noting carefully the quantity of tracks and droppings, and especially the size of both. It is a common mistake, into which hunters of some experience often fall, to count, unconsciously often, a deer to every sign or two. The beginner especially is almost certain to estimate the number of deer from six to ten times too high. The age of both tracks and droppings is quite as important to be noted. As it is nearly impossible to describe the difference between a stale track or dropping and a fresh one, this point must be left to your common-sense aided by experience. Staleness is, however, as easy to detect with the eye as it is hard to capture with the pen.

As there may be two or more deer of the same size, you may of course underestimate the number of deer. But there is little danger of this. Nearly all the danger lies in overestimating their number.

Little can be determined, however, from a small tract of ground. One deer, especially an old buck in the fall, will often track up two or three acres or more so that one would think there had been a dozen deer there; while the common expression "just like sheep-tracks" with which some ignoramus is wont to addle the beginner's head is often based on the work of two or three deer over a few acres of ground.

You must move on, then, over a considerable area of ground. And in so doing it is still more important to note the size and freshness of the tracks and droppings. For the very same deer may have marked several acres yesterday and several different acres each day before, until nearly a hundred acres may be so marked that to the careless eye it would look like the work of fifty deer.

As a rule, deer do not travel far if undisturbed. And they generally travel less in timber than in open ground. With the exception of a buck in the fall, deer in timber seldom have a daily range of over half a mile in diameter, and in open ground seldom over a mile. In brush it is often much less. This is, how-ever, on the assumption that food, water, and ground for lying down are all near each other. For if these are not near together a deer may travel very far. I have known them to go three miles for acorns, a mile or two from there to water, and a mile or two in another direction to lie down. I have known them descend five thousand feet at night for food and water, returning at daybreak to the very tops of the highest ridges in the timber-belt. Disturbance will also soon drive them to this. But where undisturbed, and where food, water, and good ground in which to lie down (of which hereafter) are close together, a deer's daily circuit is generally very limited. They will, however, often change this circuit, sometimes every day for a few days, sometimes every few days, and sometimes will spend a week or more on a thirty- or forty-acre piece of ground. This change of daily circuit is, how-ever, not extensive, being comprised often within a circle of a mile in diameter, and seldom exceeding two or three miles except for such special causes as much hunting and great distances between food, water, and cover, etc.

In thus examining ground to determine something about the amount of deer, there are certain places which require special attention. Next to the actual feeding-ground there is scarcely any place more certain to have signs and show them plainly than burnt-off ground. Why the deer resort to burnt ground is of little consequence. It is certain that the tender shoots of grass, etc., which spring up there are not the sole attraction. For often they begin to frequent it as soon as it is fairly cooled off, and continue to frequent it even in those countries where there is no summer rain to start any vegetation upon it In brushy countries this is the very best ground on which to hunt, especially when after a cold night the morning sun shines brightly into it.

Look also in the ravines and swales that lie between ridges; along the edges and in the open parts of thickets; along the bottoms and in the flats by little creeks and rivulets; in and around the heads of ravines, especially if the heads are brushy; around the edges of windfalls, especially fresh ones, as the deer will come to browse on the tops of trees and on the young saplings that have been knocked down by the larger trees. Look also in the edges and open places of the brush on the outer edge of timber, especially if it be hazel, on which they love to browse when in bud. Look also on all the highest points in the timber, on the points and backbones of ridges, the passes from ridge to ridge, and the connecting ridge of several ridges.

In inspecting open country do the same, but pay special attention to the bottoms and sides of valleys and the top of dividing ridges between them. For here, if the country be at all rough, you will be quite apt to find the trails or runways of the deer.

In those countries containing cattle running at large the cattle-paths are also good places to find deer-tracks, especially those paths leading to water or to high, rough, or brushy ground. On ground so open as to approach prairie in character, look well around the sides, heads, and mouths of all gullies, gulches, etc., and the nearest passes from one to the other across intervening ridges; also in and around all patches of brush or timber, and all sloughs or other places full of very long high grass, reeds, etc.

In inspecting ground in those countries like California and the other Spanish-American States in which there is a long season without rain, you may save time by going first to the watering-places, which will be some distance apart. But here you may easily draw wrong conclusions, as even in the very hottest and driest weather deer often go a day or more with-out drinking at all. And where it is much trouble for them to get it they will often go without it altogether. And when the browse is young, soft, and succulent, as well as when it is wet overnight with dew or fog, they will generally dispense with water even though it be close at hand. The deer is also a quick drinker, and when he goes only for a drink and not to get rid of flies, etc., generally wastes little time around a spring, especially if much hunted. In these dry countries, too, the tracks are soon obliterated by those of quails, animals, ants, and other creatures. There may also be other water-holes near at hand of which you are unaware. So you must beware how you decide from the absence of tracks that there are no deer about. Deer also often remain several days or even weeks in dense chaparral, moving very little, though this is not apt to be the case in the fall, when deer move more than in summer and winter.

On the other hand, if you find many tracks at the water you must be careful not to reckon a deer to every four hoof-prints. When several deer come to water together they may crowd and jostle each other around the edge and change their standing-places so often that the whole margin of the water is cut up. Or some may stand around while the others drink, and if not hunted or disturbed much they may linger about a while. On such ground every track shows.

In all such cases lose no time at the spring, but circle around one hundred or two hundred yards away from it, examining carefully all the trails and open places in the brush or natural passes among rocks that lead to the water. For even where deer generally have no regular runways they nearly always have certain directions from which to approach a spring, and will either make some paths of their own or take those made by cattle or other animals. Here also much ground must be examined, for upon dry ground tracks (except in trails) are not readily seen by the unpracticed eye; and to such an eye both tracks and droppings are apt to appear as fresh today as they would have seemed yesterday.

These same principles apply to examining almost any kind of ground. Deer are often found in great numbers in dense jungles of canebrake, swamp, and chaparral. But in such ground little can be done by still-hunting proper. One can only get them by driving or by hunting around the open places in the morning and evening, when they may be out.

Antelope are such rangers that this kind of inspection will not do for them. Besides, they are so sure to be on foot during a great part of the day, to be in bands, and to be on open ground, that the quickest way to find them is to ride over the country, stopping at every eminence and sweeping the country with a good glass. They will go great distances for water, seeming to need it more than deer do; and as they generally go to it in a band like cattle, the water-holes are the places to look for their tracks.

And now a puzzling question may meet the beginner-, namely. What is plenty? and are deer plenty enough to hunt?

The word "plenty" has of course different meanings for different kinds of game. One bear to the square mile would be plenty for bears, in most bear countries; yet one deer to the square mile would hardly be worth hunting except upon very favorable ground, and then you would generally need snow. "Plenty" varies also in meaning with localities. In parts of Northern California plenty - a few years ago at least - would mean forty or fifty deer to the square mile, while in San Diego we call five to the square mile plenty. In such heavy timber as covers the north of Michigan, Wisconsin, and Minnesota an average of ten to the square mile would be quite plenty, and five to the square mile would be plenty enough for the best of sport on light snow.

The word "plenty" varies, again, with the persons using it. A man finds his turnip-patch well tracked up and talks of "plenty of deer," " lots of deer," "just like a sheep-yard," etc., when in fact it is all done by two or three deer that are by daylight a mile or more away safely ensconced in some windfall or brush-patch, without another deer within two or three miles. " The deer are so plenty they are destroying the vineyards" is a species of twaddle very common in the papers of Southern California. He who lies out a few moonlight nights to watch one of those selfsame vineyards, or, failing in that, attempts to follow the tracks of the ravagers back to their mountain-home in the morning, if he is fortunate enough to get even a sight of the old doe and two fawns, accompanied perhaps by a buck or a yearling or two, that did the whole mischief, returns hot, breathless, and disgusted from a long scramble among the rocks and brush, and goes home with a vastly different notion of " lots of deer" from what he had when he came out.

One of the first and most ineradicable ideas the beginner gets is that there are about ten or twenty times as many deer about him as there really are. The consequence is a speedy feeling of disappointment. If in the course of a day's walk you start six or eight deer - that is, either see them or find where they have run away from you - and can find tracks or dropping not over a day or two old at every fifty or one hundred yards of most of your course over the kinds of ground above described, you may consider deer quite plenty enough for the best of sport.

Antelope, being banded, being on open ground, and visible at such long distances, will afford good sport on a far smaller average to the square mile than will deer. That is, on ground suitable for still-hunting. And this is a question that for either antelope or deer should be decided before you waste any time in hunting it.

Upon some kinds of ground successful still-hunting is almost an impossibility; while in ground that is suitable for it there is such a difference that five or six deer to the square mile upon one kind will give better success than twenty to the square mile upon another kind. The best kind is timber that is open enough to allow you to see at least a hundred and fifty yards in any direction, free enough from underbrush to allow you to walk without touching too much of it, yet brushy enough in places to afford good browse and lying-down covert for deer, and, above all, rolling enough to allow you to keep out of sight behind ridges and look down into hollows and basins. Ground that is very brushy or quite level is very difficult for anyone to hunt alone, and had better be entirely shunned by the novice, as his lot will almost certainly be vexatious disappointment. But, as I shall show hereafter, brushy ground may sometimes be hunted to advantage by two or more persons; and if there are openings enough through it, it may afford good sport in the season called " running time."

19

As a rule, the more rolling the ground the shorter "the breaks," and the higher the ridges, up to a hundred and fifty feet or so, the better. If it roll too much and the ridges be too high, it will make your walking too laborious and your shots too long. The best of all ground consists of hard-wood timber, well open beneath and broken into ridges about fifty feet high. Such ground generally contains acorns in the fall, has plenty of windfalls and brush to make lying-down cover for deer in the daytime, while the tops of the ridges are generally clear enough of brush to allow still movements of the hunter and afford him a good view in nearly all directions. Whether you hunt in timber or open country, the more nearly your ground approaches the rolling character of these oak ridge forests the better your chances of success.

For antelope-hunting much the same kind of ground, though built on a larger scale, is generally necessary. On a broad level plain it is now almost impossible to get within shot of antelope except by some kind of trick in the way of disguise. And even that must be an unusually smart invention. Quite rolling ground is the best on which to approach them; and if the antelope are in numerous bands or small bunches, this is the only sure ground upon which to get close shots except by such tricks as flagging, etc. But if they are scarce or all in one band, it is often impossible to look over enough of this kind of ground to find where they are without in many cases a vast amount of traveling, there being so many places where they can be out of sight in a valley or behind some knolls.

Chapter Four - The Senses of The Game and The Hunter

Having selected the ground upon which you are to hunt you will probably, if left to yourself, go wandering around the woods with your eyes fixed about fifty yards ahead of you, expecting at every turn to see a large calf-like object standing broadside to you in a nice open spot, patiently awaiting your bullet distance twenty-five or thirty yards.

The first thing you must do is to lay aside each and every idea of how a wild deer looks that you have ever derived from your imagination, from pictures even by the best artists in the best magazines or books, even when drawn by accomplished sportsmen. No picture unless of immense size and made by a thorough hunter who is also a thorough artist can convey any notion of how a deer looks on his native heath under the circumstances in which three fourths of the time you will have to see him to get a shot. There are of course cases in which a deer appears in the woods just as he does in a picture. Such was often the case in the olden days. But such is the exception now. There is an occasional deer that is either a natural fool, or has never before seen a man, or that may have dropped into a doze in the daytime and awakened bewildered for an instant at your near approach, or, owing to formation of ground, cannot make out the direction of the noise that alarms him and stops a minute to locate it. Such an one makes an easy shot.

The deer you will be apt to meet at this day are animals very different from the one above mentioned. And in order to understand them thoroughly it is necessary to consider well their senses.

You have doubtless heard and read dozens of times that the deer is timid, shy, and watchful. The trouble with all such information is that it gives no idea of the practical extent of a deer's acuteness. From all I have ever heard or read one would never dream of a deer's starting two hundred or three hundred yards away, out of your sight, beyond your hearing, etc., when you were walking " so quietly," as you thought, and against the wind too. You feel dazed when you find the tracks of his long jumps so fresh and far apart. And many times must even this be repeated before the light of the true state of affairs breaks in upon your picture-trained mind.

As a general rule, the nose of the deer is perhaps the most important sense to avoid. Not that they can smell any farther than they can see or hear; but because the smell of a man alarms them more thoroughly and completely than any sound or sight. A deer will often stop an instant to locate a noise or look at any unusual object; and when entirely undisturbed by hunting deer are so certain to do so that there is hardly ever any need of taking a running shot. But almost every wild animal knows instinctively the smell of a man. A deer seems to know it above most all others. When he catches the scent he does not have to take a second sniff of the tainted air. He has generally no further curiosity. He is perfectly satisfied as to the character and direction of the odor, and his only concern is to effect his immediate disappearance.

This delicacy of scent is developed very early and needs no practice to keep it acute. Once, while hunting on a very hot morning, I sat down to rest at the mouth of a little canon that led into a larger one. At the time scarcely any perceptible wind was stirring. I had been seated only about two minutes when a sudden crash and bump, bump, bump of hoofs brought me with a bound to my feet, and I saw two half-grown fawns bounding up the canon at full speed and a hundred yards away. On examining the ground I found that they had been lying under a thick bush of sumac about eighty yards from me, and had sprung several feet at the first bound. An intervening rise of ground showed plainly that they did not see me, and as I had been walking in a soft dusty cattle-trail with moccasins with great stillness, sat down quietly, and sat without anything moving for over two minutes (just about the time it would take scent to move to them in the light breeze there was), I feel equally confident that they did not hear me. From my knowledge of that ground I know positively that those fawns had never before met a man. I have often noticed that fawns, though they may stand and look at you, or stop when you start them with a noise only, seldom stop when they smell you.

He who has seen a good dog scent grouse against a cool morning or evening breeze on a prairie needs scarcely to be told of the distance at which a

21

deer can smell such a great gross beast as a man, especially with a cool damp breeze in a valley.

This fear of a man's scent is also more universal than the fear of a sight or sound of him. In an open country deer will often stand and watch a distant man when they know perfectly well what he is. The brush-deer often cares little for noise, and will let a man come tearing through the brush quite close to his skulking form. But let such a deer catch your scent and he tarries no longer.

Still there are times when the scent of a man does not alarm deer. But this is probably due more to the casual existence of cross-currents of air that carry away the scent than to any indifference on the part of the deer. Also when running, and even when walking, they will often pass to leeward of a man, and may come very close to him if the man keeps perfectly still. Where they seldom see a man on a horse or in a wagon, deer will frequently stand quite unconcerned within plain sight and scent of both. And where men travel much on horseback they will often do the same thing if they are not much hunted. But upon these exceptions no dependence must be placed, as where one thus stands probably two slip away unobserved.

Where much hunted the ears of a deer become the most acute and practiced of his senses. And in many sections it is his hearing that makes the most difficulty in approaching him. And often it is the hardest of all his senses to avoid. I have often seen a deer spring from his bed at a bound and run away at a racer's speed before I was within two hundred yards of him, when I was positive that a man could not at twenty yards' distance have heard the soft tread of my moccasins on the light snow, and when I touched not a single bush or twig in a way that could make a noise. Yet the fact that the breeze was coming from the deer to me showed that he could not have smelt me. And looking from the deer's bed to my own position at the time he sprang showed plainly that he could not have seen me even had he been standing instead of lying down as he was doing. Lie down upon the ground in the woods some still day about the time of your companion's return to camp and see how far you can hear his footsteps even with your dull ears.

Even when the long practiced and moccasined foot falls on the ground as softly as snow, even when the leaves or twigs are softened with long rain, there is a faint crushing, packing sound that acute ears can hear along the ground a long distance. And the lightest snow, if of any depth, makes a faint grinding noise as it packs beneath the foot. So they will hear at a long distance the snapping or brushing of twigs against your clothes and the switching sound in the air as you let them fly back. These latter are, however, not so apt to alarm a deer lying down as sounds from the feet, though the other sounds may be the more audible to you.

Deer know, too, as well as a man the distance of sounds, and also their character, and are rarely deceived. They will often lie all day within plain hearing of the noises of a settler's cabin, the sound of the ax, and the lurid vocabulary of the teamster in the "pinery." The crash of a squirrel's jump, the roar of thunder, the snapping of trees with frost, their creaking or falling in the wind, generally does not alarm them in the least. Yet the faint pressing of the leaves beneath the feet, or the crack of a twig a hundred yards or more away, may send them flying.

The direction of noise, however, often perplexes deer. And in their perfectly natural state their curiosity to know its exact location and precise character generally leads them to stop after running a few jumps. And often they will rise up and look, standing directly in their beds. After a certain amount of persecution they generally lose this curiosity, become perfectly satisfied with a general presumption of mischief, and stand not on the order of their going; though the very wildest of deer may occasionally yield to the temptation to take just one look.

Against the wind a deer cannot of course hear so well as he can down the wind. But even up wind you should relax no caution, as in such case there is generally no need of haste.

An apparent exception to this sense of hearing is in case of the skulking or hiding deer. The exception is, however, apparent only. Deer that live much in very thick brush, often depend, like many other animals, upon standing or lying still and letting you pass them. They know perfectly well that you cannot see them. The deer of Southern California is very apt to be of this character when found in the brushy regions. Even when in the open hills or in the timber-groves or in the mountains this deer is not half so shy of noise as is the deer of the Eastern woods. If deer in San Diego County were as afraid of noise as they are in the Wisconsin and Minnesota woods it would be nearly impossible to approach them in the dry season when the brush, grass, and weeds are brittle. In Southern California they depend more upon their scent and sight than upon hearing. But it would be absurd to suppose that they do not hear. Many a hunter there loses a shot through his folly in reasoning upon this point. A deer does not stand or skulk because you make an extra noise. That trick he will play anyhow if he has decided on that course. But half the time instead of standing he slips quietly off before you get in sight of him. You gain nothing on the skulker by your noise. And by it you lose the other entirely.

Another exception, which is perhaps apparent only, is the case of deer in open ground. This results mainly from the difference in the appearance of distances in the woods and in the open; distance in the woods appearing much greater. It is probable, too, that sounds can be heard a trifle farther in the woods owing to there being less wind and some cover over- head. At any rate, it seems so with noises not too distant, though the point is a hard one to prove.

To recognize an object at rest the eyes of a deer are about as dull as those of a dog. But this, again, has two partial exceptions. On open ground deer can often recognize a man quite well, especially if he be standing. And if they have taken any alarm they will be quite sure to do so. Even in the woods if a man be standing and the deer has taken alarm, the deer will be quite apt to identify him. But as a rule, if the deer is unalarmed, he will not know a man from a stump on open ground if the man is seated and motionless; nor will he in the woods even if the man is standing. If the deer is moving, and especially if running, he is quite blind to anything ahead of him, provided it does not move. Hence if some one drives a deer toward you, you need little or no concealment if you keep still. But when he gets in sight of you, beware how you move a step for a better position. You may do it, but your game is liable to switch off to one side in a twinkling.

A deer can also see a long way. I have seen them watching my companion nearly a mile away, whose motions I could hardly make out myself. It is doubtful, though, if a deer can distinguish a man at any such distance, or even at half of it.

But a deer's eyes are marvelously quick to catch a motion. And the fact that deer are generally at rest while you are in motion gives them an immense advantage over you. So keen are their eyes to detect a motion that if you once get within their eye-range and they suspect you, it is almost useless to try to get a single step closer to them. From this arises the common hunter's maxim, "When you see a deer, shoot;" a maxim demanding great qualification, however. A deer not alarmed may often be approached after you come within his sight; as we shall see hereafter.

Not only are they quick to detect a motion, but they can detect a very slight one or a very slow one, and do it, too, at quite a distance. The slow rising of your head over a ridge, the slow movement of your body across the trunks of trees, the slow motion of a creeping body along the ground they see almost instantly, unless the motion happens to be made while they have their heads down feeding or walking, etc. A deer once started watches back with an acuteness that in the woods is quite certain to baffle the keenest- eyed pursuer, and is likely to do so on open ground. And when much hunted by tracking they learn to watch their back track without waiting to be started.

The senses of antelope are about the same as those of deer. Their great bulging eyes like old-fashioned watch-crystals will catch a far slighter motion than those of a deer, will catch it three or four times as far away, and catch it, too, in almost any quarter of the horizon. My experience with them at close ranges has been too limited to enable me to determine satisfactorily whether they are as sensitive to noise as a deer. So far as I have seen they are not, though this is probably on account of being on open ground; a distinction before explained. For the same reason the question of scent seems to be less important. But then you should not presume in the slightest upon any failure of acuteness in any of their senses; and especially in their eyes, to which you must never yield a single point of vantage.

In fact, you must not presume upon any exception about the senses of either antelope or deer. If you deal with every one as if he were the most wary of his race, you will lose nothing if he turns out a simpleton. Whereas if you deal with any as if they were simpletons, you will lose not only the wise ones but many a simpleton also.

24

And now let us consider what you have with which to outgeneral these senses of your game.

I have seen one man who claimed that he could smell deer. As he could make no practical use of his power in jumping, or starting, or finding the animal, even against a cool morning breeze, it may be considered worthless even if it were not all in his fancy.

A good musky old buck in the fall, if close by, may be smelt. And so may a billy-goat. But the buck cannot be smelt far enough to keep him from discovering you first. The hunter's nose may be regarded as useless except to find camp at evening when the bacon and coffee are ready.

Your ears will often detect the sound of hoofs when you have started a deer, and are then useful as a guide to your eyes. They may also help you discover a deer moving in brush or on hard ground if near at hand. They may also catch the snort or bleat of a deer. They should by all means be cultivated.

But your main reliance must be your eyes. And these should be of the first class. If you are near- sighted or weak-sighted you may as well give up all hope of being anything like an expert. You may be a good shot at the target and see very well with glasses, but you will lack that quickness, comprehensiveness, and acuteness of sight that is indispensable to success. A deer hanging up in market, standing in a park, or stuffed in a museum is one thing. But in the ground where he is generally found, whether feeding, standing up or lying down, he is quite another. This is the reason why all pictures are misleading. A deer as he appears about five sixths of the time in his native home would make an almost invisible point on a two-by-four-foot canvas. Not only his smallness but his varying color and shape in different lights and positions, the fact that one seldom sees the whole of the body at once and sees it then only on a dim, perhaps dark, background, make him one of the hardest of all objects to catch with the eyes. Nothing in the whole line of hunting is so important as to see the deer before he sees you; and there is scarcely anything else so hard to do. In this more than in almost any other one thing lies the secret of the old and practical still-hunter's success. Sometimes a dim blur in a thicket; sometimes a small spot of brown or gray or yellow or red or white or nearly black far away on a hillside or ridge; sometimes a dark gray or brownish patch among tree-trunks or logs of the same color; sometimes only a pair of slender legs, looking like dead sticks beneath a huge fallen tree; a few tines looking like dead sticks in a distant bush; a pair of delicate ear-tips just visible above weeds, brush, or long grass; a glistening point or two where the sun strikes upon a polished horn; a shiny spot far away where the light just touches a bit of glossy hair. It takes the highest combination of natural keenness and culture of vision to detect one until just a second or two too late for a shot. I shall never forget the surprise of a certain youth who even in boyhood was distinguished among far older hunters for his acuteness in seeing squirrels hidden in trees, hares in their forms, woodcock on the autumn leaves ahead of the dog, etc. etc., when he first began to turn that eye on deer, and see them run out of a thicket through which he could see clearly; and going to

25

it, find the deer had been standing up in it all the time he was looking through it.

Very often it is impossible for anyone to see them; as where they are in thick brush, old pine-slashings, heavy windfalls, especially when lying down. So when they lie in the long slough-grass of the prairie, and in hot weather when they lie in the shade. Of course they will sometimes be in such a position that anyone can see them at once. But this is the rare exception and must not be depended on. A good glass is a great help in a large open country; but you must not allow yourself to depend on it, and should use it only when you have to. In timber it will generally be of little use, though if you must carry a lot of things it will do no harm and may be useful. For antelope-hunting it is often almost indispensable. Every spot of white or brown or gray, every hazy line, every point or glimmer like mirage for miles around should be carefully scanned with it. But for deer it had better be generally reserved to resolve doubtful things which you first catch with the naked eye. Otherwise your eye will lose the extreme keenness and quickness absolutely necessary for good stillhunting.

Chapter Five - The Daily Life of Deer and Antelope

Before one can expect any success in still-hunting he must know something about the daily life and movements of the game. In hunting antelope this is not of so much importance, as they live in country so open, are so conspicuous in color, and keep so much in bands, that with a good glass and careful searching from prominent points they can be seen at immense distances. And this must be done anyhow, for they are such wide rangers that there is little use to be made of their tracks except to get their general course; and when you are once upon their range you can employ your time to better advantage in covering as much ground as possible with your horse and sweeping it with your glass.

But the deer keeps so close to some kind of cover, is of a color so neutral, often resembling the general background upon which he is to be seen, that one may often pass within easy shot of a dozen without seeing them at all unless they run. There is little trouble in seeing antelope, on rolling ground at least, provided you get within a half-mile or so of them. The main difficulty is to get a shot after you do see them. With deer it is not only difficult enough to get a good shot, but almost as hard to find them at all. The general whereabouts of antelope being known, it is little trouble or rather it takes little or no skill or knowledge to find their particular whereabouts. But, given the general whereabouts of deer, it generally, on bare ground, remains a highly intricate problem to find the clew to their particular whereabouts. To do this, on ground where it is not possible or advisable to track, a pretty accurate knowledge of the deer's life is necessary. This varies so 'much in the details in different countries, and even in different parts of the same country, that all that any writer can do within the limits of a general work is to mark out the outlines and leave them to be filled in by your own experience and study in the woods.

The deer is an early riser. He is generally up before daybreak, and often up the whole night except at short intervals. But by daybreak he is nearly always on foot. About the first thing he does in those countries where water is scarce and where the season is dry and hot enough to make him thirsty is to start for water. This he may do very leisurely, though; feeding along the way and taking plenty of time to look about him, so that he may not reach water until sunrise or long after. Or he may go straight to it and walk away quite as rapidly as he came. Or he may come directly to it and then lounge away from it, feeding and looking as he goes. How a deer will act in going to water or leaving it, as well as his time of watering, are things that cannot be reduced to rule. When entirely undisturbed they will in hot weather water at any time of day, and when flies or mosquitoes are bad will spend much of their time there if there are large bodies of water. But where there are simply small drinking-holes they will rarely stay there, and if disturbed much will water only at night or very early in the morning. And they will be apt to do the same when watering very near a house or spring where they may see people passing, even though they are not shot at. In the forests of nearly all the Eastern States, especially in the mountains, water is so abundant that little use can be made, in still-hunting proper, of the question, When and where does a deer water? For fire-hunting, etc., the question has its importance. And even in those dry countries where the water-holes are scarce one must beware for the reasons heretofore given of placing too much reliance upon a deer's habits in regard to drinking.

A deer is, however, quite certain to feed more or less after daybreak, even though he may have been on foot the greater part of the night. The deer belongs to that class of animals like the horse, the ox, etc., that can see tolerably well in the dark and always do a certain amount of moving about at night, but nevertheless prefer a little more light when it is not too inconvenient to get it. So that, though he may be never so well fed during the night, he is quite likely to take a little more browse or a few more acorns at daybreak.

Like a cow or horse in good pasture a deer may do all of his feeding on an acre or two of ground, or he may straggle over fifty or a hundred acres of equally good feed. Which he will do it is impossible to determine except approximately. When in heavy brush he is apt to feed close. So when he has been much on foot during the night, as during full moon; so when he is hunted much. On the contrary, in thin brush or during the dark of the moon, or when little disturbed, he is more apt to straggle about while feeding. The quantity of food at hand seems to make little difference. A deer will often wander on over ridge after ridge well covered with acorns, picking up one or two here and there and going on a few yards for more, or eating half a dozen here and there and going on a hundred yards for more. In such particulars he is governed mainly by whim.

A deer may straggle over fifty acres, feeding and finishing very quickly, or he may take three or four hours about it. The same when feeding on a small space. He may stand and browse half an hour on one bush, or after one or two bites leave it for the next one, which perhaps is not half so good, and spend an hour in trying fifty bushes. In all these respects he is a provokingly aggravating beast, governed largely by caprice and often upsetting your best calculations. And it is often very important to make these calculations correctly, especially in hunting open country, where you see a deer feeding a long way off and need some time to get within good shot. But in general, the length of time a deer will feed will depend, as in case of the space over which he will wander in feeding, upon the moon and the amount of persecution he has. It will depend also upon the weather. In very hot weather he will, as a rule, finish feeding and lie down sooner than in cool or cold weather.

In nearly every case in which deer are foraging in a garden, a turnip-patch, or other cultivated crop, they understand perfectly what they are about. Daybreak will nearly always find them gone or departing. When feeding in such a place they must generally be sought far away from it in the daytime.

But when feeding after daybreak there is one thing a deer rarely fails to do, and that is to keep up a pretty constant watch for danger. Every moment or two the head comes up and scans at least half the circle of vision, while the big ears flare impatiently for the faintest sound. Sometimes this looking is continued so long and suspiciously that you feel positive that he suspects you. Yet if you have perfect patience you may soon find that he suspects nothing, though he may have been looking never so keenly and directly at you. When the head is thus up and the animal watching, it is unsafe to make the slightest movement if you are near, as, even if you are out of his sight, his ears are then keener; if within fair shot, you should shoot notwithstanding the movement necessary to do so, as a deer thus watching is liable to vanish at any moment, and, even if suspecting nothing, is liable in a second to slip out of your sight behind a bush or tree or rise of ground.

Having finished feeding, the deer generally proceeds to lounge a while. He is a gentleman of elegant leisure, and has all the deliberate ease of aristocratic dignity. He stands a while and surveys the landscape or the dark rotunda of tree-trunks around him. Then perhaps he scratches one ear with a hind-foot, wiggles his tail, and stands a while longer. If there are any fawns, they are apt to skip and play a little. A year- ling is also apt to feel a little frisky, and even a dignified old doe or buck may romp a minute or two with some young deer.

But there is generally at such times a decided tendency to move on. This is generally done by easy stages. The deer walks slowly a little way, and then stops a while. Why he stops he probably does not know himself. He may nibble a twig or two during these pauses, or he may stand half an hour by a bush full of succulent and savory twigs and not touch one. He may stand two, five, twenty, or thirty minutes and do nothing; or he may move slowly on, making numerous short pauses. If the weather be cold or very cool he will be almost certain to stop in the sun- shine. If it be hot he is quite as certain to tarry in the shade; generally on the shady side of a bush if on open ground. As he often postpones drinking until after feeding, he may all this time be tending toward water; though, as a rule, when going to water after feeding that is, unless feeding toward water the deer walks fast and stops but little. While thus walking or lounging along the deer is generally not as watchful as when feeding. He will often stand a while with head down like a cow, especially in a rain or snow storm, and often when in the shade on a hot morning. When the sun-shine feels good on a cold morning he is more apt to have his head up. But, as I have before remarked, never presume upon a deer's carelessness if you can help it.

This lounging spell may be continued for an hour or two or three hours, depending, like his feeding, much upon the length of time the deer has been on foot during the night, the temperature of the morning, and amount of still-hunting.

All this time he is either tending toward the ground where he will lie down, or when he finishes his lounging he starts for it. In a previous chapter, under the directions where to look for deer-tracks, I have given the places over which a deer will be most apt to pass during his feeding and lounging time; though there is scarce any place over which he may not pass. In a subsequent chapter I will give the kind of places to which he is most apt to go to lie down.

The length of time deer will remain in bed during the day is also impossible to determine. Sometimes they will lie until four or five o'clock, and sometimes rise by three. I here mean rise for the rest of the day. In very hot weather, if a deer has a cool shady place away from flies and mosquitoes he is very apt to stay there during all the heat of the day. And if much hunted and he finds good comfortable and safe cover he is also likely to stay. But in cool, cloudy, or windy weather, especially if little disturbed, he is quite apt to be on foot two or three times during the day, browsing a little, lounging a little, shifting position a little, or merely getting up for the sake of lying down again. During the dark of the moon, if little hunted he is apt to feed a little during mid-day. In rainy or snowy or cold blustering weather he is quite apt to be on foot the greater part of the day, standing most of the time in some brush-patch, wind-fall, or sheltered ravine or little gulch, with head down like an old cow.

In the afternoon, if the deer rise early he is quite apt to lounge about a while as he did in the morning. If he rise late he is quite apt to go directly toward his feeding-ground, though he will doubtless browse some on the way. He will then feed and lounge about in much the same way he did in the morning until dark. In hot weather, if he is little disturbed he is quite as apt to go to water between sundown and dark as he is to go there in the morning.

For a long while after dark the deer is still on foot. If the moon be full he may be on foot most of the night. If he has any mischief to do he can find his way to it without any moon. Sometimes he will lie down and sleep a large part of the night in one bed. Sometimes the same deer will make three or four different beds in one night. When very much persecuted he will do nearly all his feeding, watering, sleeping, etc., during the night, without regard to the moon or anything else, and spend the day in close concealment.

These movements are varied somewhat in what is known as the "running time;" a matter we will consider hereafter.

How much antelope move by night I cannot say. But they certainly move far more by day than deer do, and it is therefore probable that they move much less at night, if they move at all. Though they lie down during a large part of the day, they are still much longer on foot than deer are. And generally some of the band are on foot while the rest are lying down. All that I have ever seen watered in the morning from sunrise to nine or ten o'clock. Their habits may, however, vary in this respect with places. They are much more apt to feed ahead on a straight course than deer are, and cover a much greater area of ground in doing so. They go- many miles for water if necessary. In fact in nearly all their business they travel a mile where a deer goes two hundred yards. But whatever they are doing they are watching, watching, watching; trusting more to their great eyes and less to nose and ears than a deer does to his.

Chapter Six - Looking for Deer That Are on Foot

Since it is generally so hard to catch sight of a deer until it is just too late to shoot, and since lying down is a position in which it is generally next to impossible to see one at all, it follows that far brighter prospects of success lie on the side of finding a deer on foot. So much is this the case that in many kinds of ground it is almost useless to try to get a shot at one in any other way. Such is the case where deer are keeping in heavy swamps, canebrake, tule, chapparal, or other stuff that is too high and too dense to afford a fair shot at one when running. There your only chance of success is to find them on foot along the edges, or from some piece of rising ground see them moving or standing in the covert. You may in such kinds of ground find enough eminences to give you some fair running shots at deer started below you; but such is not generally the case.

And now we are about ready to take the field. But let us first see whether the day will do for still-hunting. For, recollect, there are some days when you might almost as well stay at home. Such are the still, warm days of autumn, when you can hear a squirrel scamper over the dead leaves a hundred yards away;" When not a breath creeps through the rosy air, and yet the forest leaves seem stirred with prayer."

Such are the days when the snow is crusty and stiff or grinds under your feet, while the trees snap and crack with the frost; in short, all days when you can- not walk without making a noise that a man could hear at forty or fifty yards; though even on such days it will pay you to go out and study the movements of deer and the " lay of the land." And if it should be very windy, by moving against the wind you may get a shot, though when the trees are creaking and rattling with wind the deer are often in a very nervous condition all day; but against a strong wind they cannot smell you and cannot hear you as well as usual.

But when the autumn rains have softened down the dead leaves and sticks, or during or just after a gentle rain, or when the ground is covered with an inch or more of soft snow, then is the time, especially if a gentle breeze sighs through the tree-tops, when your heart may well bound high with hope.

We will first consider hunting on bare ground.

To find a deer on foot you had better be in the woods about the time the morning star begins to fade in the first smile of coming day. This exactness is not always necessary. But if deer are not very plenty, or if they have been much hunted, or if the moon is near or past the full, the earlier you are in the woods after it is light enough to see a deer at all, the better.

Let us first try the oak ridges, as these form the easiest ground upon which to take your first lessons.

The first questions that arise are, from which way shall we approach the ridges? and, in which direction shall we traverse them?

In determining these points, the first thing in importance is the wind. Be cautious how you decide that there is no breeze yet. If you can notice it in no other way, wet your finger, and holding it up see if you can feel one side colder than the other. This test on a cold morning in dry air is quite delicate, the faintest movement of air making the side toward the wind cooler from increase of evaporation.

There being no perceptible wind, the next thing in importance is the elevation of ground and its freedom from brush, etc. It is best in hunting such ridges to walk where you can move with the least noise and can get the best view of all the other ridges and the intervening hollows. We will therefore wind along the highest ridges; they being in most places quite free from brush.

And now we must move with great caution. Avoid, when possible, walking through any brush that your clothes will touch. If you cannot help touching some twigs, ease them off with your hand so that they do not scrape on your clothes, snap, or make a switching noise in flying back. Above all beware of treading upon dead or dried sticks or piles of dead leaves, and feel the ground cautiously with each foot before you rest your whole weight upon it.

But none of this care must take off any of the attention of your eyes. For these must ajl the time be sweeping the whole ground as far ahead as you can see and covering the whole arc of a semicircle in range. Do not look as a child or woman does at only one thing at a time but let your gaze be comprehensive as well as keen, taking in at one view the near and the distant, the front and the sides of your field of vision.

At the same time beware of going too slowly. To traverse sufficient ground is quite as important in the long-run as anything else in still-hunting. You must rid your mind at once of the besetting sin of the tyro the idea that nearly every bush contains a deer. It is true that a deer may be in any bush. And you must hunt and look upon that assumption. But it is equally true and often equally probable that there is not one within quarter of a mile of you. And the speed of your movements must be often based upon that assumption. Between these two conflicting principles you must learn to make a happy compromise; yielding sometimes almost entirely to one, sometimes almost entirely to the other; sometimes taking the golden mean between the two.

Here we are on the ridges at last. And you at once see signs of deer about you. Here, there, and everywhere are places where sharp-toed hoofs have pressed down the dead leaves. In some places they have cut through the leaves. In some places they have pressed a damp leaf into the ground so that it forms a lining to the track. Pick up a few of the dry leaves and see if any of those lying next the damp ones below are moistened any on the underside. Here is one with a distinct trace of dampness where it has been pressed against a wet one below. The leaf has had no time to dry since it was done. Here, too, close beside it are droppings that have had no time to dry (or freeze, if it be cold weather). Put your fingers in several of these footprints and see if they are not of different sizes. Observe the size also of the droppings. Let nothing escape you that will indicate the number of the deer, so that you do not mistake the work of one for that of half a dozen. Here is a bit of ground that is quite bare. And upon it are plainly visible three different-sized tracks. One is that of a big buck. The others are tracks of a doe and fawn. The "edges of the tracks and the bottom of the depressions are clear-cut, smooth, and fresh-looking, in that appearance so impossible to describe. A little more inspection shows that the droppings, too, all vary in size.

Look carefully now all around as far as you can see. But do not look for a deer. Remember this singular advice. Do not forget it for a moment. One of the greatest troubles that besets the beginner is looking all the time for a deer. If the artist's deer is in sight you will see him quickly enough. Never mind that beast at all. Spend all your time in looking for spots and patches of light gray, dark gray, brown, or even black. Examine all you can see from only the size of your hand to the size of a small goat. Never mind the shape of them. Examine, too, everything that looks like the thick part of a thicket, and every blur or indistinct outline in a brush. No matter how much it may look like a bit of stump, fallen log, shade, or tangle of brush, or how little it may in shape resemble a deer; if it is in brush, or anywhere where you cannot see clearly what it is, give it a second, even a third, look. Look low, too, very low, along the ground. And be very careful how you run your eye over a bit of brush, deciding that it is too low for a deer to be in without your seeing him. Not only does a deer in the woods generally look entirely unlike the deer that stands in Imagination's park, but it does not stand half so high in the woods as it does in that park. When un- suspicious, a deer often has his head down, and this, too, makes him still lower. You need not be looking at this time of day for a deer

32

lying down, but look just as low along the ground as if you were looking for one lying down.

There are numerous such spots, patches, and blurs in view. But under a keen scrutiny they all fade into stumps, pieces of log, etc., and you are satisfied that there is nothing in sight.

Before going on, now, stop a moment and take a very important lesson. You see that the ground in every direction is dented with tracks. There is scarcely a square foot anywhere without two or three or half a dozen prints in it. You see, too, droppings in every direction. Now nearly every tyro, and a great many who have hunted enough to know better, will think at once of not less than forty deer. They will not so express it in words. And if asked directly how many they thought had made all these tracks, they would doubtless tone it down to eighteen or twenty. But the latent idea that remains in their mind is of about forty deer.

Now all these tracks and dropping were probably made by only three deer* There may have been five or six; perhaps another doe and fawn or two fawns. Or perhaps another old buck and a yearling or two-year- old buck. But if you examine the age and size of the tracks and droppings, you will see how three deer visiting this ground every day could in two or three weeks make all this amount of indications. You can- not say positively that they alone did it. But they could have done it. And the probability is that they did. You cannot see the proof of this now. For that you must wait until snow comes or until you can get on bare ground where you can track welt and can see just how a few deer can mark ground. Until then take my word for it. For a proper idea of how many deer there are about you will save you a large amount of wondering, disappointment, and vexation, as well as help you direct your steps to the most proper places to search for what they are. Few things so perplex the beginner and make him go wandering so aimlessly about the woods, expecting to see deer every minute yet ever fretting with disappointment, as exaggerated notions of the quantity of deer around him.

Here you see where the buck has gone down the side of the ridge we are on and across the flat below. He has doubtless crossed the next ridge. Although it is generally not worthwhile to track an old buck at this time of year, especially when the ground is bare a thing almost impossible where tracks are so numerous as they are here yet at this time of the morning fresh tracks are an excellent guide, and it is often best to take a look in the direction in which they have gone. Remember what I told you about the quantity of deer. You will see the expediency of doing this instead of roaming idly off in any direction.

In moving across this flat between this and the next ridge you may now go quite fast. But be still cautious about noise. And above all things tread on no dead sticks.

Here, you see, is the track again where the buck has gone up the next ridge. But it turns off and goes toward the neck of land that joins this ridge to the one we just left. No matter, though; he may have turned again. Now look over the ridge just as keenly as if you knew he were in the next hollow.

Slowly now! very slowly! For your head is about to rise over the crest of the ridge and come in plain sight of everything on the next ridge beyond and in the hollow between. Drop your gun, too, from your shoulder.

Here are two important points, the neglect of which causes even quite good hunters to lose many a deer. Many a one brings half his body into view at once before he fairly begins to look. Then his gun remains on his shoulder, flashing in the sun perhaps, swinging as he turns his body to look from right to left, always making an unnecessary amount of plainly visible motion if it should be necessary to lower it to shoot. You remember what I told you about the quickness of a deer's eye to catch a motion. Should you happen to bring your head in view of the deer at the time when he happens to have his head up and be watching which is at least one half and often two thirds of his time when on foot he is almost certain to see you unless you raise your head as little as possible and do it very slowly. This is extremely important in antelope-stalking; but its importance in deer-hunting, even in heavy timber, must never be underrated. Therefore make this a habit, so that you come to do it unconsciously to drop your gun always in going up the crest of a ridge; to show no more of your head than is absolutely necessary; to inspect the ground beyond, layer by layer, beginning with the farthest ground on the ridge beyond and running gradually down into the hollow. An exception to this would be when you know the game is in the hollow, when you know it to be alarmed or moving, or when your scent can blow over the ridge into the hollow. In such case it may be best to get on your hands and knees to look over instead of showing your whole body to anything that may be on the slopes beyond. And you never need your gun on your shoulder at such times. Cultivate this habit at once. It will cost you a minute or two of time only, requires no extra work, and will secure you many a good standing shot where you would otherwise get only a wild running one or too long a standing one.

A long and careful look over the ground beyond shows you no game. You however notice plenty of tracks on this ridge also. And careful examination will show you that they were made by the very same deer that tracked up the last ridge.

Here, too, are three or four smooth, oval depressions in the ground about two or two and a half feet long and about half as wide. The leaves in them are pressed down nice and flat, and there are some quite fresh tracks in them made after the occupant rose. I need hardly tell you that they are beds; but I do need to tell you that they are night beds. Therefore you need not expect to see a deer lying at the foot of the next tree or under the next bush.

The distinction between beds made by deer at night and those made by them during the day is important, and one almost certain to be overlooked by the unassisted beginner. And it is almost certain to make him waste much time and temper in searching for deer on ground where they lie only at night, while they are lying down perhaps a mile away. This subject properly belongs to another chapter, but I call your attention to it now that you may lose no time with these beds. The distinction is this. Deer will at night lie down almost anywhere; but if disturbed by hunting or otherwise they will hardly ever lie down by day on or near their feeding-ground, or near their watering-place, or on any ground except such as, in a subsequent chapter, I shall describe as " lying-down ground."

Instead of crossing this ridge and going to the next one, keep along the side you are now on, but just enough below the crest to see over and along the top of the ridge. Follow it along in this way until you reach the neck of land that connects this ridge with the one you were last on. Then peep as cautiously over this as you did over the last ridge.

You see several new ridges leading away in various directions, with nice little hollows between them containing charming places for a deer to stand in or feed in. But you see nothing resembling a deer. Pass on, then, along the main backbone of the ridges, and keep a keen watch from side to side, being careful about showing too much of yourself or showing even the upper half of your head too quickly to anything that might be in any of the hollows; and examine the tops and sides of every ridge as carefully as you can.

Here, you see, are some more beds; and the tracks in two of them are of different size from those we saw before, which shows that within a quarter of a mile there have been since last evening at least five, probably six and per- haps seven, different deer. These, too, are only night-beds, and the occupants may now be half a mile or more away. But as it is not yet time to lie down, they may be only a hundred yards away. And now you may 'walk still more slowly, for the chances of being near a deer are increasing. Of course the more plenty deer are, the more carefully you must move.

But see here! What is this? Down the sloping side of a ridge the ground is torn up and the fresh dirt and leaves thrown about. There are four such places nearly together. In some of them there are plain marks of two long split-hoofs and two prints of dew-claws just back of them. Here is another set of such marks fifteen feet farther on, and again about twelve feet beyond these last. The dirt thrown out is dark, soft, and damp. The bottom of the torn-up place is in some spots clean, smooth, and even shiny^ You need not be told what mean these long plunging jumps of sharp-edged hoofs. But to take a good les- son, follow the track back a few jumps.

It leads back to the top of the ridge and stops at a small clump of bushes about waist-high. Here, you see, are some fresh tracks and droppings of a pretty large deer. Here, too, are the ends of many twigs all freshly bitten off. Mark, too, the direction of the tracks the biter made as he stood here brows- ing. You find that they point toward where you were a minute or two ago. "It could not have been possible," do you think? It does indeed seem strange that a deer could have been standing in brush so low and thin as this and you not see him. But that he should run away in full bounding career without your seeing or hearing him does seem incredible.

35

Now put a piece of paper on these freshly bitten twigs and then take your track back to the place where you first come in sight of the paper.

Following your track back some sixty yards along the ridge, we reach a point where the paper first becomes visible. And behold! you can almost see through all that brush, and it appears not over two feet high!

Now mark well your error, and never forget it. It is not at all likely that he either heard or smelt you, for you were going with extreme caution, and a gentle breeze was rising and was in your face. But you passed your eye too carelessly over that brush just because it was so low and thin. You thought of course you could see everything there. You were hunting in Fancy's park again and forgot that you were in the woods; and when you raised your head more and were looking around to the right he saw you, and two jumps took him out of sight. Remember again what I told you, that a deer is not six feet high in the woods, and does not spend his time in posing for a sculptor or artist.

It will be quite useless now to go in the direction in which he ran; for not only do you stand little chance of seeing him, but he will probably stampede all deer along his course.

You now wander along for nearly half a mile, seeing plenty of fresh signs of deer, enough, combined with what you have already seen, to justify the conclusion that at least fifteen deer have fed on these ridges this morning; and that is quite plenty enough to satisfy any reasonable being. You begin to feel a strong hope that you will soon see something.

You do see something, but it is another set of long, plunging jumps. Follow them back and see how you lost the deer. As long as you hunt, no matter how old you may grow in experience, make it your custom whenever you lose a deer to study how you lost him. This may occupy a little time at first, but in the end it will well repay you.

Following the jumps back, you find that the deer was standing on the clear open top of the ridge when he started. The direction of the wind shows that he did not smell you; it is not at all likely that he heard you, for you were moving very quietly and were also down the wind from him, just as in the other case; and a glance back at the ground over which you came shows that you could have seen him at least a hundred and fifty yards off.

To one having much pride in his acuteness of sight this would seem good proof that some other cause or thing had startled the deer. But you had better lay aside all your pride, and remember that this fact may also prove that a deer in the woods can see you and run away without your ever seeing him run. And this can happen in woods and on ridges much more open than these are. You probably passed your eye directly over a small, dim, dark-grayish spot far away among the tree-trunks without a suspicion of what it was; and as your eye wandered on around the circle of vision you never noticed its disappearance. Your trouble is that you cannot yet comprehend in the concrete what you already are beginning to realize in the abstract the difficulty of recognizing your game under the circumstances under which you are most likely to meet it. Your scrutiny of the woods is as yet entirely too general, and is not one half as keen as you flatter yourself it is.

You now pass over nearly half a mile, when suddenly you see a grand old buck standing in a thicket a hundred and fifty yards away. There he stands in all the majesty of the buck on the powder-flask, with his big antlers, big neck, big body, and all.

No; do not shoot from here. He suspects nothing, and will stand there a few minutes. You can easily get close enough for a sure shot. Back off from this ridge and work around its point. That will bring you to that large fallen log that lies within seventy-five yards of him.

With chattering teeth, quaking heart, and crawling hair you finally reach the fallen tree. Taking a cautious look, you see nothing; a still more keen and cautious look reveals only a greater intensity of nothing. After more looking and carefully advancing you reach the place where he was. But there is nothing there, and there are no fresh tracks, signs, or jumps to show that a deer has been there within two days. You lean against a huge piece of fallen white-oak that has lodged in some brush among some upturned roots and of charred trunks of fallen pine, and wonder where your deer is.

Well, go back to the ridge and look at the log against which you are leaning, and take a lesson quite as important as any you could possibly take to-day; namely, how a deer does not look in the woods. At that distance and among that kind of stuff a deer would not be one third as large or distinct as what you saw; and if he were standing there motionless it would take the very keenest of eyes to detect him.

The sun is now getting so high that most of the deer have probably left the ridges and gone off to lie down; and we will leave them for another time. But be not discouraged in the least by the fact that you have seen no deer. You have learned far more than if you had shot one. For if you had killed one you would probably have sat for a week beneath a cataract of joy and conceit, perfectly blind to all one could tell you. Few things are so fatal to ultimate success as an early germination of the idea that you are "a pretty smart chap on deer." It is almost as ruinous as the idea that you are a poet. The teachers you need are disappointment and humiliation. If these cure you of still-hunting, it is well; for it proves you were not born for that, and the sooner you quit it the better. But if there is any of the true spirit in you, defeat will only inspire you. You will learn more from your failures than many do from success, and they will arouse you to double care, double energy, double keenness, and double hope.

The analysis of error is a far better source of instruction than the analysis of truth. For this reason we will at first study failures more than successes. And this will be rendered all the more easy by the fact that at first you will probably have little besides error to study.

Chapter Seven - Looking for Deer Lying Low

Having failed to see deer on foot during their feeding or lounging time of the morning, the next best thing is to seek them where they have gone to lie down during the main part of the day. It is sometimes more easy to find them in this way than when they are on foot, though it is generally harder. It is generally so very difficult to see one in bed at all that you are mainly confined in this kind of hunting to what is known as "jumping a deer;" that is, starting him from his bed, and firing at him as he bounds away or waiting until he stops to look back a moment, as deer generally do if little disturbed.

From the loose talk among hunters and the careless pens of writers about "jumping" deer the beginner is very apt to fancy it something like kicking up a hare from its form and rolling it over with a charge of shot as it scuds away. He is very apt to go marching confidently about expecting to see a deer hop out of any bush within twenty or thirty yards. This will occasionally happen, especially if the wind be right and the ground soft enough for silent walking. But three times out of four "jumping" a deer is what you shall soon see for yourself.

When entirely undisturbed by man deer will lie down in the daytime as they do at night - almost anywhere. But even then they show a decided preference for the following kinds of ground:

1. The points and backs of ridges, especially if brushy.

2. The brushy heads of little ravines and hollows.

3. Windfalls and choppings, especially when old and brushy.

4. Thin thickets containing fallen logs or trees.

5. Heavy thickets without fallen logs or trees.

6. Patches of heavy fern or willow in little valleys.

7. Little plateaus, knobs, or terraces on hillsides. In open country in addition to the above named places, if there are any, they will take -

8. The long grass or heavy weeds of sloughs or swales.

9. The brushy edges and center of patches of scrub timber.

10. Hill-sides with scattered trees or bushes.

11. The bottoms of cañons, gullies, and shady ravines, with the side pockets, etc., connected with them.

12. Brushy basins and the brushy bottoms of creeks and rivers.

13. The shade of big rocks, etc.

14. Bare ground under a tree on a hill-side, ridge, or in a valley, lying there just as cattle do.

There are many other places in which they spend the day, such as swamps, heavy chapparal, etc. But in all such places it is not worthwhile to hunt at all in this way.

If little disturbed they will not generally go far from their feeding-ground or watering-place to lie down. I have, however, known deer that scarcely ever saw or heard a man go as far back as three miles and as high up as five thousand feet from their feeding and watering place. It is only in very high and quite dry mountains that they are likely to do this, though flies, heat, and other causes may make them sometimes go far back anywhere.

Much hunting is, however, almost sure to drive them farther back, to make them take the thickest brush and the highest ground. And in mountainous country it is quite certain to drive them to higher ground, from which they will descend only at night. And there is then little ground too high or too rough for them. They are apt, too, to go farther back about the full of the moon, though I find the moon makes little practical difference about the distance deer go back. It affects more the time of going.

In winter deer are quite certain to lie in the sun. In summer they are quite as certain to lie in shade. In autumn they often do both, lying in the sun during the cool part of the morning (though they are then more apt to stand in the sun), and changing to the shade when it becomes warm. They seldom lie down where they will be disturbed with noises that make them get up often and look, such as wagons, cattle, etc. Yet they care nothing for the plain noise of people if it be distant.

Just when and where a deer may be expected to lie down it is, of course, impossible to say. Like many other kinds of game, they are provokingly irregular in their habits, and do not appreciate your kindness in picking out nice lying-places for them, but prefer to make their own selection. If you cannot track, you can only travel on, on, on over such ground as is above described and have patience until something starts.

The same caution that was needful before must be Still observed. In regard to noise from your feet you must be even more cautious than when looking for deer on foot; since they will hear noise from your feet more readily when lying with head near the ground than when standing.

Though a deer cannot smell or see you quite so readily when lying down as when on foot, he can still do either quickly enough. A deer lies generally with head up and sometimes with it laid over on one side; but in either case is nearly always listening and watching. Occasionally a deer falls in the daytime into a light doze, and once in a while you may thus get very close to one before he springs. In such case he is very apt to stop after a jump or two. But the times when a deer thus loses himself in the daytime are very rare, and nearly all his sleeping is done at night. And even if he were sound asleep in the daytime, it would not allow of any carelessness in approaching him. His senses are not to be trifled with under any circumstances. So that the question of a deer's sleeping by day is of no practical importance.

Sometimes a deer will purposely lie still when he hears a person. This kind of lying close will rarely or never trouble you on the kind of ground we are now considering. All your trouble will be the other way.

Sometimes it is quite easy to see a deer while in bed; as where they are in open timber or open bluffy country with little heavy brush, but with snow on the ground and the country rolling enough to allow you to get well above them so as to look down upon them. At such times every dark looking oval spot, no matter how much it may resemble a stump, requires close inspection. Where they are lying under trees on open ridges, along hill-sides, or in valleys, it is also quite easy to see them; as in much of the ground that deer frequent in California and countries of similar mountain formation, before they are hunted too much. But in the Eastern States a deer will now be rarely or never found lying by day in such a place.

You must be careful, therefore, how you waste much time in trying to see deer in bed. Where the ground is very rocky, brushy, or covered with windfalls, if there is no snow, or even if there is snow unless the ground is quite rolling, it will not be worth while to try to see them so. In such case your object should generally be to get over the greatest amount of ground with the least noise, depending entirely upon starting one close enough for a shot. And even on ground where deer can be seen you must strain your eyes to the utmost, for it is even then no very easy matter to see one in bed.

Very rarely does a deer lie twice in the same bed. A fat old buck late in summer or in early fall, before he begins to roam much, will sometimes do it. Any deer may sometimes lie for several days on a piece of a few acres, though roaming a mile or more away from it at night. Fawns and does, as well as barren does and yearlings, will sometimes lie twice in the same bush and even in the very same bed of the day before or beside it. But the rule is very decidedly the other way. Though deer often keep for years in the same orbit of a mile or so in diameter, they change their special whereabouts so often that as a rule it will never be worth while to hunt around old beds; and when you have started a deer from a particular bed you need not, as a rule, expect to find him either there or very nearby it for two or three or four days and often more.

One of the most natural blunders a beginner will make is to spend the middle of the day hunting around the oak ridges or wherever he sees the most tracks, when in fact most of the deer are half a mile or a mile away. I have already noticed the distinction between night-beds and day-beds, and between ground where deer feed and where they go to lie down. You must bear this ever in mind or you may lose much time in hunting where your game was two or three hours or more ago and a half-mile or more from where it now is.

Let us therefore leave the ridges, as it is ten o'clock and the majority of the deer are now lying down. Half a mile to the north are some very brushy ridges and windfalls, and just beyond them is a large piece of ground from which the pine has been cut out. This is known to the woodsmen and hunters as a "slash" or "chopping." A pine "slash" is about as rough a piece of ground as is possibly consistent with still-hunting. It is covered in all directions with tree-tops, logs too small or too broken by falling to make good lumber, small brush and trees crushed by the larger ones, stumps and branches of all sizes, and the whole is well covered with briers, saplings, and brush. But there is no other ground that the deer so loves to lie down in during the cool bright days of autumn and the sunny days of winter.

Here is a large windfall just ahead. It will bear inspection. Mounting one of the huge fallen trunks on the outside, we see nothing but great shafts of timber lying headlong in ruinous confusion, mixed throughout with great upturned roots, crushed tops, and shattered limbs, and throughout all a rank growth of briers and young brush. But wherever we see the bare ground distinctly there are signs of deer. See that smooth oval depression in the ground on the sunny side of those great upturned roots of a pine. A deer lay there yesterday; and if he has not been disturbed it is not at all unlikely that he is here now.

Hark! Did your ear catch that faint crack of brush about a hundred yards off? No. Yet dull and untrained, your ear did not notice it. And if it had noticed it, it would doubtless have taken it for a squirrel or a bird.

We reach the other side of the windfall without seeing anything. Let us, however, take a circuit around the edge and see if anything has gone out. What is that mark on the ground about twenty yards ahead? Some leaves are upturned. They look moist on one side. The dirt, too, is dark, damp, and soft, and shows plainly the imprint of four feet that have come plunging into it from above. Look back over this log and see if you do not find some more tracks there.

You find them readily. And several feet farther back toward the main body of the windfall you find more.

Well, we have "jumped" a deer at last. Let us try another and see if we cannot get at least a view of him as he jumps.

Do you see those brushy ridges with the ends pointing this way, some two hundred yards away, just visible in the distance? The backs and points of those are worth examining when deer are so plenty as they now are here. Make a wide circuit to the left so as to reach the backbone of the first ridge a hundred and fifty yards or more from its point. Then go carefully out to the point. If you see nothing, retrace your steps and take the next ridge the same way.

Too much trouble for an uncertainty, do you think? Then by all means have your own way and go straight to the point. You may learn more in that way. But you will yet see the day when you will take far more trouble tharf that for an uncertainty.

On you go to the first point, travel down that ridge and across to the next one. Up that and down the next one you think you will go, when suddenly you find some more tracks of long plunging jumps. They look so fresh that you had better follow them back to where they came from.

They lead you to the very point of the second ridge, and there, in a bunch of thin brush, you find a fresh warm bed about fifteen feet from where the occupant's hoofs tore up the dirt at the first place he struck the ground. Now stoop down in the bed until your head is about eighteen inches from the ground. Do you notice now how you can see over nearly the whole of the low ground over which you passed in coming to the other ridge? The deer might possibly have heard you. But as he could have seen you, we need not seek any other explanation. Now if you had followed my advice, he could not have seen you until you were quite close; you would have had the same advantage of the wind, for it is blowing across the ridges; you might have got a shot at him as he was running away over the level ground; and if he had run around either side of the ridge you would probably have heard his hoofs, and by a quick dash to that side of the ridge you might have got a shot at him. At all events, you would at least have seen him, which would be no small pleasure to one who has never yet seen a wild deer in his native woods.

And now we are in sight of the old "chopping" or "slash" a clearing with an occasional tall dead, burned or blasted tree standing amid a general solitude of logs and brush.

You must now study four things in the following order of relative importance :

1. To avoid noise in walking.

2. To avoid going down the wind.

3. To keep on as high ground as is consistent with quiet walking and the wind.

4. To keep the sun on your back.

The first three of these we have already considered, and you know their importance. For hunting open ground the fourth often becomes of great importance; and it is sometimes an advantage worth all the rest together. In hunting ground as open as a "slash," it is sometimes quite important, especially if there are any deer in it still on foot, which is often the case, as deer do not reserve a slash exclusively for siestas. And on all kinds of ground it is an advantage that should always be taken where it can be done without sacrifice of the others.

Under the head of shooting with the rifle we shall examine the difficulties of shooting toward the sun, especially when it is near the horizon, the time when you will be most apt to get shots at deer. Now to hunt toward the sun is often to have to shoot toward the sun. And the more you can avoid this the better. So much is this the case that if you are hunting down a narrow shallow ravine or gulch from which you expect to jump a deer and will have to take a running shot along or up one side or across the ridge or open ground on the other side, you had better walk on the side toward the sun even though it be the windward side and be the most difficult one upon which to move quietly. This principle holds with more or less force in all cases where your game will be likely to run toward the sun, especially if uphill.

But there is another reason quite as strong which is of immense advantage in such kinds of open ground as prairie, table-lands, etc., where you often see deer at a long distance. If you have the sun on your own back and full on a deer's coat, he will strike your eye twice as far or twice as quickly as if the case were reversed. When the sun is the other way you may sometimes see at a long distance the sheen as the sun glances from the hair on a deer's back. But as a rule, the practical effect of having the sun beyond the deer is to make the deer stand in shade. You need scarcely be told that this makes him much

42

harder to see, aside from the dazzling effect of the sun upon your eyes. And when you are in the sun and the deer has it be- hind him, it is as much easier for him to see you as it is easier for you to see him when you have the sun on your back and it is shining full upon his jacket. And there is so much sunshine in these old choppings or slashes that you should give this point all the attention possibly consistent with a due regard to the others.

For an hour you toil through the bristly beard of the old clearing, picking your way through old logging-roads or other open places, when you come to another series of tracks made by plunging hoofs and ten or fifteen feet apart. Examination shows that a doe and two full-grown fawns have just vacated a bit of brush among some old logs in a manner savoring decidedly of expedition. And yet you have seen and heard nothing. But you are doing something of much more ultimate use to you than seeing or even bagging a deer could possibly be. You are learning at last what it means to " jump a deer." It means generally out of shot, often out of hearing, frequently even out of sight

Well, let us move along. The ground is getting higher and more broken and is nearing a creek bottom. This bottom is covered with "hard-wood" timber, and some of it begins to appear upon the ground we are now on.

But hark! What is that? A sound like the distant hoof of a horse in slow gallop, coming from the side of the hill toward the creek bottom.

And now see how naturally you will do just the very thing you should not do - a thing the beginner is almost certain to do at first if left to himself. You sneak cautiously to the edge of the hill and peer keenly over in the direction from which the sound came. You think you see about everything there is to be seen. And you are about right. For that dark, dim spot in the edge of the timber that faded away with a single whisk into the dark depths of the timber was hardly to be seen by even the keenest eyes until just too late to shoot.

While you were sneaking so cautiously a deer was getting swiftly away, and stopped in the edge of the heavy timber to look back. He then saw your hat rise slowly over the edge of the hill. As he was standing still and you were moving he had every advantage of you. He saw you at once and left before your eye got around to where he was. But you probably would not have seen him even had you turned your glance at once upon him, for a deer in such timber is very hard to see. And even if you had seen him he would undoubtedly have seen you first, and would probably have started before you could take a shot. Now if at the first sound of hoofs you had run at top speed for the edge of the hill you would have re-versed all this. You would have come in sight of him before he stopped running. If you had then stopped instantly, you would have had either a running shot or a good standing shot as soon as he stopped. For, not seeing you if you were motionless, he would have paused a moment or two before going on. In such a case don't stop even to reload your rifle, as you can run to the edge and then load with much more chance of success than by loading first and then going.

This is a principle that must never be forgotten. The advantage that one of two persons or animals at rest has over the other one moving, is immense.

And if a deer in any way gets this advantage you will rarely get him, if very wild, except by a long running shot. With antelope it is still more fatal to success. And even to the tamest deer this advantage must never be given, but should be always retained by the hunter. There are many cases in which you cannot prevent a deer from having it, and such constitute a large part of what is known as the "luck against you."

It is now getting toward the middle of the afternoon and is time to work toward the oak ridge's again. In hunting them observe the same rules that you observed this morning. But remember that as night approaches it becomes very hard to distinguish a deer among the tree-trunks, even though other objects still remain quite distinct.

Night drops at last her dark pall around your hopes. You wend your way homeward with gloomy face and heavy heart.

Yet why despond? You cannot expect to learn an art in a day or two. You have made progress enough already. You have learned what deer-hunting is not You do not yet realize in a practical form the excessive amount of caution necessary. You still step too hard; let your clothes touch too much brush; your eyes are yet too dull; and you make many mistakes of strategy.

But there is no ground for discouragement. It took me just eleven days, where deer were plenty, too, but very wild, to get sight of my first deer. Humiliating to confess, but I confess for your benefit. The causes were books, dry leaves, still days, and totally erroneous notions derived from pictures, hunting-stories, old hunters' gabble, etc., without any book or friend to help me.

Chapter Eight - The First Sight of Game

By the first shimmer of light from the eastern arch you tread again the oak ridges. Disappointment instead of discouraging you has only spurred your spirits to the prancing point. The woods, too, begin to seem more like home than before, and your eyes take in with swifter and more comprehensive glance the various sights of the forest far quicker and farther than ever before and with only a side glance you detect the tip of the squirrel's bushy tail or his little ears as he peers inquiringly at you through some fork of a tree. Almost without looking you see the ruffed grouse spread his banded fan-like tail and walk over the dead leaves in the heavy thicket along the creek. And far faster and more keenly your eye darts down the long forest aisles and among the dark colonnades of tree-trunks, and sees everything very much more plainly than before. All but the thing you wish to see! All around you are tokens enough of its recent presence, but it seems a kind of spiritual slipperiness that eludes all your senses.

You will now observe all the precautions given you before and wind along and over the ridges, sometimes crossing them directly, sometimes quartering over them, sometimes traveling behind the crest, some- times moving directly upon the top; according to shape of ground, direction of wind, and facilities for quietly moving.

Suddenly your eye rests upon a dim spot of dark gray on a ridge a hundred and fifty yards off. A strange feeling overwhelms you at once, for there is about it a something - an indescribable something - that never would have caught your eye before, but now does most decidedly catch it. But then it does not look in the least like -

Ha! It moves, and in a moment slides slowly out of sight over the ridge.

Why, that must have been a -

Of course. What other thing of that color would be there at this time of day? Its head and legs were out of sight beyond the crest of the ridge, so that you could distinguish nothing that looked much like an animal.

And now what will you do about it? Seeing a deer is by no means getting a shot at it, and getting a shot is often a long way from bagging it. I will leave you to yourself and let you see how naturally you will do the wrong thing.

With stealthy step you cross the hollow directly in line with the spot where the deer disappeared. By the time you get half way to the top of the ridge a faint thump'k'thump comes from the other side. Remembering your experience of yesterday, you dash to the crest and arrive there just in time to see - nothing. You had just a little too far to run; it was up hill also; and the deer needed but a few bounds to disappear in the heavy timber of the flat below.

And how did you lose him? Well, he was feeding slowly along, and was just below where you last saw him when you came to the foot of the ridge. You went quietly enough; that is, about as quietly as anyone could go on such ground. But the ridge was both narrow and low, and it would have been nearly impossible on leaves, and would have been hard enough even on snow, to approach close enough to see him without his hearing your steps. Now the wind would have allowed you to swing around the point of the ridge toward which he was feeding, which would have brought you eighty or ninety yards ahead of him and directly on his course. From that point you could either have shot or have lain and watched his movements, and perhaps have had him feed toward you. Or you might have swung around the other way and have come in behind him. But this course would have been unsafe if the deer were moving at any speed, as it would have brought you in too far behind him, and the deer is such a fast walker that you could not have overtaken him without making too much noise. You might also have waited a while in the flat to advantage. For he either might have appeared on the ridge again or would have had more time to get off the other side or farther along it, so that you could have got in sight of him without his hearing you. As it was, you would have had to get within fifteen or twenty yards of him to see him at all; a thing extremely hard to do even on soft snow.

Four or five more ridges are crossed, and as you are winding along the back of another one there is a sudden flash of white among the dark tree-trunks two hundred yards ahead; another second and it flashes again, but more faintly; another dim flash, and it is gone.

45

There is no need of desponding, however. You are doing finely. You are making progress enough in getting sight of them at all. And never shall you see the time when, in spite of all your care, the white flag will not occasionally wave you such a farewell. You were not to blame; for there are times when a deer will see the hunter first and no amount of skill or caution on his part can prevent it. Still, you might as well allow this escape to intensify your caution about walking quietly, as well as your keenness of vision.

Old Phoebus has his wain hitched up at last; its glowing axle is climbing fast the eastern sky; the tree-tops begin to whisper in the rising breeze. It is time the deer were beginning to move toward their lying-down ground, and we might as well work that way. But let us not go too fast.

Stop! There is one just below the crest of yonder ridge; just in the edge of a little clump of brush; about ten feet to the left of that tall basswood.

You cannot see any deer? Do you not see that dark low thing shaped nearly like a piece of log - right in the edge of the brush?

That is no deer? Well, if you cannot take my word for it, go on and satisfy yourself. Show more of your head and shoulders, of course. Smash a stick or two while twisting your head around for a better view.

As you raise your head for a better view there is a sudden change. Something like the deer of the artist is suddenly standing beside the bush, looking rather small, it is true, but an unmistakable picture-deer, vastly different from what you saw a second ago and very pretty and sculpturesque. It stands just long enough to allow you to think of your rifle; then there is a graceful undulation of white banner over the ridge; and in a second you are again gazing sadly at vacancy.

We are now nearing the old pine-chopping or "slash," but before going into it let us inspect that mass of wind-fallen timber on the right. Swing around to the leeward side, mount a high log and go on through the windfall, moving as far as possible upon tree-trunks and logs.

One third of it is thus passed when there is a sudden crack of brush and over a distant log whirls a curving mass of gray. As you raise your rifle with convulsive jerk, down goes the gray over the log with an upward flirt of a snowy tail. Up it comes again, and curving over the next huge trunk goes plunging out of sight behind it, just as you try to catch a sight with the rifle. Away it goes over log after log, with the white banner flaunting high as the curving gray goes down; in an instant it clears the last log; glimmers for a second on the open ground beyond, and fades in a twinkling over a little rise.

No occasion for desponding now either. You did just right. No one could have seen that deer standing still or lying down in there. The only chance was to "jump" him and take a running shot. And such a hurdle-leaper is one of the hardest things in the world to hit. You actually did better to stand and watch it without shooting at all than you would have done had you fired without seeing your rifle-sight or making any calculations for the deer's up-and-down motion.

And here we are at the slash. Now remember the points about hunting it that you learned the last time.

For nearly an hour you thread the open places, picking your way with care. But this gets tiresome, and you conclude to go to yonder point and sit down a while. A harmless idea enough; but be just as careful in going to it as you have been at any time yet.

No, no. Keep out of those briers. Attempt no short-cuts. Walk around to that ridge on the right and take that, for it is high ground and is not brushy.

You listen, however, to your weary legs and take the short-cut. You finally reach the point, and are about to sit down when your attention is suddenly arrested by three small objects careering away nearly a quarter of a mile off. They look but little larger than rabbits; and their woolly tails bob up and down in much the same manner, as, on a gentle rolling canter, they dissolve in the brush and briers.

Only a doe and two fawns. They were lying just over the point and heard you enjoying the luxury of that short-cut. By going that way you made an unnecessary cracking of brush which you could have avoided by taking this old logging-road that leads to that other ridge. That ridge connects with the one on which the deer were, and is not brushy enough to prevent quiet walking. Thus you would have made no noise and would have been all the time in a position to see anything that might run, instead of being in the brush and briers where you could see nothing. You may sit down now, but spend the time in pondering this moral: Beware of short-cuts in still-hunting.

But deer do not always lie upon the ridges or their points, either in a "slash " or anywhere else. There is some old hunter's talk about "bucks lyin" up on the pints a-hardenin' their horns." But my experience has been that even an old buck at the time his horns are hardening - late in the summer or very early in the fall - is just about as fond of a nice little brushy basin as of the points; especially when the sun is hot and there is little cover on the points. And at this time - when the acorns are falling and the deer's horns are fully hardened - I never could observe that either bucks, does, or fawns had any preference for points, though of course they will often lie on them. Now there, some three hundred yards to the right, is a nice little basin well filled with old logs and grown up with brush, which will probably repay inspection.

You go over to it, and before you get a fair sight of the bottom of it you are startled by a hollow- toned phew long-drawn and penetrating. Instantly there is a crash of brush, the thump of heavy hoofs, a gleam of dark gray among the yielding bushes, a sudden glistening of the sun on sharp-pointed tines, and in a twinkling bursts from the brush into the open ground the stately form of the buck that made those big tracks you saw leading into the "slash." Away he goes, with sleek coat bright and glossy in the morning sun, his shining horns carried well up and his long snowy tail waving up and down. Just as you begin to remember what you came for he wheels around a jutting point and is gone.

And now, why did you forget the lesson you so lately had about short-cuts? It was too much trouble to go a little way around, so you came directly down the wind, perhaps without thinking about it at all. It was also too much trouble to get on the ridge instead of entering the basin so low down as you did. Now if you had made a circuit of three hundred yards, and got upon this ridge to the leeward, you might have still had to take a running shot, but you would have been almost certain to get as close again before starting the buck, and would have seen him three times as long after you did start him. Unless you are more careful you will not only get through that brush instead of around it. nothing but running shots, but will get only very long and bad ones even of those.

Half an hour more brings you in sight of a piece of low ground along a creek. And here a slight movement in some brush some two hundred yards away arrests your eye.

Drop at once out of its sight and see what it is. In a moment two delicate gray ears appear above the brush, followed by the head and slim, graceful neck of a fawn.

Pshaw! Only a fawn! Surely no sportsman ever butchers a little baby-deer.

No; not with the pen. It is always that everlasting "old buck," the biggest, oldest, fattest, and heaviest ever seen. He never weighs under two hundred and fifty pounds, dressed and never flourishes less than seven or eight tines on his horns. Such a number of these fall annually before the unerring quill-shots of our country that I have at times felt inclined, in the interests of natural history, to offer a reward for any really reliable information about the killing of a small doe or a fawn.

The idea that a fawn is necessarily easy to kill is the offspring of an ignorant head. The spotted fawn generally is, and few sportsmen ever kill one if they can see exactly what it is. But when seven or eight months old a fawn can often slip through the fingers of skill and experience in a style so deeply impressive that the older one grows in experience (with the rifle instead of the pen) the more his respect for a fawn increases. Fawns are wilder to-day than full-grown deer were twenty years ago; they grow still wilder with a little hunting; and they are always wild enough when alone and not running with the mother to be highly worthy of the tyro's bullet.

It would not do to shoot from here. It is too far entirely for a sure shot by any one, and a tyro would be sure to miss. Therefore the very first thing you must do is not to be in a hurry. Find out what the fawn is doing; examine all the surroundings; see which is the best way to approach it. But above all things, positively no hurry, for in still-hunting Hurry is the parent of Flurry. There is no occasion for haste, for the fawn will probably not leave that brush at this time of day. It probably has not yet lain down and is about to do so. Or it may have been lying down and has risen to change its bed to the shade, or you know not what at any rate, it is not alarmed, and will probably stay there until afternoon if let alone. It is browsing a little, you see. A deer is very apt to nip a few twigs at any time of the day he happens to be on foot. Every time it nips a bud or two it raises its pretty little head above the bushes and takes a good long look. You must get within at least a hundred yards, and even fifty if you can; for it will be no easy matter to tell where its body is, and the head will be too fine a mark for a beginner.

Slipping backward and going down a little ravine, you reach the low ground without being seen by the fawn, and soon reach the patch of low brush in which you saw it. You take unusual care about every step; you stoop quite low; you felicitate yourself upon your acuteness and caution. Arriving within a hundred yards of where it was, you rise up and take a look; but seeing nothing, you move on twenty yards more and take another look. Nothing in sight yet, and twenty yards more fails to reveal anything.

Twenty yards more are passed, and your heart begins to labor heavily, for the crisis fast approaches. A long look. Nothing stirs. The silence becomes painfully suspicious. A moment more and you reach the edge of the bushes. The bright sun filters through them; the bluejay jangles his discordant notes in the tree above; the raven wheeling on high grates his dismal throat; but of venison there is neither sight nor sound. Going around the bushes, you find on the side toward the creek those marking so refreshing to the soul of the weary hunter whose internal economy has for half an hour been running under the superheated steam of anticipation - fresh tracks of plunging jumps twelve or fifteen feet apart.

I have seen men who would blame the deer for all this and start for home, declaring still-hunting a fraud and vowing vengeance on anyone who ever again mentioned the pestiferous business. I have known others who blamed themselves for it entirely, sat down and meditated the causes of their failure, and arose with increased respect and admiration for the deer, double determination to conquer him and his tricks, and redoubled ardor for the chase. For the first class this book is not written. The Adirondack guide who holds a deer by the tail in the water for his patrons to shoot from the boat with a shotgun, or the owner of the scaffold at some salt-lick, can give such all the information they are likely ever to need or appreciate. But you, for whom this is written, can learn a good lesson here.

You took care to keep the wind in your face; you went quietly enough and slowly enough; you also looked keenly enough. So far very well.

But you forgot two very important things.

1 st. That the deer was standing in brush of almost the height of its head.

2 nd. That a deer in brush can see out of it far better than you can see into it.

In such a position a deer has every advantage of you. Your only chance to see him is to get upon high ground where you can see down into the brush; or wait until he moves; or else approach the brush in such a way that you can get a good running shot in case he starts. Now there is a knoll on the side toward the creek, and it is only sixty yards from where the deer was. If you had made a circuit and got upon it, you would have seen the fawn's neck and head when he raised them. You would also have seen him if he moved. You might have waited there an hour or more with safety, for at this time of day a deer not disturbed will not move far. He might have come out of the brush and

49

browsed around the edges a while, or even have come toward you. At all events, you would have known just what he was doing; and if he had lain down, by approaching from this side you might have had a fair running shot; for the ground on the other side, you see, is rising and open, whereas this is falling and so brushy that you did not even see him when he ran.

On your way homeward in the afternoon you suddenly discover two slim gray sticks just under the trunk of a large fallen tree. A few days ago you would hardly have noticed them, but now you at once see a curious color, shape, and slant about them not shared by common sticks.

But stop do not try to get any closer; that will never do. You are almost too close now. Higher up and farther around, so as to see the other side of the log, is where you want to get. If you go directly toward those logs the owner of the "sticks" will be sure to hear you, or see your legs under the log, before you can possibly see his body. Back out as silently as death, and circling around behind that ridge, go to its top from the back side. That commands a view of the other side of the tree-trunk. If you should start that deer now, you would not get even a running shot; at this time of day he may stand there so long that it will not be advisable to wait for him to move; if he does move, the chances are against his moving into your eye-range, as there are many other big logs close by.

A detour of some two hundred yards brings you to the top of the ridge. You look down at the fallen tree and see nothing. You look several seconds, and yet see nothing. Concluding that you were mistaken or that he is gone, you come over the crest of the ridge. And in a twinkling

"Venison vanisheth down the vale
With bounding hoof and flaunting tail."

You were too impatient. He had moved only a few steps while you were going around, and stood in a thin bush a few steps to the right. You should have thoroughly scanned every spot within fifty yards of the log, and looked for several minutes, instead of several seconds, before showing even your head over the ridge. So important is patience in general that I shall have to reserve it for a special chapter.

You wind your way homeward over the oak ridges, and through the darkening timber see a white hand- kerchief or two beckoning you on, and hear once or twice the sound of bounding hoofs. But you reach home without seeing anything upon which you can catch sight with your rifle. You have seen plenty of deer to-day, but all going, going, going, glimmering through the dream of things that ought to be. Yet somehow you feel a supreme contempt for the exploit of your friend who last year sat by a salt-lick and bagged two in one night with a shot-gun. You feel rich in a far higher and nobler experience, and feel that to him who has within the true spirit of the chase there is far more pleasure in seeing over a ridge or among the darkening trunks a flaunting flag wave a mocking farewell to hope, than in contemplating a gross pile of meat bagged with less skill than is required to wring a chicken's neck on a moonlight night.

And you have learned at last the first steps in what is the most important part of hunting very wild deer, and about the last thing about which the tyro is likely to imagine any difficulty; viz., to get sight of a deer at all.

Chapter Nine - The First Shot at A Deer

We will suppose that several days of blighted hopes have passed over your head; that some days you have seen nothing but tracks and occasional long jumps, and on others only a tail or two glimmering out of sight in the dark depths of timber or over a ridge. We will suppose this because it is most likely to be true, and nothing should be concealed from you. On the contrary, it is far better to know fully the obstacles before you, so that you will know the want of progress is your own fault, and one which you share with all beginners.

We will suppose - what is quite certain to be true if you have any spirit of the chase in you - that these days of disappointment have been days full of profit and rich in experience; that your eye has become keener, more widely ranging and comprehensive in its glance, more familiar with all the features of the forest, detecting instantly shapes and spots before unnoticed, and penetrating thicket and brush which at first appeared almost impenetrable; that your step has become lighter and more elastic, your foot at once feeling a stick beneath it while your eyes are fixed far away; your coat and legs avoiding brush as if instinctively; your ears more keenly alive to every noise, and your whole being worked up into a combination of watchfulness and caution. We will suppose, too, that you have duly studied the lessons you have had, and are getting quite an idea of the kinds of ground on which a deer may be expected to be found at any particular time of day, as well as of those kinds upon which he will probably not be found. With this improvement we will try the woods again.

Already the east is flooded with enough silvery sheen to allow you to see a deer in the woods, and again you are gliding along the acorn ridges. The morning is cool and fresh; there was a fine rain yesterday, and all the leaves and twigs under foot are soft and quiet to the touch; the breeze is strong and fresh, and by walking against it this morning you shall have good prospects of game, you think. Very correct. But relax not an atom of either vigilance or caution on account of these advantages. Mark this well. In still-hunting you have never an advantage to spare. It will do you no harm to retain every one, and you may lose by throwing away a very slight one that you think quite needless.

And what sort of a beast is that on yonder ridge a hundred and fifty yards away, just dimly visible through the cloud of twigs and branches of intervening trees? It can hardly be a deer. It looks small and dark and lacks all that graceful outline of the deer engraved on the lock-plate of your gun. Its head, too, is low down and projecting like that of a long-necked goat, while its nether extremity looks awkwardly angular like that of a cow. It is not a very en-chanting piece of symmetry, and seems lacking in that feature so essential to the regulation deer - a pair of ten-pointed horns. But then it is an animal of some kind and must be inspected. And to tell you the truth, you had better lose no time in inspecting it. For it is walking, and the deer, if this should be one, is a fast walker.

At a glance you see the folly of shooting at a walking mark of such a small size at such a distance. Moreover, there are many twigs and small branches in the way that can easily deflect a ball. You see, too, the impossibility of crossing in time the flat be- tween you and the ridge the deer is on; and very properly doubt the policy of so doing even if you could cross it. But you also notice that it is walking with the wind and along the top of the ridge it is on. You see, too, that some two hundred yards in the same direction the deer is taking, the ridge you are on connects with the one the deer is on.

Quickly and quietly you back off of the ridge you are on, run down along it to where it joins the other, and then going carefully to the top you raise your head with great caution and look down along the other ridge. But you see nothing.

And now beware. You are coming now to the trying point. You have done very well so far, but are now at the point where a little haste often dashes to the ground the cup of success just as it has reached the lip. You want to go ahead. You feel a burning anxiety to see that animal. Your foot is already raised to go ahead.

But stop and consider a moment. Suppose that just at the moment you move ahead the deer should happen to be standing still. Have you forgotten how hard it will then be for you to see him, and how easy it will be for him to see you? Recollect that it is only daylight; that the deer is undoubtedly feed-ing, and is in no haste to move away; and that you have the wind from him to you. If it leaves that ridge at all, it is much more likely to come to this point of junction with another one than it is to cross that flat. That is probably just what it is now doing. At all events, the chances of its doing that or else staying on the ridge are greater than the chances of your moving far along that ridge without being seen by it. Nevertheless you may move out a little farther, be-cause you got here so quickly that the deer is probably little over half way here. But stoop very low; go very carefully; go no farther than is necessary to give you a good view of either hollow in case the deer should cross one of them; and then stop behind a tree, stand upright behind it, and move your head in looking as little and as slowly as possible.

And there you stand while a second seems a minute and a minute seems the grandfather of an hour. How restless your feet become to move on again! But yield not an inch to impatience now. Recollect that there is not one chance in fifty that that deer will retrace his steps; there is not one in five that he will cross either flat, or one in ten that he can do it without your seeing him and getting a tolerably fair shot at him. Remember, too, that there is not one chance in ten of your seeing him first if you move on. That deer is probably within seventy-five yards of you and feeding slowly along the ridge.

If patience ever brings reward, it is to the still-hunter. And here at last comes yours - a piece of dull dark gray slowly moving in some brush forty or fifty yards ahead.

No, no; do not shoot yet. It will surely come closer and make a more distinct mark. But watch it closely, for you have no idea of how easily a deer can slip out of sight even in pretty open brush. So keep your eye on that dark gray while I tell you a little story about a friend of mine, a dilettante sportsman:

Twas on a clear and frosty morn,
When loudly on the air were borne
Those weird and deeply thrilling sounds,
The clanging tones of clamorous hounds.
"How sweet" said he, that music floats
And rolls in wild tumultuous notes;
Now ringing up the mountain's side,
Now waxing, waning, like the tide.
Or swinging loud across the dell
Like Pandemonium's carnival."
Hot bounds his blood in swift career,
When bursts the uproar still more near.
And hope and fear alternate play
With bounding joy and dark dismay.
As louder, nearer, bays the pack,
Cold shivers dance along his back;
From tip to toe his nerves all tingle,
His knee-pans seem almost to jingle.
All o'er his skin hot flashes amble.
And on his head each hair doth scramble;
He feels his heart erratic beat.
He nearly melts with inward heat.
And grasps with quivering hand the gun
As nears the pack in rapid run.
And now there comes an ominous sound
Of hoofs that fiercely spurn the ground.
Close followed by a sudden crash,
As through the brush with headlong dash
There bursts in view a lordly buck.
"Ye gods!" he chattered, "oh, what luck!
But oh! ain't he a splendid sight!
Those spirit-eyes! How wildly bright!
What graceful form! What glossy vest!
What massive neck! What brawny chest!
What proud defiance seem to shed

53

Those antlers o'er his shapely head!
How in the sun they flash and shine
From rugged base to polished tine!
"Phew! " said the buck, with lofty bound
That scattered dirt and leaves around;
Then skipped across the field of view.
Waved with his flag a fond adieu
To his admirer's ravished eye.
Just as the hounds came foaming by.
"But Where's my gun? He's gone! Oh, thunder!
How could I ever make such blunder!
It looked so fine to see him run I quite forgot I had a gun."

Here now is your animal in plain sight. It will pass you on a slanting course about twenty-five yards to your right. If you were an experienced shot you could hit it while moving; but being a novice you had better make it halt so as to be sure of it. Say Mah! plainly and distinctly, but not too loudly.

Presto! what a change I Mah! is about the sound of a deer's bleat. At the sound the awkward-looking thing is resolved, as by the stroke of an enchanter's wand, into all the grace and symmetry of the artist's deer. It stands in the light of the rising sun with sleek and shiny coat, rotund with fatness; its dark eyes are turned inquiringly toward you; its delicate ears are turned forward to catch the slightest sound. It is a fine, full-grown doe, only thirty yards away, and broadside at that. The picture-deer exactly!

The little story has had its intended effect, and has kept off that form of what is called "buck ague."

With hand quite firm you raise the rifle; your eye glances along the sights and sees they are in line with the beamy pelt; with a thrill of delight you press the trigger.

At the crack of the rifle the doe rolls away in billowy flight, her white flag riding like a white-cap each wave of her course, until in a moment it sinks into the sea of timber and brush around you.

Too close. That's all.

How can a thing be too close? Well, a deer nearly always is for the first few shots. It looks too big, makes you feel too sure of it, and prevents your sighting as carefully as you should do. Even an experienced shot occasionally misses a deer in this way. A trifling amount of overconfidence is enough to do it. You did not take a fine enough sight. You flattered yourself that you were cool and saw the sights of the rifle plainly. So you did, after a certain fashion. But you still aimed very much as you would have aimed with a shot-gun at a rabbit, whereas you should have aimed precisely as you would aim to hit a two-inch bull's-eye on a target at that distance. So take this as your first lesson in shooting; namely, a deer at a distance where one can almost hit it with a stone may be missed with a rifle in perfectly cool hands by a very trifling lack of care in aiming.

But after shooting at a deer you should always examine the ground where it stood for blood or hair, and should follow its tracks for some distance, looking for blood or indications of staggering or unsteadiness in its gait. It will generally suffice to follow them to the first place where the deer stops to look back. If no blood shows itself here, you may feel quite certain it is not hurt enough for you to secure unless upon snow; though one mortally wounded may run half a mile or more without showing it even upon snow. On one occasion I found a stale and bloody trail of a deer in snow one afternoon with no hunter's track upon it. I soon tracked it up, and found the deer dead with a bullet-hole through the neck. As the hole corresponded in size with the ball I was then using, and as the deer looked like one I had shot at that morning, I concluded to follow the trail back to where it was shot. Nearly half a mile back from there I came to the place where I had given up the trail in the morning. I had followed it about a quarter of a mile, and it was nearly one third of a mile to where blood first began to spot the snow. Many deer are lost by neglecting a thorough examination of this kind, especially when they are shot with rifles of such small caliber as those in which the American heart most delights.

You spend another hour upon the ridges without seeing anything but the tracks of some more plunging jumps of deer that you have started unseen. As this is a difficulty that you can never entirely overcome, you need not feel very bad about it. No matter how carefully one may hunt, or how keen one's sight may be, a deer will often escape in this way, even when one has the aid of snow to tell nearly where the deer is. The advantage which a deer is often sure to have in being at rest while you are moving, in being on ground where it is impossible for you to walk quietly, in being at one of those turning-points in your course where you must walk down wind for a while, or in being in one of those eddies or cross-currents that carry your scent where you least expect it, will often turn the fortune of the day against you even if you are the very best of hunters.

It is now about time to visit the old " slash" again. Here is a long low creek-bottom covered with black-haw, thorn-apple, wild-plum, and other bushes and scrubby trees amid the heavier timber. And this is the very kind of ground on which a deer will often lounge about an hour or so on his way to the "slash," windfall, or brushy ridges where he will lie down. And often, especially in stormy weather, he will spend the whole day in such a bottom, standing around most of the time in the thickets or openings between or in them and often lying down in them. And when they are not hunted much you will be quite apt to find some deer in such a place at any time of day.

And now stop. There is a dark, dim spot in yonder brush a hundred and fifty yards away. It may be a bit of stump or log, but it is worth investigation. But you cannot go ahead and do so. If it is a deer, it is one at rest; and on ground so level as this you have no chance of getting close enough. But here is a ridge on your left that runs within fifty yards of the suspicious spot. Stoop low and retrace your steps until you can get around behind that ridge without being seen, go about a hundred and fifty yards on the back side of it, then cautiously ascend and stop the instant you catch sight of the flat where the spot is. And remember not to show too much of your head.

All this you do quite well. But when you come to look over the ridge there is nothing to be seen but trees and brush, through which you can see quite distinctly. You have learned, however, that here is a critical point, and that there is great danger in deciding too quickly that there is nothing in sight. You stand some five minutes carefully scanning every spot in sight and studying every bush. And your patience is at last rewarded. For suddenly you see a slight movement and a delicate head nips off some twigs from a bush you were looking directly at a moment ago, and which you then thought you could see entirely through. And now you see the body and the points of a pair of small horns glisten on its head. Astonishing, is it not, to see how quickly the outlines of a deer begin to develop the instant you know it is one? A fine young spike-buck that is. And now do not forget your last shot and what I told you about holding a fine sight.

Bang! goes the rifle. The buck takes two jumps and strikes an attitude a sculptor would envy. He is evidently lost in wonder, and looks about as if in doubt which way to run, or whether in fact there be any occasion to run at all. A rustic youth, perhaps, that has never before heard a rifle; or he may be wild enough, yet be bewildered by the conformation of the ridges, making it impossible for him to tell whence the sound comes.

Bang! goes another shot. The buck runs a few jumps and again stops and looks about half dazed.

Bang! goes another shot from the rifle that now trembles like a leaf in your hand. The buck takes a few more jumps, stops for a second, then disappears in a high rolling wavy line of dark gray and white.

You think you took a good aim that time and were quite cool?

Well, it was a decided improvement upon the last shot. But you were the victim of an error into which the expert often falls - overshooting on a down-hill shot. The tendency to do this is one of the curious things about rifle-shooting on game. Even on a long shot, where one would suppose the natural drop of the ball from the line of sight would overbalance any error of elevation, there is continual danger of it. This is no optical illusion, nor is there any deflection of the lines of light to cause it. It is simply from catching too much of the front sight without knowing it, and from holding too high upon your game because you are looking down upon it. The next time make the front sight the most prominent object of your attention, and get it very low on the animal - not more than one third of the way from the lower edge of the body.

At last you reach the old chopping, and after a long tour among its various beauties are about to return home disappointed again, when, in coming along an old logging-road that leads through a little basin in one corner of the "slash," you are suddenly riveted to the ground by an unexpected apparition. Within twenty-five yards, standing full broadside toward you and looking directly at you, is the great-grandfather of all the big bucks you ever heard or read of. He stands like a statue of glossy fur, with neck as thick as a water-pail, wide-branching, full-tined horns all glistening in the sun, bright staring eyes, and great flaring gray ears turned directly at you. Where he came from or how he got there you know not. You heard nothing move and saw nothing move. He probably rose directly out of his bed, and you may find it beneath him. This is one of those occasional visitations of pure good fortune which may come to the most verdant of bunglers and delude him with the idea that he is a mighty hunter. Even the oldest and wildest of deer is liable once in a while to get out of bed slightly dazed. Perhaps he has fallen into a doze or into one of those reveries that all animals appear to indulge in at times, and the sudden alarm has turned his head a bit.

However he is here, and something must be done; and rather promptly, too. A cold shiver descends like a shower-bath upon you, your hand trembles like an aspen leaf, and the sights tremble all over the body of your target as you raise the rifle. Your previous misses; the necessity of making this last chance for to-day count; and, what is worst of all, the thought of the large amount of toothsome tidbits beneath that shiny fur, - all these make you tremble still more.

Put down the rifle and take a second's breathing- space. Precious as time is, there is a stronger prospect of his standing than of your hitting him in your present state of tremor.

You cannot wait? Go on, then. But shoot at the lower edge of his body, just where the fore-leg appears to join it.

Bang! goes the rifle. The buck gives a sudden start and plunges away through the thickest brush and briers with the speed of a race-horse.

You had another form of "buck ague," a little different from the kind I told you of in the story, but often quite as effective. It is quite common to suppose that the "buck ague" does not trouble one after one or two shots. But it is liable to occur for a long time, and you will have to shoot many a deer and miss many another one before you can shoot steadily. Even then you cannot always do it, for a certain amount of tremor is liable to attack any one on a long or very fine shot, especially when very anxious to get something for a vacant larder. I doubt, too, if any one of fine sensibilities, and who hunts only for the love of hunting, can ever acquire the butcher's coolness when in the imposing presence of noble game. The only remedy for this when excessive is to stop and rest a while whenever you can. But if the game is on foot and alarmed, you have little time for this. You must then shoot with a trembling gun, and your only safety will be to shoot at least six inches lower than you otherwise would. Because you are in such case certain to see twice as much of the front sight as you should see. This will not do, however, on a long shot. There you must wait for your hand to get steady, unless you can get a rest without moving too much in sight of the deer.

But do not give up to despair just yet. Remember the advice about following a deer you have shot at. Did you not notice a convulsive jerk about that buck's manner of getting under way? Did you not notice that instead of the white waving tail you have before seen adorning a glossy rump, it was carried down and close to the body? Did you not notice a plunging heaviness in his gait very different from the airy elasticity you have seen in the gait of others? Did you not see that he tore through brush when there was enough open ground for him to chose, and that he made as much smashing of brush as a wild bull could have made? It will certainly repay you to follow those tracks.

The ground where he stood reveals neither blood nor hair. But never mind; your rifle is small. His shoulders are thick; the ball may not have passed through. Let us take the track, which will be easily followed as long as he keeps on running.

Here is the first jump beyond the bush where he disappeared. But there is no blood. The next one is eight or nine feet beyond - a good sign, for if unhurt he would have cleared twelve or fifteen feet on such a down-hill slope as this. The next one, and the next, and the next, for eight or ten jumps, are all right, but only eight or nine feet apart But the next one is closer, and the hoof-prints in it are wider apart from each other than they were a while ago. Aha! Look at the next. He is staggering as surely as you live. Hold your rifle ready and look well ahead, for it is just possible that he is still on foot; or if he has fallen, he may possibly rise. But he is probably dead.

And now the marks of jumps grow closer together, while the four tracks composing them are wider still.

And now they cease, and the trail becomes a trot, long-plunging and staggering. A few more yards and your buck lies dead against a log he could not get over. He is shot in the shoulder, but nearly a foot above the lower line of his body. Do you see now how you would have fared if you had fired at your own sweet will instead of aiming where I told you?

Chapter Ten - Running Time

Still Hunting is not a system of any special tricks any more than sparring is. The art of self-defense consists in the rapid, almost automatic, application of a very few principles deeply founded in commonsense. Any one knows that a quick blow is better than a slow one; that a straight blow is better than a curving one; that a slight parry that merely turns aside an opponent's blow is quite as effective as one that knocks it aside, and much more easy to make quickly; that dodging a blow is often better than stopping it; that the left hand can strike as hard and quickly as the right, etc. etc. Yet, strangely enough, a man left to himself falls naturally into the clumsy, awkward methods of the rural boxer. And to get him into the most natural, easy, and common-sense way of striking, parrying, etc., requires an immense amount of instruction and drilling. It is the same with still-hunting. The trick part of it amounts to almost nothing. The principles are all natural, founded in common-sense, and simple. You must first learn what they are, and especially what they are not. Then they must be followed until you follow them unconsciously and become a bundle of good habits.

We have now gone through all the leading principles involved in still-hunting in the woods before snow falls. And many of these I have repeated even at the risk of being tedious; for I well know their extreme importance, and how easily one forgets them just at the critical moment. The principals involved in tracking and in hunting open ground will be given farther on, and the same effort made to impress them upon the memory. Any more illustration of plain hunting in the woods before snow would now be too tiresome on account of the repetition of the leading principles we have already seen. Moreover, to follow out in de- tail all the varying scenes of the still-hunt and all the special modifications of general principles rendered necessary from time to time by change of ground, wind, light, actions of the deer, etc., would swell this book to a size that would seal its fate at once. We will therefore pass on to what is known among hunters as the " running-time."

The expressions "rutting-time" and "running-time" are generally used to mean the same thing. But the " running-time" is really only the climax of the "rutting-time."

The "rutting-time" begins at different times in different sections, depending upon climate and elevation. And even in any one place it is difficult to say just when it begins and when it ends. But at periods varying from September to December, inclusive of those months, the does will be in season. And in the North and West this is about the time of the first heavy frosts.

For several weeks before the does are ready the bucks begin to get uneasy. Their necks swell to an unusual thickness, as you noticed in the one you shot yesterday. They keep on foot later in the morning and start out earlier in the afternoon. They roam more widely than before; so much so that it becomes a tedious task to track them unless the track be very fresh and it be quite late in the morning. You have doubtless on your last few hunts noticed places where the ground had been pawed and scraped bare in spots two feet or more in diameter, and that on this bare spot were unmistakable tracks of a big hoof. You saw, too, some bushes that had been bent, twisted, and broken by horns, very different in appearance from the marks you saw some time since of frayed bark on sapling brush, etc., and which was done by the buck rubbing the velvet from his horns late in summer. The brush now looks as if worsted in a fight with a pair of horns. And such is the case.

These signs show the beginning of " running-time." But as yet there is no difference of which you can take advantage.

Though a doe is still occasionally seen in company with a buck, the majori-ty of them now keep away from him. And he spends a large portion of his time traveling about in search of them. This he generally does on a walk and with head well down. At first he does this only early in the morning and late in the evening. But as the season advances his ardor increases, and for ten or twelve days he follows them, often on a half- walk and half-trot, varied at times with a clumsy gallop very different from the graceful canter with which he vacates the vicinity of danger. And at the height of this time he often spends the greater part of the day in this amusement.

During the height of the season it is no uncommon thing for a doe to be pursued by three or four and even more bucks, one after the other. They are not together, but a short distance apart. Generally the biggest one is ahead, and the procession tapers off to a two-year-old or so, keeping a respectful distance in the rear. But sometimes they come together, and then there is a clattering of horns, flashing of greenish- blue eyes, and an elevation of hair that is decidedly entertaining to one who can keep his finger from the trigger long enough to "see it out."

If at the time when a doe is pursued by one or more of these ardents a hunter happens to be upon her course, either before or after she passes, he may be overwhelmed with a perfect avalanche of success before he knows it. A deer running on a gallop is always blind enough to anything ahead of him that does not move. But when thus inflamed with passion the buck is so much so that he often does not care even for a thing that does move a little, and will sometimes charge past or nearly upon the hunter in spite of all bleating, whistling, or any other noise with which the hunter may try to stop him. The havoc wrought in a 'novice's nervous organization by such an onset may well be imagined; and fortunate is he if he has any nerve left by the time the others arrive, which is generally in a very few minutes, or even seconds.

I have myself never seen more than three bucks after one doe, and that but once; but I know several well-authenticated cases of four and five, and one case of seven being killed behind one doe in less than fifteen minutes, so well attested that I feel obliged to believe it.

But all such cases as even four or five are now the rare exception, and one might spend the whole running-time without ever getting on the course of a buck following a doe either in company or alone.

And if you do not thus get on their course you are no better off than if it were not " running-time."

I have seen some very silly stuff in print about the ease with which any blockhead can kill a deer in " running-time." This always comes from the advocates of driving deer with hounds men who generally know nothing of still-hunting, but think it necessary to defend hounding by condemning still-hunting. If one happens on the right runway and does not get flurried when the procession comes, this is true enough. But unless he happens upon the course of a doe, he can do nothing more than at any other time.

It is said " all one has to do is to lie along a runway and shoot."

Now unless deer are extremely plenty the chances of getting on a runway likely to be used that day for such a parade are all against the hunter. And there is absolutely nothing by which the most experienced hunter can decide what runway deer will take at such a time unless he has already seen them in motion.

The habits of deer in forming and traveling in run- ways or paths are peculiar, and vary with localities in a way difficult to reduce to rule. In nearly all countries deer will form runways when the snow gets deep, but by that time they are generally so poor that only the brute will molest them. On bare ground deer will generally form runways in very hilly, rocky, brushy, or swampy ground. But it is equally certain that on such ground they often do not form them.

They also, on some kinds of ground, change their runways so often that when you find one you cannot feel certain that it will be traveled again at all. And they often have so many that you cannot decide whether the next travel upon any one will be to-day or next week. Again, a road made by a small band of deer passing only once over a piece of soft ground may have all the appearance of a runway and yet never again be used. The best thing to do with runways, except for hounding, is to let them entirely alone. One can do an immense amount of aggravating waiting at even the best of them. And if deer are plenty enough to make it worthwhile to watch a runway at all, you can generally do better by keeping in motion, as you have done before "running-time." Though the "rutting-time" is long, the part of it that will be of much aid to the novice is very short; while the ease, advantages, and pleasures of lying by a run-way and taking in a string of bucks are most absurdly exaggerated. Moreover, the does, yearlings, and fawns are just as wild now as at any other time. And even the old buck, though he may be a crazy fool while actually running, yet that same buck, when he cools down and goes off to feed or lie down, is just about as wary and hard to approach as at any other time of year. When the leaves are dry and stiff, or from any cause the woods cannot be traversed quietly, then runway watching may do.

Otherwise the best way to utilize "running-time" for both sport and success is to hunt just about as we did before, but with a slight change of ground. In this way we shall lose no other advantages and retain all the advantages of the " running-time." And it certainly has advantages which can neither be ignored nor despised.

As in your other still-hunting, you must not let the sun tread upon your heels, but should be in the woods early. And you might as well go, as before, directly to the oak ridges, because the does and yearlings and fawns will not neglect eating, as the buck now sometimes does, and they will be found in about the same places as before. Moreover, as a matter of fact, aside from any foolish notions about the superior glory of bagging a big buck, or having a "head" to mount as a "trophy" genuine "vanity of vanities" the does, fawns, and yearlings are apt to be far the best game. A big buck is now far more apt to be an old fool than a fawn ever is to be a young fool, and the adage " No fool to an old fool " never had a truer application than when applied to an ardent buck when running. So that when you kill a fawn of six or eight months old at this time it is a much greater achievement than to kill a buck when after a doe. The bucks, too, at this time are apt to be strong and musky in flavor. Some of them become intolerably so and cannot be eaten. It is a common idea that the removal of the scrotum and penis prevents this. But this is mainly an idea. It may do some good; but the fact is that some bucks, even with thickly swelled necks, are not at all strong flavored, while others are as rank as a muskrat all over, in spite of the instant removal of the genital organs, and this flavor cannot be eliminated in any way so as to make it palatable to any one but a city snob who eats venison for style.

Still, some of the bucks are good, and the younger they are the more apt are they to be good. And to find them you should keep a keen watch around the heads of big ravines and along their dividing ridges; also along creek-bottoms, flats, and hollows where there is some brush, but not too thick. But other ground must not be neglected, and a good watch should be kept everywhere; for a buck is apt to get on the trail of a doe at any point and overtake her anywhere.

If the ground be very broken, the ridges high, and the ravines deep, you will be apt to find runways along the bottoms, up the sides, and around the heads of ravines, especially crossing the dividing ridge be- tween the head of one ravine and that of another running towards it from an opposite direction. You will also find them along or crossing the "divide" be- tween ravines running in the same direction. If you find runways numerous or well traveled, you might as well spend the day in lounging around such places, taking a seat from time to time upon some ridge that commands a good view of both ridges and hollows and their heads. And even where deer do not form runways, if you find them plenty it will be worth while to do the same thing at this time of year. But do not allow any affinity that may spring up between you and a comfortable log to become too lasting, unless there are well-traveled runways and deer are quite plenty.

When moving on a runway look frequently behind you as well as ahead, for a deer is as liable to come from one direction as from another. When you see fresh tracks of the size of a doe's hoof it is well to wait there some time, for a buck may be from five to thirty minutes behind a doe as well as close to her. Should you see the doe and shoot her, or should she escape, remain there fifteen or twenty minutes, keeping a keen watch in the direction from which she came. It by no means follows, though, that a doe has a buck behind her, or that there is more than one buck behind her. Where deer are plenty the chances are the other way. Should you see a buck coming towards you, be in no haste. If you are on the course of the doe, there is no probability of his sheering to either side if you keep still. Let him come directly towards you. If walking, you can generally halt him with a bleat. But if you can shoot well enough, and are cool enough, it is best to halt him with a ball, for there is some little risk of his getting away if you try otherwise to halt him. When you have shot one buck, remove the scrotum and slit him at once in the chest like a hog cutting the throat does not half bleed a deer and then go back a few paces on his course and wait for a successor, etc.

It is better in the long-run to keep slowly moving for the most of the time. And your eye must be as keen as ever. A deer, even when moving, is often very hard to see. They are not only low along the ground, but are very fast and silent walkers. Even after you see one it can slip out of your sight with wonderful ease, and this, too, where it suspects nothing, but its disappearance is entirely accidental. You must remember this in all cases where you once get your eye upon a moving deer, and either try to get closer to it or try to get ahead of it upon its course, so as to wait for it. A very big buck can slip out of sight, horns and all, in brush so thin and low that you would never dream of his escape.

As a rule, the following of tracks in " running-time" is not remunerative. The bucks roam for miles, and the does travel farther than at other times. Still, where you find fresh tracks leading to a " slash," toward the middle of the day it will be well to go there if you have snow to make the tracking easy. And yearlings and fawns you may track as at other times.

Chapter Eleven - Hunting on Snow

The climax of pleasure and generally of skill is reached in tracking up your game so as to get a good shot at it. Many of the best still-hunters will not hunt at all until snow comes, and in the Eastern and Northwestern States the season may be said to commence only "when snow flies," as they say in the woods.

Tracking upon snow and upon bare ground are generically the same, but specifically so different as to require separate treatment. And tracking upon snow being the easiest, we will consider it first.

To follow a deer's track upon snow is so easy a matter that almost any one of any tact at all can do it with a trifling bit of practice in judging of the freshness of the marks and the snow thrown out ahead of the footprints. As we go on we will notice the prominent features of a fresh trail.

Two very natural mistakes are, however, apt to be made by the novice who hunts upon snow:
1st. That a fresh trail is to be followed as a matter of course.
2nd. That he is to follow directly upon it.

The advantage of snow for still-hunting lies not alone in enabling one to locate a deer and come up with him. It lies quite as much in softening the ground and deadening the sound of your steps; in making a background upon which you may the more easily discover your game; in enabling you to speedily ascertain the quantity and quality of the deer about you, the direction they have taken, what they were doing, and how long since they passed, etc. etc. To follow up tracks is often folly. An old buck in " running-time" will often lead you too long a race. A doe may then do the same. If tracks consist of jumps or half-jumps, or half-trot or half-walk and half-jump, it generally shows that the deer are alarmed, especially if there are places where they have stopped and turned around or sideways to look back. It will then be quite useless to follow them except as hereafter directed. If the deer are much hunted by still- hunters, they will be so likely to watch their back track even when lying down that it will be quite vain to keep on the track. Where the ground is very brushy or very level it is rarely advisable to follow a trail unless the deer are very tame or you can use a cow-bell or horse. And where deer are plenty and you are well acquainted with the ground, knowing all the ridges, passes, feeding-places, and lying-down ground, it is often better to let tracks entirely alone and hunt as you have done heretofore to find them on foot at feeding-time, or standing in or around thickets during the day, or lying down. This is the course pursued by many of the best hunters quite as often as tracking. They use the tracks only as a general guide, and depend mainly upon the other advantages of the snow above mentioned.

But whether you follow tracks or not, there are some points ever to be remembered:

1st. That while snow enables you to see a deer much farther as well as more quickly and distinctly than upon bare ground, it also gives the deer precisely the same advantage over you, an advantage which you cannot in heavy timber avoid by all the white clothes and hats you can invent.

2d. That though snow deadens the sharpness or distinctness of sounds, yet dull sounds, like the crushing of dead or rotten sticks beneath the foot, will be conveyed along the ground as well as ever, and perhaps even better if the snow be wet.

3d. That it may make an entirely new noise by grinding or packing under your foot when deep and dry, unless you work your foot into it toe first; or when a little stiff or crusty from thaw or rain, it may make a noise worse than any it hides. And both these new noises being conveyed along the ground, and being unmistakable in their character, will frighten a wild deer farther and more effectually than any other kind of noise. And in no respect must any of the caution to be observed in hunting on bare ground be relaxed.

Not only is it a great pleasure to work up a trail, but where deer are scarce it is often essential to success. And as hunting on snow without tracking does not materially differ from what we have already been over, we will pass at once to tracking.

About all the descriptions of tracking deer that it has ever been my lot to see were nothing but exaggerated rabbit-hunts, such as when a boy I used to take before breakfast on the first " tracking-snow" of the season. They all depict a man sneaking along on the trail until he comes up with the deer, which he knocks over as a matter of course. The deer is bigger than a rabbit; its distance from the hunter is a few yards greater than the distance the rabbit generally is; and a rifle is used instead of a shot-gun. In all else they are par excellence rabbit-hunts. Where deer are very tame, one may sometimes be tracked and bagged almost as easily as a rabbit. But even then it is the rare exception. And where they are wild, the exception is so very rare that it may be thrown entirely out of consideration. In no way can you get so good an idea of what tracking very wild deer is as by seeing what it is not. And in accordance with our plan we will see first what mistakes you will naturally fall into, and how to avoid them.

A light feathery snow of about two inches in depth which fell last evening now covers the ground. And again we tread the woods by the time it is light enough to distinguish a deer. For the earlier we get upon a track the less the distance we shall have to follow it, and the more likely we shall be to find our game on foot instead of lying down where we may have to depend upon a running shot.

Here is a track already. But it will not be best to follow it, as it was made last night soon after the snow ceased falling. Compare it with your own track and see how the snow thrown out ahead of the hole lacks the sparkle of that thrown from your track. You see, too, that the edges of the hole made by the deer's foot do not glisten like the edges of the one you have made. All this is because the crystals of snow have lost their keenness of edge by evaporation a process that takes place in the very driest snow and coldest air. Stoop low and examine the deer's tracks closely, and notice a little fallen snow and a few faint particles of fine dust from the trees in them. This dust is always falling even in the very stillest weather. But you need nothing more reliable than the mere appearance of the snow around the edge and in front of the track. With a few days' practice you can tell a trail five minutes old from one five hours old, even in dry snow. But we will leave this trail, for we shall surely find fresher ones.

Here we come to one that is quite fresh. But the size of the footprints, as well as their distance apart, shows the trail to be that of a large buck. As it is the height of running-time we will let him go.

Ah! Here is what we want a trail of a doe and two fawns. They are going, too, toward the acorn ridges a good place to catch them.

With watchful eye you steal cautiously along the trails. These lead to the acorn ridges, and here they begin to separate. The deer evidently have stopped traveling, and are now straggling about here and there. Your common-sense now tells you that they have probably stopped to feed a bit here and may be very close, perhaps just over the next ridge. Therefore you redouble your caution about noise, and look more keenly than ever at every spot that can possibly be a bit of a deer's coat. All of which is very well.

In a moment or two you reach the top of the first ridge, and a good long look at all the ground in sight shows you no deer. But you find where deer have pawed up the snow for acorns. The trails, too, cross and recross each other here, so that you can follow nothing. And they become mixed, too, with other deer-tracks until you are quite confused. You consider yourself fully equal, however, to this emergency, and resolve to cut the knot by the very simple device of the rabbit- tracker a circle.

This plan is correct enough in itself. But why do it now? If the deer are still on these ridges you need not follow their tracks at all, but look for them just as you would do if the ridges were bare, as in your previous hunts. Your chances of seeing them in that way are quite good enough. And by the amount and variety of tracks you see there are other deer about, and some are probably feeding on the ridges this very minute. Never mind the tracks now, but slip around to the leeward of the breeze that you see is just beginning to sift down a little fine snow from the tree-tops above. Do not lose the advantage of the wind for the sake of following tracks now. You can follow those tracks in two hours as well as you can now; and if the deer have gone away to lie down or lounge, they will then be little farther away than they now are. Keep to the leeward and remain on these ridges at least an hour more.

But your anxiety to follow them is too great, and you start on a circle to find their trail again. In five minutes the circle is completed. Yet your stock of information on the subject of those three deer remains unchanged. You find only confusion worse con- founded, a complete network of trails. You should have made your circle four or five times as large as you did make it.

You see this mistake, and set out upon a much larger circle than before. And while doing this, one of the first things you discover is a series of long jumps down a ridge to the left. Following these back as before advised, to find how you lost that deer, you find that he was feeding just over a ridge only a hundred yards from where you began your first circle, and that by the time that circle was half completed, you with your eyes fixed upon the ground, where they had no business to be, came directly into his sight.

Two hundred yards more of your second circle brings you to another object of peculiar, often painful, interest to anxious hunters two more sets of long jumps where two yearlings have scattered the snow, leaves, and dirt with their plunging hoofs. In the excitement of your circle business you quite over- looked the little matter of wind, and they probably smelt you. Or they may have been stampeded by the running of the other one, for he must have passed somewhere near here. And the running of a deer will nearly always alarm every deer within hearing of the sound of his hoofs. So generally will they take alarm from any other animal.

By the time your circle is nearly completed you find that the doe and two fawns have left the ridges and gone across a flat creek-bottom. This does not, however, prove your circle enterprise a profitable one, for you could easily have discovered this in time without throwing away the prospects you had for a shot at the other three deer.

You follow the trail of the doe and fawns across the creek, where it turns and goes up the creek-bottom some twenty or thirty yards from the creek. Thus far they have been walking along nearly together, and at an ordinary pace. But now the trails are separating and the steps get shorter and more irregular. Here one has wandered off a few rods to one side; here another has stopped at a bush and nibbled a few twigs; there the old one has been traveling rather aimlessly around and through a patch of black-haws. All these signs tell you to be very careful, for they may be within sight at this instant, though they may also have gone on half a mile or more. On the way to lie down deer will often stop an hour or two in such a place to browse and stand around a while. That is what these have been doing, and as it is yet early they may yet be here.

66

Priding yourself upon your caution and acuteness you move quietly along, with rifle ready and eyes piercing every bush far into the distance, for some three hundred yards. There on the other side of a thin patch of wild-plum bushes you find that refreshing sight with which your eyes are already so familiar, the long-jumps. There are three sets of them, and all beautifully long. At first you are inclined to ejaculate; but your chagrin yields at once to wonder, for a glance into the brush shows you that they were all on foot in it when they started. Yet the brush is so thin that you can see plainly all through it, and you recognize the plum-patch as one at which you looked very keenly some two hundred yards back and thought then that you could see distinctly through it.

And you naturally wonder how they got started. Well, when your head first arrived in sight of that brush they were standing in there, two of them browsing, the other looking back in the direction from which they came. You have already been told of what an advantage the animal that is at rest has over the one that is moving. You have also learned that an animal in brush can see out much better than one outside can see in. And I must again remind you that a deer standing still in brush is, even with the aid of snow as a background, one of the hardest things in the world to detect with the eye.

But you cannot comprehend how they could have run without your seeing them at all. If they saw enough, of your head to take the alarm, how could their whole bodies escape your eyes, especially when that bit of brush was the first thing on which your eyes rested when you came in sight of it at all? It is rather a puzzle, it is true; but its only solution is this: a deer's eyes, when watching his back track, are as keen to detect a motion in the woods as are those of the wildest antelope on the plain. Some people who had never hunted very wild deer would doubt this, but as you have an hour or two now of time that is not very precious I will show you how extremely true it is. It will reduce your opinion of yourself considerably below par, but it will reward you well in future, and also give you a good idea of the general futility of following upon the track of a deer that you have started.

Let us follow, then, the trail of these three and see if we can again get sight of them. Do not try to get a shot; be content with even a sight. Go right ahead on the trail and look into the woods as far and as keenly as you can. Nearly half a mile you follow them, the long jumps still continuing. Here they have skipped a high fallen log, and in three places the snow is switched from it by their descending tails. Here one has smashed through a bush, scattering snow and dead branches around, and there another has struck some boggy ground and splashed mud and water around in fine style. But suddenly the jumps slacken to a trot; in a few yards that stops, and you find where they have stopped and huddled up, one standing sideways, the other two turning all the way around. And then the long jumps begin again, still longer now than before.

And yet the ground is all quite open. They stopped behind no brush, no logs, no rising ground, .nothing to hide them from your sight. Yet it is evident

67

that they stopped here and looked back, and that they then started again in sudden alarm. Yet the wind and the distance are such that they could neither have heard nor smelt you. They must therefore have seen you; yet you saw nothing of them, although they were under full headway. Do you think this impossible? Does it seem that the second run must have been only a continuance of the first run? Then by all means follow them to the next place where they stop to look back and see what they do there.

On, on, on, on, nearly half a mile farther go the tracks, as if the deer were in a hurdle-race over the biggest logs to be found. Then they suddenly stop and huddle up; and then as suddenly go on again in jumps as long as ever.

And so you might keep on the livelong day, seeing perhaps two or three times a faint glimpse of dark evanescence among the distant trunks, but seeing nothing long enough to raise the rifle upon, and four fifths of the time seeing not a trace of game at all. And yet all the time it is evident that the deer have each time seen you. And five times out of six such will be your experience with very wild deer, whether they be old bucks or young fawns. The sixth time you may perhaps get a long standing shot or a closer running one in the course of half a day's chase, but neither will be good enough to give you much prospect of hitting.

The principal difference between these and deer that are not very wild is that you will generally get sight of the latter, but rarely until they are running away. And when you do see them standing it will rarely he long enough, nor will they generally be close enough, for anything like a certain shot. This applies to the latter deer only when they have once been started. Deer that are not very wild seldom or never have the trick of watching back upon their track before being started.

You passed a fresh track of a big buck a few moments ago that led toward the slash. He has gone there to rest a bit after his morning travels. You had better try him, for " anybody can kill a buck in running-time." At least that is what they say.

You start off upon his track with much more care than you did upon the trail of the others. But this is only time wasted. The woods here are quite open for several hundred yards, and as far as you can see there are no windfalls, brush-patches, or brushy ridges.

There is no probability that he has stopped anywhere along such ground as this when, if you remember the woods as you should do, the old slash is less than half a mile in the direction the track is leading.

Reaching the slash you find the trail winds over a ridge and down into a little basin. You look very long and carefully into the basin, thoroughly inspecting all the brush it contains. Seeing nothing, you descend and follow the trail across it and up the end of a ridge that juts into it. On the point of this ridge, in a clump of low briers, you find a large, fresh, warm bed, with the well-known long jumps leading away from it.

Now stoop low in this bed and you can still see every step of the way you came for a hundred and fifty or two hundred yards back. While your eyes were intently fixed upon the track he saw you and departed.

Now what was the use in keeping your eyes so much upon the track? Can you not tell well enough about where it is going to be able to go at least fifty yards without looking at it? And if you must look at it, can you not do so with an occasional side glance of the eye that does not take your attention from anything beyond? And where the necessity of treading so constantly in the tracks? And what was the use in going into that basin at all? Could you not just as well have wound around it out of sight behind this ridge to the right? And by so doing could you not have found out whether the buck passed out of the basin, and just where he left it, quite as surely as you could have done by having both eyes and feet half the time in his tracks? Had you done this he would not have seen you so soon; and when he did see you, you would have had a good running shot at him.

Turn off now to one side and keep down along the edge of the " slash" and see if any more deer have come from the timber to lie down in here.

A few moments' walk brings you to the trail of two yearlings. These you follow for quarter of a mile into the "slash," using all your care, skill, eyesight, and caution about noise, moving not over half a mile an hour, working each foot toe first through the snow so as to feel any possible stick or brush that may crack beneath it, easing off any twig that could possibly scratch on your clothes, and looking, looking, looking oh so keenly! You reap at last a common reward of honest, patient toil a sight of two sets of long plunging jumps leading away from two fresh warm beds. The sun smiles sweetly as ever down through the bracing air; the lonely pines are as dignified and solemn as usual; the luxuriant briers embrace your trowsers as fraternally as ever; and the old logs and stumps loom up around you more smiling and bigger than before. But sight or sound of venison there is none, and you are the sole being in a dreary microcosm of snow, brush, briers, stumps, logs, and dead trees.

Chapter Twelve - The Surest Way to Track Deer When Very Wild

Your high opinion of the merits of a " tracking-snow" for deer underwent yesterday a very serious modification. And if you had continued hunting a few days as you did yesterday you might have concluded that snow was no better than bare ground for hunting deer. Your error was a very common and natural one, yet one that you might hunt a long time without even suspecting.

You have already seen how deer, when once started, watch their back track so keenly that you not only stand no chance of getting a shot, but can rarely get even sight of them again. And a single deer can do this just as well as a dozen could. All deer are so nearly alike in this respect that it will rarely avail you to follow tracks of those you have started. But deer that are little hunted, especially when not hunted by tracking, generally pay no more attention to their back track than to any other direction; that is, previous to being alarmed. But when much hunted by tracking they finally drift into a state of chronic suspicion of their back track. Hence they will learn to watch it with as much care before being started as they do after being started; and they will select places to lie down in from which they can see back upon quite a portion of their trail. And this instinct is transmitted by descent until even the fawns will watch back.

I do not mean that all deer, even very wild ones, will always do this, but so many of them will that it is best to hunt on the assumption that all will. The greater includes the less, and you will lose little or nothing by dealing with the very tamest deer as if they were the very wildest. On the contrary, the use of care and skill even in the highest degree will repay you heavily even when hunting the tamest deer that are now to be found.

Let us now try another style of tactics. Here is the trail of a doe and two yearlings that have left the ridges about half an hour ago. They have done feeding and have gone off to lie down. As you al- ready know they may lounge about an hour or two before they go to lie down. And during this hour or two they may go a quarter of a mile only or a full mile, but probably will not go over half a mile.

You are in a part of the woods that is new to you. But never mind that. Glance over the ground as far as you can and see if you cannot get a pretty fair idea of where those deer will go. You know that somewhere on the north is the " slash," and that there are windfalls and brushy ridges to the east. All the better to know this. But let us suppose you have no idea of the " lay of the land " beyond what you can see from here.

Far away in the direction the tracks have gone you can make out the dim outline of a long strip of brush such as generally lines a little creek. Along that creek there is likely to be a flat with more or less brush in it. It was to such ground that your doe and fawns went yesterday. There is plenty of such ground in nearly all woods, and it is a favorite place for deer to while away an hour or two at this time of day.

Such ground, too, is apt to have a ridge on the farther side of it. There was a ridge on the side of the creek-bottom where you started the doe and fawns yesterday, but you never thought of getting behind it. Now the chances are four to one that these deer are going to that creek-bottom, and once there the chances are four to one that they will remain there a while, and in leaving it will go either up or down it for some distance.

Suppose now you let this track entirely alone, strike the creek-bottom some three hundred yards ' below where this trail will probably cross it, go across the bottom and over the ridge beyond. If the deer have gone down the bottom you will cross their track; and if you do not cross any you will have their location partly determined.

70

Now travel along behind the ridge, and out of sight, for some hundred yards or so. Then look carefully over and examine all the ground in sight. Back off and go along behind the crest of the ridge another hundred yards or so and then take another look. You see at once the advantage of this an advantage so great that even the advantage of wind had better be subordinated to it, especially as scent blowing over a ridge is not so apt to reach anything in a valley; at all events, not until you first have a good chance to see the game.

But how do you keep the track all this time? Per- haps they have recrossed the creek.

And suppose they have; is it not probable that they will still continue up the creek-bottom as before? And are not both sides of the creek-bottom in sight of the ridge where you are? And even if it is, in places, quite far, are not your chances of seeing the deer at least as good as if you were directly on the track again, and on low ground too? It is difficult to see how, next to following the track itself, you can do anything more certain to find them than what you are now doing. You know they have not gone below; if they cross the ridge you are on you will meet their track; if they keep on up the creek-bottom you will be on a parallel with them; and if they recross the creek and go in the direction they came from, which is highly improbable, you will only lose a little time in finding it out. And such time will not be important, for such a movement will generally indicate that they have gone to lie down, in which case there is certainly no haste. And no matter what your opinion may be about where they have gone, until you know they are off this ground be in no haste. Let your motto in tracking always be, Positively no haste, except on such kinds of ground as clear open woods, etc., where deer so rarely stop that it does not repay you to lose time.

For three hundred or four hundred yards more you keep behind the ridge, which is sometimes low, sometimes high, sometimes near, and sometimes far from the creek, and sometimes cut with a hollow. Yet you see nothing, though you stop at every seventy or eighty yards and take a good look. The creek-bottom goes on some distance yet, and they are probably still ahead.

Yet wherever it is possible, without too much danger of being seen, to slip in and see if you are still parallel with the track, it is better to do so. And here is a good opportunity to do that very thing, for just ahead of you a little streamlet runs into the creek. Its bottom is low, and its sides are so fringed with brush that you can steal down to the main creek with little danger of being seen.

You reach the main creek and find no tracks. They must then have crossed it. The ridges on the other side are now nearly as close to the creek as those you have just left. Might it not be expedient to get be- hind them instead of going back to the others? Undoubtedly it would be if you can get behind them without being seen, and that you can easily do by going back two hundred or three hundred yards or so. The loss of that much distance amounts to nothing, and you can there cross the track and find its course as well as here.

But stop; not that way. Go back behind your ridge again and retrace your old track. It looks like unnecessary particularity, I admit, but then it takes little time. And take my word for it when I tell you that a fair percentage of your failures in still-hunting comes from leaving in your net a few loose knots^ to tighten which would have cost you only a trifle more of work, care, and time. And mark another thing. While going back do not neglect to look the creek-bottom over again because you have once examined it.

Back you go nearly two hundred yards, looking over the ridge from time to time as before. Over across the creek upon -ground you thoroughly scanned before something catches your eye. It is only a spot about the size of your hat, but in shape it is marvelously like the haunch of a deer that is almost hidden by the upturned butt of a huge fallen tree. The tree has lain there a long time; brush has grown up around it; its trunk and branches alone would hide a dozen deer standing behind it. Therefore be very careful.

Several questions now crowd and jostle each other in your mind.

1st. Is it a deer?

2nd. If so, is it not too small a mark to hit at such a distance (at least a hundred and fifty yards)?

3d. If too far, shall I try to get closer or wait for it to move and present a fuller mark?

4th. Which way shall I go to get closer, directly toward it or go up the creek a way and come down?

5th. If I wait for it to move, may it not move out of my sight as well as into it?

All these are very pertinent, but are easy to answer.

1st. It has the unmistakable outline of a deer's haunch. The shape of the lower part and leg settles that sufficiently to make it worth while to risk a shot. It is very dark in color, but then a deer nearly always looks dark upon a background of snow.

2d. It is too small a mark for a novice to shoot at from this distance. If you raise your sights or hold over it you are very liable to miss it. If you draw a fine sight on it you are liable to miss it or only break a leg. It is a shot which none but a skilled marksman skilled in the field on game can make with certainty even with a rest.

3d. Even if it moves and shows its full body, it will still be too fine a shot for a beginner to make, so you had better get closer.

4th. The farther you can keep from the deers' back track in approaching them the better. The other two are undoubtedly there watching, and may be on this side of the log, and standing up, too, although you do not see them.

5th. It is just as liable to move out of your sight as in it. But then another one is just as liable to move into your sight as remain out of it, as at present.

On the whole, your best chance is to go back to where you came to the creek a while ago, cross it, and, stooping low, swing around in line with any little rise of ground, windfall, or heavy clump of brush, etc., you find between you and the deer, get behind that and wait patiently. For if you try to get close enough to the fallen tree to see the deer, you will be quite apt to see nothing but the flip of their tails as they make off in line with it. And if you wait a while they will be quite certain to move and perhaps come towards you. And if they lie down there, you will then be able to approach much closer than you now can, and get a much better running shot since you would probably have to take one anyhow than you now could.

A very slight change of circumstances would modify all this advice. If you were a good cool shot it would be better perhaps to shoot from where you are; and so it would be better even for a poor shot if he had to approach that tree from the trail-side, or from open ground above. And if there were a ridge near by on the other side it would be better to get behind that. And all these considerations might be changed again by the question of wind. It would be impossible within the limits of a readable book to go through every case of this sort with its modifications. But when you are once familiar with the representative cases or leading conditions, nearly all the modifications will soon suggest themselves. There are of course certain kinds of ground where it is safe to walk on the trail; but wherever you can keep away from it without losing it, it is better to do so.

So far we have had no trouble in keeping the course of the trail. And after you once get well acquainted with a deer's habits about feeding, lounging, and going off to lie down, you will have little trouble in this respect. And you will have far less when you once know the ground well. But sometimes you will have some trouble with it, especially in brushy timber, in heavy pine where deer are apt to meander more in their course. And so during a storm, or in such timber as it is hard to keep your course in, such as heavy pine in a cloudy day. In all such cases you will have to swing in frequently upon the trail, taking advantage of course of any hollows, etc., to do so.

We have also had no trouble this morning to keep out of sight. We shall often find ground where there is little shelter from friendly ridges. As I advised you before, such ground is generally unprofitable to the still-hunter. But if you happen to be on it you will find the advantages of side-tracking very great. The better way there, is to make half-circles, going far away from the trail, then coming down at right angles to it and keeping a most careful watch on both sides, then backing out and swinging around again. You can sometimes see the track at quite a distance, but rarely from a distance that is safe. You had better always depend upon your knowledge of the deer's course and upon occasional coming into the track.

Sometimes a deer will make a circuit before lying down, and then lie down on one side of his main trail. In such case he is almost certain to see you if you are directly upon the trail, as you travel too much in his sight. Whereas if you circle it you may come in upon him from the side that he is not watching. Or if you happen on the other side of the main trail you will perhaps be so far off that he cannot see you, and when you finally miss the trail you may swing around the doubling point and come in upon him from be- hind. At all events, if a deer does play this trick on you, you are in no worse condition than if you were on the trail. And you may be in a much better one.

Where a trail runs toward a heavy windfall into which you can see no better from one side than from the other, you may feel an inclination to keep close to the track because you feel that the deer, if inside the windfall, cannot see you. This is in a measure true.

But he may have stopped just in the edge of it. If he has, you will be quite certain to lose him by a direct approach. Whereas if you circle around and come along the edge he will be much less apt to see you. And if he runs he will probably give you a much better shot by running away from it instead of plunging directly into it, as he would probably otherwise do.

A hunter may picket his horse with a "granny- knot" on his neck and a slip-knot on the stake and may find him fast there in the morning. If he use a bow-line-knot and a clove-hitch he will find him fast if nothing breaks. Yet the two latter knots take no more time or trouble to tie than the other. So there are many cases where it is as easy to follow the very tamest deer away off on one side as directly on the track. On the track may do; but the other way is vastly surer.

How far this plan of side-tracking or circling will avail with antelope I cannot say. But they are such rangers that where it will be worth while to follow their tracks at all too much time would probably be lost by circling. Their eyes are moreover so keen when they are much hunted, and they keep such a constant watch upon every quarter of the horizon, especially when there are many together, that it may be doubted whether anything can be gained by the mere direction of approach.

Chapter Thirteen - Tracking on Bare Ground

In tracking deer upon bare ground a difficulty meets us which is practically unknown in tracking upon snow; namely, recognizing the footprints. On snow one can generally watch the trail with an occasional side glance of the most careless kind, keeping all his attention directed toward catching first sight of the game. But on bare ground not only is keener sight necessary to detect the game, but a large part of the attention so necessary for that purpose has to be diverted toward finding and recognizing the footprints of the trail.

I have read some very weak stuff about the stupendous difficulties of tracking upon bare ground. I have read very able articles by eminent sportsmen in our best magazines in which the tracking of a moose weighing nearly a thousand pounds was depicted as a vast 'and wondrous achievement, the ability to do which was reserved to the gifted Indian and denied to the poor Paleface. There are indeed some people who could not track an elephant through a dew-covered clover-patch; but there is not a backwoods boy of sixteen who ever has to hunt up a lost yearling calf in the woods, not a young vaquero in California who ever followed an animal over the rugged hills, who would not laugh at those articles and declare the author a gosling. The authors of such articles are, however, no such thing, but simply careless writers who allow their admiration of the Indian to run away with their pens. But the effect of all such stuff is bad. It deters from attempting tracking many a one who might easily attain, not great skill, but enough for good sport.

There may be a hereditary tendency in the Indian which makes it more easy for him to learn tracking; but he has also vastly more practice. And herein lies the main secret perfect sight and practice, practice, practice. And with practice the average white man is fully equal to the average Indian. There will be a difference in individuals just as there is in the knack or facility of doing anything, and consequently some Indians will excel some white men. But if the average Indian excels the average white man, it is in what he will do and not in what he can do. He will run all day with nothing to eat, keeping a dog-trot nearly all the time for a single deer. The white man has more regard for the day of reckoning, and will rarely throw away his health or prematurely use up his strength for such a paltry reward as a deer. And just so the Indian will cling to a trail and eventually secure the game when the white man would give it up as involving more patience or work than the game was worth. The Indian hunts for food; when he sets out for it he is bound to have it, and he will continue the chase as long as daylight allows him. Here he undoubtedly excels. And, so far as I am concerned, he is triply welcome to all the glory of this superiority.

Tracking on bare ground is, however, very often difficult, and is never any too easy. On some kinds of ground it is impossible for either white man or Indian to track an animal as light and as small-hoofed as a deer fast enough to be of any avail; and often where it can be done it is too tedious even for the Indian. He rarely tracks a single deer on most kinds of bare ground un- less it is wounded or deer are very scarce. Where a single track goes through heavy timber; where the ground is covered with dry dead leaves or dry dead grass; where it is very dry and hard, or is stony or frozen; where it is thickly covered with brush, dry weeds, canebrake, etc., rare is the hunter, either white or red, who will have patience to follow a track. And often they could not if they would. More often, however, they merely skip such places and. depend upon picking up the trail on better ground; but where the whole or greater part of the ground is of the nature above described, nearly all hunters let the tracks alone, unless they be tracks of a traveling band.

But, on the other hand, there are some kinds of ground on which a deer can be followed with almost as much certainty as on snow, and so fast as to require little patience on the part of the hunter. Such are the bare hilly regions where the ground is not too rocky, and where little or no grass grows and the brush is not too thick. Such is almost all open ground when very wet and not too much covered with dead grass, weeds, etc.; such is most open ground covered with green grass, especially if the dew is on it; such is ground on which wild cattle range, and where the deer often follow the cattle-trails and make runways of their own from one trail to another. On these and various other kinds of ground it often is worthwhile to work up a trail of even a single deer;

but just when and where this will be worthwhile depends so entirely upon the nature of the ground, the size of the deer, the distance it is likely to travel, the age of the track, its direction, the time of day, etc., that it is quite impossible to lay down any useful rule. It is a thing to be decided by the circumstances of each particular case.

But though it may not be worthwhile to track a single deer on bare ground, the case is often quite different when there are several. A band of five or six deer is quite easy to follow, and even a doe and two fawns will keep so close together that where the track of one is extremely faint that of another nearby it is very plain. So long as they keep near together, so that one fills up the dim part of the trail of another, a band is quite easy to track; but when they begin to straggle out and wander here and there they get harder to follow, and, as before, in tracking on snow, it is now best to leave the tracks for a while and look out for the game from behind some ridge. Still it will not always be advisable to follow even a band, if deer are plenty enough without doing so; for though it is easier for you to see some of them, it is also much easier for them to see, or hear, or smell you. So if the ground is very level or brushy, with no good lookout-places or facilities for circling well, or if the wind be wrong, it is often best not to bother even with tracking several deer if others are plenty enough to give you a fair chance elsewhere.

If you only expect to hunt a little at long intervals it will not be worthwhile to study tracking on bare ground, for to acquire sufficient skill to do it rapidly enough, and with certainty enough, requires unquestionably a large amount of practice. But, on the other hand, if you intend to do any considerable amount of still-hunting you should by all means practice it. And to begin this it is not necessary to wait until the necessity arises. The first steps in the art can be learned by practicing on your own trail.

To do this go first upon ground that is soft enough to take the impression of your foot. After walking a hundred yards or so, circle around backward and look for your trail. Then follow it, not with your eyes upon any one track and then shifting to the next one, but with eyes fixed as far away, as possible, and with a gaze that takes in at once twenty-five or thirty feet of the trail. After trying this for a few days you will discover a marked difference in the speed with which your eye catches each footprint, in the distance at which it will catch them, and in the number it will take in at once. On each day look also for the tracks of the preceding day and days before that, until you can no longer find them; and note care- fully the difference in the appearance of freshness, a very important point. When it becomes easy to find and follow your trail on such ground, change to more difficult ground. Unless you live in a large city all this kind of practice may easily be had near home. A cow or horse track, off the road, is also good to practice on. But remember to always try and see as far ahead as possible on the trail. Tracking does not, as some might suppose, consist in picking out each step by a separate search, but in a comprehensive view of the whole ground for several yards ahead.

Sometimes it is necessary to grope one's way from step to step like a child in its primer, as where the trail gets very faint or turns much; but generally the experienced tracker reads several yards of the trail at a glance, just as the fluent reader does words in a book. The gaze is fixed quite as much on the surrounding ground, and the trail appears almost to stand out in relief.

The appearance of a deer's track upon bare ground varies very much, and a trail may in a quarter of a mile run through a dozen or more variations. All appearances may, however, be included under the following heads, and the great majority of tracks you will see will correspond exactly with the description of the class :

1st. Distinct impressions of the whole hoof.

2nd. Faint impressions of only the points of the hoof.

3rd. A slight rim of dirt or dust thrown up by the sharp edge of the hoof.

4th. Slight scrapes upon hard ground, recognizable only by the change of color, being made by a faint grinding of the finest particles of the surface without any impression.

5th. Mere touches or spots showing only a faint change in the shade of the color. There is scarcely any air so dry that the ground during the night will not absorb a trace of moisture. The least disturbance of the top particles of such soil, even without grinding them over each other, will make a difference in the shade of the color, which will be visible under some point of view though invisible from others, depending upon the direction of the light.

6th. Crushing or grinding of the surface of friable rocks, and mere scrapes or scratches on harder rock or frozen ground.

7th. Depressions in moss, grass, dead leaves, etc.

8th. Dead leaves, sticks, etc., kicked or brushed aside or overturned, or broken or bent, etc.

9th. A plain bending or separating of the spears of grass or weeds. This is generally caused by the feet treading down the stalks at the bottom and not as the next (No. 10) is.

10th. A bending of the spears of grass or weeds, etc., by the legs of the passing animal. In this case the bend itself of the spears is hardly noticeable except by the change in the shade of light cast by them. In such case a faint streak of differently shaded color will be found running through the grass or weeds, visible only from some directions.

11th. Change of color from brushing dew, raindrops, or frost from grass, weeds, etc.

12th. Upturning of the under surfaces (generally moist) of stones, leaves, etc.

These twelve classes include about all you will need to study. There are of course some others, but generally so accidental and rare that you had better skip such places and seek the trail farther on, such as the under surface of dry leaves pressed against wet ones beneath but not upturned. It will not be worthwhile to spend time on a trail in looking for such signs.

Where the animal has run or bounded it is of course easy to follow. But this generally shows that you have alarmed it, or that someone else has. You already know your prospects in such v a case. About the only tracks worth following are those where the animal was walking, and these are the very hardest.

I should deem it unnecessary to mention the peculiar shape of a deer's track had I not known the tracks of both hogs and sheep frequently taken for those of a deer. Both hogs and sheep have more round and uneven pointed hoofs than a deer has. A hog, too, spreads his toes out, and a sheep generally does more or less. A deer always keeps his toes tight together except when running, and sometimes when walking on wet and slippery ground. There is once in a great while a deer with spreading toes, and once in a great while a sheep with a foot almost like a deer's foot. But these are too rare to give you any trouble. The feet of an antelope are still sharper, if possible, than those of a deer, though there is often resemblance enough to deceive nearly any one judging by the mere footprints without regard to the nature of the ground, the number of animals, etc. A calf has also a spreading foot and much more rounding toes than those of a deer, as well as a larger hoof. The goat makes a solid track, very uneven in front. The difference in the distance of the step will generally settle most cases of doubt, as a deer has a much longer step than a sheep, hog, or goat. The feet of these animals also drag more in snow than do those of a deer.

When the track runs over ground where it becomes hard to recognize it is best to skip that part and look for it farther on. And this must also be done where you can easily follow it but cannot do so without some danger of alarming the game; as where the trail runs down a hill-side in plain view of the valley or basin in which the game is likely to be, or turns down wind, etc. etc. And where it is necessary to circle the trail when deer watch the back trail, etc. etc., it must be found again in the same way.

In order to do this a knowledge of the deer's habits and movements is indispensable. So is a quick and comprehensive grasp of the features (or " lay of the land ") of the country where you do not already know them. You must know the kind of ground to which a deer is most likely to go at any particular time of day, the length of time he is likely to remain there, how far he is likely to travel, etc. etc., and be quick to see the most advantageous way to approach such places as the game may probably be in, as well as the best and easiest place to regain the trail. All of which will so vary with the locality and the wildness of the deer that little advice can be given about it except generally, as has been already somewhat done and will be continued farther on. And even where the trail is easily followed this kind of knowledge will enable you to make many advantageous flank movements, etc.

The freshness of a track is generally less easy to determine upon bare ground than upon snow, though it can be done with far more certainty than one would suppose. It is indeed often more difficult than it is upon snow to distinguish a track five minutes old from one two or three hours old. And sometimes a difference of several hours cannot be noticed. But it is generally very easy to tell with certainty the track of to-day from that of yesterday.

There are places, however, where sometimes even this can hardly be done, as in coarse dry sand, dry dead weeds and grass where the stalk does not straighten again, but the slant remains and continues to make a different shade of light, etc. etc.

Where dew, frost, or rain-drops have been brushed from grass or weeds the freshness is of course unmistakable. So where wet leaves, stones, etc., have been upturned, if the air is dry the freshness is also easy to determine. The beginner will find little trouble with anything but dry ground, rocky ground, etc.

And here he must learn to note the shade of color in case of mere scrapes, and the smoothness and fineness of the outlines in case of distinct impressions. Where tracks are not deep they are often obliterated in a few days, and this even without any rain or strong wind. There is always more or less moving of ants and birds over them; there is always more or less dust falling from the air, the bushes, etc., and the faintest breeze stirs up more. If they do not in a few days obliterate a track all these things will quickly give it an appearance unmistakably old. The brighter color, too, of any track on dry ground will generally by one night, however dry the air may apparently be, be restored to the color of the ground around it, though the outline, if any, may yet remain distinct. On the dry hills of Southern California I have time and again noticed that tracks that I had followed with ease, and where the imprint of the hoof was perfect, were gone in four or five days, and this where there were no quails trooping over the trail. This same obliteration takes place there with the droppings during the dry season, though this occurs more slowly. They are not merely bleached out, but they disappear. This will sometimes happen in a fortnight or so, though more often it takes months. Where there is rain they will often go sooner. But color and gloss will generally determine their age anywhere.

I have confined myself in this chapter only to very general hints, as nothing will supply the place of practice, and practice will supply all I have omitted. Without practice, and considerable of it, much success in bare tracking is out of the question. It is not half as hard as it is generally represented, but it is still no child's play. As long as you have to grope your way from track to track it will be too slow. You must study the ground until you can see tracks almost stick out from it, and see the line of the trail yards and rods ahead.

The besetting sin of most trackers when upon bare ground is allowing the trail to take too much of their attention. And often while they are looking at the trail the game is looking at them.

Sometimes it may be best to skip the whole of the trail, using its direction only as a general guide; as where you find it leading from a spring toward some brushy basin upon the mountain-side, which is a favorite resort for deer during the day. And sometimes if you find a fresh trail coming down from such a place to a spring, but can find no trail returning, it may even be worthwhile to back-track the incoming trail, as the deer may have returned to the basin by a roundabout way, over ground or through brush where it is too hard to follow them. The size and character of the basin and the quantity of other good lying-down places must determine such questions.

Sometimes you get personally acquainted with a certain deer or set of deer so that you not only know them by sight, but know their tracks at once; know where they will keep, where they will run if started, where they will be to-morrow if started to-day, etc. You come to know them perfectly, but there is always something the matter when you find them. They are too far, or jumping too high, or well, in short you have not yet got them. The tracks of such deer are a pretty sure guide to their whereabouts without adhering to the tracks themselves.

Chapter Fourteen - Still-Hunting on Open Ground

Much of the best deer-hunting now to be found in the western half of the United States is upon ground either quite bare or entirely bare of timber. Not only are many first-rate deer-ranges nearly or totally destitute of timber, but even where there is plenty of timber the deer will sometimes leave it and take the open ground. In summer and early autumn they will often be found on the prairie miles away from timber (though they may go to the timber at night), lying during the day in the long grass of the sloughs and swales, feeding and standing at evening and in the morning along the 'slopes, on the knolls, in the hollows, or moving toward the timber or away from it. The bluffy ground along Western rivers and streams; the brushy ground that often lies between the timber and the prairie; open table-lands cut with ravines; the brushy foot-hills of heavily timbered mountains; barren rocky-looking hills studded with boulders; even bare-looking hills on which you would think at a distant glance nothing could live, all these often afford excellent hunting.

You must not forget that by "open country" I mean country bare only of timber and not clean or clear ground. On such clear ground as antelope generally love the deer will rarely be found. And when the deer does go upon such ground it is generally for only a portion of the day. Antelope will, however, sometimes go upon ground containing considerable brush or scrub timber if it is thin enough to allow them to pass through it without touching it too much, such as the cactus and sage-brush covered parts of plains and deserts. And on such ground the deer may be sometimes found in the company of his handsome cousin. But the open country that is generally worth hunting at all for deer is too brushy for antelope. It is generally covered with brush, long grass, or something from knee-high up to above the height of your head, with plenty of cover in the sloughs, swales, gulches, basins, pockets, and valleys. If cover be wanting on the ridges these sloughs and gulches, etc., must contain it or there will be few or no deer, as the animal will have cover somewhere.

Upon all such ground that is worth hunting at all there is generally far more cover that can completely conceal the body of a deer than there is in such timber as is worth still-hunting. So that ground which, if timbered, would afford very poor still-hunting may, when open, afford very good; the reason of which we shall see as we go on. But to insure such result the open ground should be quite rolling, even more rolling than is necessary to success in timber. Or if it is of the nature of table-land it should be well cut up with brushy gulches, valleys, basins, and pockets, etc. If the ground be too level the deer will have the immense advantage of being in cover that conceals all but part of his head when it is upraised, while the whole upper part of your body is often in his plain view. And his head is often so nearly the color of the brush that it is hard to see, and it will be generally too small a mark to hit if you do see it.

The daily life of a deer in such ground varies little from his life in the woods. He is, however, more apt to lie in valleys and under an occasional tree along an open hill-side than when in the woods, and will often take denser brush to lie down in. But as a rule, deer will move from their feeding and watering ground to higher, rougher, and more brushy ground to lie down on. And much hunting will surely drive them to higher and rougher ground and thicker brush.

Upon such ground deer are much more apt to travel in paths. In the Spanish-American States and Territories there are numerous cattle-trails which deer are quite certain to travel; on which tracking is mere play as long as they keep the trail; and where there are no cattle they are apt to make trails or run-ways of their own up the bottom or along the sides of valleys and across or along the ridge between two valleys. In open ground one can still-hunt often summer and early fall, while in the woods he would have to await the falling of the leaves for good success.

Here, too, water is often much scarcer than in timber, and often the water-holes are the very best places to go to first to find the direction deer have taken. Sometimes this kind of ground will have bush acorns, but if there are none the deer will find food enough in the leaves and twigs of the brush; so that if there is enough green bush in sight you need not allow the question " What is there for them to live on?" to trouble you in the least. But should there be any groves of oaks or other nut or fruit bearing trees, the fruit of which deer love, such groves will be quite sure to concentrate the game when the nuts or fruits are ripe.

Even at the risk of being considered tedious, I have tried to force upon the learner the extreme importance of seeing a deer before he sees the hunter, and the extreme difficulty, in the majority of cases, of doing this. If the learner thinks me tedious, I know not what he will think of experience if he waits for that to force this truth upon him. Now in open ground this importance and this difficulty are not a whit less than in timber. Where deer are very plenty the wider and longer range of view may enable one to see something sooner than in the woods; but where they are only moderately plenty, or at all scarce, it generally becomes, in such open ground as is worth hunting at all, quite as difficult to see them as it is in the woods. And often, as in case of the chaparral deer, it is even more difficult.

To see deer well in open ground involves not only all the care and acuteness of sight necessary in the woods, but needs some special care.

Some natural mistakes are often made by the hunter trained in the woods when he first tries the open ground.

1st. He does not look far enough away.

2nd. He does not look close enough by.

3rd. He forgets that the advantage he has of wide range of vision is enjoyed also by his game.

He is apt to be scanning the ground too much from one hundred to two hundred yards away, and lets a little dark or brown spot of life on a hill-side half or three quarters of a mile away entirely escape his eye. And many a deer standing in brush within fifty yards of him may either stand still and let him pass by, knowing that he does not see him, or he may slip quietly out of it and, with head and tail both down low, vanish down some little ravine like a snake gliding over velvet.

A deer, too, on this kind of ground can see a man almost as far as an antelope can, and often nearly as quickly. And he can here distinguish a man at rest or motionless much quicker than he can in the woods. Hence caution in showing your head over a ridge becomes even more important than it does in the woods.

Some of the advantages that the hunter here has over a deer are very great. Aided by a glass, or even by his naked eye if he takes proper care and hunts when the game is on foot, he can discover a deer before it sees him at a distance so great that there is little danger of immediately alarming it. He can then decide what are his prospects for getting closer, and settle upon the best modes of approach. He can tell what the game is doing, how long it will be likely to remain where it is, which way it will be likely to go, and about where to find it if it shall have moved while he is approaching it. He can calculate its distance better, get a better opportunity for a good rest for a long shot, have a better prospect for several shots, and can see more of the missing balls strikeground, and by their aid correct his errors of elevation, etc. He has also a much better opportunity to head off game that has been started, or get a shot at it by a sudden dash, and to put himself in the path of game that he sees moving anywhere toward him. His prospects, too, for following up game that has been started are often so good that it often rewards his pains, where in the woods certain failure would be the result. But the great advantage, especially for one who has arrived at that period of life when he discovers that work is not an indispensable ingredient of the pleasure of hunting, is in often being able to hunt a vast number of acres with the eye while the body is in a state of blissful repose upon some sunny rock or shady point; the spirits meanwhile being kept in a state of elegant tranquillity by the reflection that just at hand is a saddle for which to exchange that rock when you wish to move on.

On the whole, it may be said that the open ground is generally the best for the lazy hunter and the bungler, and out of an equal number of deer to the square mile much the best for success. On the other hand, the woods give scope to the greater skill and care, and give a deeper satisfaction to him who values game more for the skill required to bag it than as a thing to eat or boast of.

On this kind of ground you will be very apt to be the victim of a new trick. In the woods you found that evanescence was the invariable rule of action with all deer as soon as they discovered you. But you will now meet a deer that will hide or skulk silently away in brush quite as often perhaps as he will try to avoid you by running. All kinds of deer when inhabiting very dense cover learn, as nearly all wild animals do, that skulking out of sight is just as effective as running, and much cheaper. The reason we have so far seen no skulking deer was that in woods open enough for successful still-hunting there is not enough thick cover to hide a deer from a man only a few yards off. But on such open ground as is worth hunting there is generally considerable of such cover, and in many places you cannot get high enough above it to see down into it. This cover a deer knows at once. Hence the same deer that in the woods will start at the faintest crack of a twig two hundred yards away, when he goes to the dense brush on the edge of the timber, the long slough grass of the prairies, or the chaparral of the open hills, may let you walk within ten yards of him without moving. He may be lying down and continue lying perfectly still, as a wild-cat, fox, or coyote often does in cover. He may be feeding and simply drop his head and neck out of sight and stand still. Or he may be running with high elastic bounds, then suddenly, on reaching the right kind of brush, drop into a low sneaking trot, then come to a walk, and then stand still with head down and body motionless. In Southern California deer that will weigh a hundred and fifty pounds can almost sneak out of sight in a potato-patch. Well as I know the trick and their capacity for playing it, I am yet occasionally amazed by seeing them disappear in brush scarcely waist-high. In following up wounded ones in brush not over waist-high I have frequently been unable to catch sight of them, although I could hear them start and run only a few yards ahead. And yet the natural gait of these deer is a bound, or rather bounce, so high that a buck will often throw his whole body, legs and all, clear of brush five or six feet high. This is a trick that there seems no good way of circumventing. Where you know a deer is hiding from you, you may sometimes get on higher ground and see a bit of his jacket; or you may sit down and wait for him to move. But there seems no way to make him stir unless you send a dog in after him. Breaking of brush, slapping of hands, bleating, stone-throwing, etc. etc., will seldom avail. Sometimes giving them your scent will .move them; but when they once get in good brush with the intention of hiding they will rarely move for anything but a dog. Consequently you gain nothing in such ground by making a noise in walking. For you can move nothing that has intended to hide, but may move several deer that would have known nothing of your approach if you had kept still. It is impossible to estimate the proportion of deer that will thus hide, as in most cases we know nothing of them. A deer, too, may hide to-day and let you pass within five yards of him that to-morrow, on ground equally good, will start two hundred yards from you and run a mile without stopping. Nor do deer always confine this trick to dense brush. On tolerably open ground where the only brush consisted of isolated clumps of sumac and other bushes fifteen or twenty feet, or even as many yards, apart I have repeatedly known them lie without moving in these clumps of bushes while I passed all around them in their wind, sight, hearing, etc. A thoroughly trained dog that can be trusted a few yards from your heels is the best thing for such cases, as often you cannot rouse the deer without kicking in the very bush where it happens to be. There is no reason why a well-bred pointer or setter cannot be broken to point deer as well as birds. I broke a fox- hound puppy to do it, and have seen him make as fair a point as ever a dog made on a woodcock, except that he sat up instead of straightening out.

While you must always, in hunting such ground, bear in mind the possibility of deer thus hiding, you must still govern all your actions and movements by the presumption that they will act as you have seen them do in the woods. For this will be the greatest difficulty you will have to meet. The deer that hide may as well be counted out. Your bag must be made up from the number of those that would run away or which you can catch without giving them an opportunity to consider what they will do.

It is still more expedient than in case of timber- deer to hunt these open-country deer during the time of day when they are on foot. For they are a beast of exceeding perversity and scorn all the hundred and one nice places that you select for them to lie in. Moreover, they will, especially when much hunted, lie so much in heavy brush that you can rarely get a good shot if you do start one from his bed. Besides this they are much more apt to skulk if lying down when they hear you than if standing. Nevertheless, when deer are keeping on ground covered only with isolated clumps of high brush, whether on the ridges or in valleys, excellent sport may often be had by jumping them. Especially is this so where one is a good tracker on bare ground, or there is snow enough to track by.

Much more advantage can be taken of the running-time in open ground because a running deer can be seen at so much greater distance. Good speed must, however, be made, if you have any distance to go, to get ahead on the course of a running deer.

On open ground it is quite as essential to distinguish the night beds and tracks from those made by day as it is in timber. For at night a deer is seldom afraid to go anywhere, and will jump the fence of a garden that he will be a mile away from at daybreak.

So, too, noise must be avoided as far as possibly consistent with proper speed. A careless walker will indeed get shots at deer in Open country where in the woods with the same amount of noise he would not get even a sight of them. So even the best of hunters must often make a noise in the brush of open ground. But though, on account of the greater distances of game, etc., in open ground, noise is not so fatal to success as in the woods, it still does no good and may do harm. Where a noisy hunter sees one deer, two slip away without his dreaming of their existence.

The question of wind is sometimes more important and at other times less important than in the woods. A canon, valley, or even a hill may alter the course of the wind that a moment ago you thought you had in your face. And a cafion carries the wind farther and faster than any current in the woods. On ridges, etc., it is of not so much consequence, as the currents of the intermediate valleys will generally keep the scent from crossing from ridge to ridge. The distance, too, at which game may be seen often makes it of less importance than it is in the woods where the distances are less.

The question of sun is here of more importance than anywhere else. And where your game must be seen at very long distances, as on long rolling prairie- or table-land, or long wavy hills without much elevation, everything else should often be sacrificed to it.

The "lay of the land" is here quite as important to learn as it is in the woods. And what is known as "the run of the deer" is even more so, for it is more variable. You must be careful how you decide that there is no game until you have searched not only different kinds of ground, different kinds of brush, but especially different elevations. I have often found fine-looking ground bare of deer, and a mile away found plenty on the same kind of ground. But they were a thousand feet higher up. In the cold nights of fall and winter the elevation often is very important. The belt or stratum of warmest air lies between five hundred and two thousand feet above sea-level, the valleys being very cold as well as the very high land. During the night and during the time deer stand in the morning sun they will be more apt to be found along this belt than anywhere else.

Chapter Fifteen - Deer on Open Ground

Perhaps the most important question in hunting open country is where to walk, on high or low ground. This must not be confounded with the question of where to hunt, on high or low elevations a question, as we have seen, can in general be satisfactorily answered only by an actual inspection of the ground itself as all ground worth hunting must be examined. But having selected the elevation of ground which contains the most game, then arises the question, where shall I walk, on high or low ground?

Very good authority says, " Always keep on high ground." As we have seen, this is nearly always the best plan in the woods. But for open country the advice is bad, because stated without the exceptions, which are fully equal to the rule itself. As watch- towers, as shields behind which to approach your game without it seeing you, ridges and hills are so essential that if there are none you may generally pronounce the ground worthless for still-hunting game at all wild, especially antelope. But it by no means follows that one should do most of his walking on the high ground.

Where the ridges are low and the valleys narrow, it is generally best to keep upon the ridges nearly all of the time, certainly during the time the deer are on foot. And where the ridges are low and the intervening valleys are so narrow that you will not have to take too long shots at anything running from the valley up the opposite ridge, then it is better to remain on the ridges even during such time as the deer are lying down. But when the ridges are high and the valleys broad between them, then it may be folly to hunt upon the ridges at all, even during the time when the deer are on foot.

Two things must determine your choice of elevation for walking:
1st. Where are the most deer keeping, in the valleys or on the ridges?
2nd. From which ground can I the more easily approach and get a shot at them, the high or low?

If the valleys are of any breadth at the bottom say from forty or fifty yards upward and contain good feed or browse, which, as well as water, they will be quite apt to contain, then the greater number of deer, if not much disturbed, will often be found in the valley at all times of the day. Especially will this be the case where the valley is several hundred yards and more in width. So also they may often be found all day in valleys so narrow at the bottom as to be mere ravines, as is often the case in stormy weather.

On the other hand, if the hills are well broken into brushy gulches, basins, and pockets, the deer will be quite likely to prefer them to the valleys, and if much hunted will be quite certain to do so. The warm belt mentioned in the last chapter, and other questions heretofore discussed, will go far to determine this matter, although it cannot be definitely decided in any way; and there will nearly always be some deer in both places, the only question being as to the preponderance.

Suppose now the deer are in the valleys and the hills are high; the deer are on foot and you are on the hills. You see a deer feeding in the valley, but he is at least a hundred yards from the foot of the hill, and the hill is nearly two hundred yards high.

This makes the distance too long for accurate shooting even on a level, and a down-hill shot of that length is the very worst you could have.

You will get closer then, will you? Very good. But you will rarely do it by going down the hill on the valley side. Of all ways to approach a deer the worst is down hill in his sight, unless the hill be such that you can slide yourself down it sitting or lying down. And even that is bad enough. Either deer or antelope can see anything above them about as quickly as they can anything below; at all events, quickly enough. In sneaking down hill you show more of your body than in crawling up hill, make quicker motions, cannot hide behind trees and bushes so well, and cannot stop yourself so quickly when a deer raises his head as when you are going up hill. Another very important point is that a deer on low ground can often notice any motion above him quite as well when his head is down as when it is up. But if you are below him on a hill-side he can rarely notice you when his head is down. Deer cannot, indeed, either smell or hear you so well when you are above them, but the difference is not enough, in case of high hills and long slopes, to outweigh the difference in the advantage they have for seeing you. On the whole, never try to creep down hill upon deer, and especially upon antelope, if you can possibly get a shot in any other way. Your chances are but little better, even when the hill-side is covered with timber, unless there are very thick trunks behind which to move. Going down hill one is apt to think himself unseen because he does not- see the deer. But the deer, meanwhile, sees his legs.

So you conclude, then, that you will go down the back side of the hill and get into the valley in that way. This is well enough; but stop a moment. That valley is some three hundred yards in width at the bottom. It is covered more or less with bushes higher than your head. There are indeed plenty of openings in all directions, the bushes being only scattered clumps. But when you get down there all will look alike. Before you can find your deer he may move or get into cover, and while looking for him you may start another one or two that you have not seen from the hill. So you see that, everything else being right such as the wind, quiet walking, etc. you might about as well have been in the valley at first as to have taken all the trouble to climb this high hill. And such you will find to be the general rule where deer are at all plenty and the low ground is suitable for walking. Of course if the low ground is brushy, and especially if noisy, or if it is too bare of cover to protect you from a deer's eyes, or if you cannot get the wind in your face, you should keep the high ground. And where deer are very scarce the high ground is best, as your chances of seeing one at all are so slender that you need every advantage to see it. In hunting among isolated clumps of thick bushes with good openings between for easy walking and a view of a hundred or a hundred and fifty yards in most directions, one has, even on level ground, a fair chance to catch deer on foot feeding before they see him, This is in fact about the only level ground worth still-hunting at all. And even there the clumps of brush must be thick, and there should be a good breeze in your face. Then the valley will generally be the best place to walk.

So far we have considered deer on foot in the low ground. Its advantages for walking when deer are lying down are often much greater. Unless you have the aid of snow as a background it is almost impossible to see deer lying down in a valley; for if the day be warm the deer will certainly lie in the shade either of a bush or trees, in either of which cases you will have a task to see them if you are on the hills. Moreover, if the hills are high they probably will not start from their beds even if they see you. And if they do start you are at a great disadvantage. You probably will not jump them close enough for any sort of a shot, and they will be almost certain to run across the valley or up or down it all bad shots for one on the hill. On the other hand, if you are in the valley you will be quite certain to start them, and they will be quite apt to give you a fair shot; for a deer running from something in a valley is quite apt to run up hill, and when running up hill a deer is quite apt to stop two or three times in going up, and is almost sure to stop at the top for a final look. If you are on a hill and start a deer, it is because he sees you and knows exactly what you are. He has no more curiosity, and is concerned only about effecting his disappearance. But if you are in the valley and he starts, it is nearly always because he hears you. In such case he does not know certainly what made the noise and has a strong desire to know, to which desire, if not too much hunted, he will be apt to yield.

In a valley, however, the wind is quite certain to be moving one way or the other, and you may have to go around to the head of it and come down it a proceeding that may not be profitable unless you are certain that deer are in there. If a deer escapes you in a valley, you have no chance to get another shot with a quick dash as you often have in the hills; and you are also often deprived of that wide range of vision so essential when deer are scarce. But then you have a full view of the hill-sides, which, even when very bare, steep, or rocky, are often fine places for deer to stand and sun themselves.

But suppose the valley to have broad sloping sides, furrowed with little ravines, sprinkled perhaps with occasional bushes or trees. It may now be best to take the hill-side part of the way up, where you can get a good downward view, and a good forward and upward view along the slope. This will generally be far the best place to walk, for then the deer will be as apt to be on the slopes as in the valley. Especially is this the best place when the main valley splits up into little side-valleys, and these again into smaller ravines and pockets, or when there are little plateaus along the slopes. And even when the hills are quite steep, if the walking be good it is often best to wind into all these small valleys about half-way up the hill. For the wind almost invariably draws into such places from the main valley.

If the deer are in a table-land where the ravines and basins are not too deep and wide then the edges of these will be the best places to walk, and one need rarely go into them unless when the deer are lying down, in which case (unless the ravines are narrow and shallow) your best chance is in them. Not only is bare tracking generally easier on open ground, but much more use can be made of tracks. You can see at a much greater distance the particular kinds of ground which deer are apt to frequent at different times of day. You can see far away the "divides" over or along which trails will be apt to pass, and can take short-cuts to them. When you reach that part of the trail that shows the deer are near at hand, you can sit down and wait for them to show themselves. When you find tracks leading to a certain basin of any size, and see no other ground near it better adapted for lying-down ground, you may feel a certainty that they are there. Not only are the tracks themselves apt to be much more plainly visible than they are in the woods, but you have an immense in- crease in the ease of following tracks by direction. When deer start on a general course, as from a spring, you can tell very nearly where they will pass half a mile away although the trail itself may meander considerably. And where trails are hard to follow, or it becomes necessary to leave the trail often to avoid noise or being seen, or because the deer watch back, or because the trail has reached a place where they may have stopped and you want to get on the highest ground to look, such advantages are immense. A person of quick comprehensive mind for topography will soon use most of these advantages in timber, and in fact they must be used by the successful tracker. But even such a person will find the advantages of the open ground immense.

In hunting open ground you must, quite as much as in the woods, avoid looking for a deer. But spend all your time in looking at spots, patches, shades in brush, dark shadowy spots by the side of bushes, everything gray, yellowish, reddish, brownish, or blackish. Even white spots must not be overlooked, for some varieties of deer show considerable white behind, and all show a little even with tail down. Nothing must be passed by with a careless glance because its shape is not that of a deer. If it has the color of a deer, give it a second and third look no matter what the shape. If it has the shape of the game, give it a second and third look without regard to its color. If you are in any doubt whether a thing be a deer or not and have no glass, either get closer without its seeing you or wait a while and see if it moves. But beware always how you decide that any dubious thing is not a deer. The chances are hundreds to one against any particular spot or shape being a deer. Yet all the danger of error lies in deciding in the negative. The novice is quick to say, "Oh, that's no deer," and pass along. It takes the experienced hunter to say, " I really believe that's a deer." Once in a while a shot may be thrown away upon a rock or stump or shade, but such is a far better course than to be always too prompt with a negative decision. This presupposes due care to see that the object be not a person a mistake no good hunter ever makes unless someone is fool enough to be out hunting with a deer's hide or head, etc.

When the sun is out nothing that shines or glistens should escape your notice. When you are between the sun and the deer, as you should be if possible, there will seldom be any sheen from his coat or horns, though you can see him then much more plainly. But if he is between you and the sun, especially when the sun is near the horizon, a shiny spot where the sun strikes his back may be seen half a mile or more away when the body itself would not be noticed.

So where a buck is standing in brush you may see nothing but two or more glistening points where the sunlight tips his horns, or you may see a faint line of light where it strikes the side of a tine. But do not forget that you may not be in position to see this sheen or glistening appearance, and consequently must not assume that where nothing shines toward the sun there is therefore no deer.

In hunting antelope not only should every white and cinnamon spot as far away as it can be seen be investigated either with a glass or by waiting for its motion or going closer, but even gray and dark spots should receive attention. The head and neck of an antelope lying down are quite hard to see at a distance, none of the white of the body may show at all, and the cinnamon part may cast a far darker shade than you would expect to see.

The habits of deer in open country will be found more variable than the habits of the timber-deer; mainly because the nature and face of the country varies more, as well as the nature, quantity, and accessibility of food, etc. Their habits will generally be varied more by hunting, there being generally a greater variety of cover, etc., in which to spend the day. In some places their daily range will be far greater than in others. Such things must be learned by inquiry from hunters or from careful observation in hunting, and often cannot be learned at all until it is too late to profit by them. But all such things I must pass by, even where I know them, as the general information necessary to be known will demand too much space to allow anything special or local to be stated to any extent.

Chapter Sixteen - A Day in The Table-Lands

Having examined in the abstract still-hunting in open country, let us now consider it in the concrete. We will select for our hunt to-day the mesa, or tableland, that lies along the coast and covers much of the interior of Southern California. I select this because the deer that live on this are essentially open-country deer and not timber-deer happening in the open country. There are various theories here about deer shifting from the lowlands to the mountains and vice versa. But although this is true as to some deer, it is not as to the majority of the deer of the mesas, or table-lands, especially near the coast. Most of these deer remain there the year round, although they are of the same variety as the deer of the mountains. Like all deer they are, however, subject at times to a migratory mania without any apparent cause; but as to the majority of deer it is only at long intervals and without any regularity. This is a variety of the mule-deer, but somewhat smaller and shorter-legged than the mule-deer of the Rocky Mountains. This deer is often called the "black-tail," but Judge Caton, of the Illinois Supreme Court, a naturalist whose opinion is of more value than that of all the hunters in California, says it is a 'variety of the mule-deer, although having a black tail. Its usual gait when alarmed is a perfect ricochet, or bounce, all four feet being grouped close up as it rises and all striking the ground, not one after the other, but all at once, not with a touch as do the feet of the white-tailed or Virginia deer, but with a violent blow that sends the animal three or four feet in air in a twinkling. Though this is a tiresome gait, this deer will hold it with surprising speed for half a mile or even a mile or more. All ground is about alike to these deer, and either up or down hill, across gullies, over rocks, among boulders, through brush, or along steep hill-sides, they can accomplish a hundred per cent more of disappearance per second than any other animal that lives.

90

Owing to the entire absence of persecution in the past and the comparatively small amount to which they are subjected now, these deer are mere block- heads compared with those of the Eastern woods, whose ancestors have been harried until wildness becomes a second nature transmissible to progeny, and whose natural wildness thus acquired has, from the spotted baby-jacket upward, been kept at the finest point of cultivation by the incessant crack of the still- hunter's rifle. Nevertheless they are wild enough by nature to make some care necessary; they become wild surprisingly quick when hunted a little, and even with the tamest of them the most scientific hunting is the most profitable. I shall therefore adhere to my general plan and consider them as if all very wild.

The table-land we shall try today is quite bare in places; in other places it is covered with a dark cedar-like brush from waist-high to as high as your head. Here and there run valleys from fifty to four hundred feet deep. Some are narrow at the bottom; others are two hundred yards or more in width. Some are half a mile long; others are several miles long. All of them have plenty of arms and branches. And the top of the table-land contains numerous little ravines and swales leading into these valleys, and numerous brushy basins and plateaus along their edges caused by washes and slides in years of excessive rain.

The first question is, Where shall we walk, upon the high ground or in the valleys?

We shall have little trouble to decide this question today. For the table-land is in many places too bare to contain any deer. -And this brush that you see is just dense enough to stop all the breeze yet admit most of the sun, so that at this time of year August, a month as good as any for still-hunting here the deer will not remain in it during the day. The deer are now in the valleys and the brushy basins and ravines leading into them. But the greater number are doubtless in the main valleys or their large branches, as they are very little disturbed here. Moreover, this brush is so high and level that we could not see a deer in it unless it were jumping, and we should probably see few in this way, as the greater number would simply skulk.

Then how shall we hunt the valleys? By walking in them or along the edge of the table-land?

If it were no later than eight o'clock I should say keep the edge of the mesa here. For this valley before us is neither wide nor deep, and a hundred and fifty yards will be about the longest shot you would have to make. You can see everything in the valley so much better from the high ground that your chances there would have been best two hours ago. But we have come out too late today; the deer are now lying down in the valleys, and you cannot see them as they are in the shade. You might walk along the edge of the high ground and pass half a dozen lying close in the dark green shade of the sumacs and fusicas in the valley, watching you all the time and knowing that you do not see them. Now if you go down the valley you will be far more apt to start them; for though they will occasionally lie concealed in scattered brush and let you pass near them, the prevailing rule is quite the other way, provided you come close, say fifty or sixty yards. Though they will often lie in a bush and look at you at a hundred or a hundred and fifty yards away, they will seldom let you get as close as they often do in very thick brush.

But even in this wild country there is such a vast number of acres to the deer and such exceedingly liberal measure given for an acre that it will not do to go rambling aimlessly about, trusting to fortune to start a deer. We will therefore go to a water-hole about half a mile down that valley and see if any deer watered there this morning, and, if so, which way they went when they left it. But as there is a chance of some deer being in this end of the valley, and as the wind blows up it from the sea, we will go down it just as carefully as if we knew some deer were in it.

Winding down an old cattle-trail at its upper end we find ourselves in a little valley about a hundred yards wide at the widest points, about half filled with green bushes from four to eight or ten feet high, but containing plenty of open places, and a cattle-trail down the center that allows, quiet and easy walking.

Here, you see, are deer-tracks and "sign" already, but they are yesterday's. Here have been a big buck, a doe, two fawns, and a smaller buck yesterday. Now be careful, for they may be here again to-day. Here, you see, are signs of two or three days ago, showing that they have spent several days here. But that very fact shows that it is just as likely they are not here today, for deer seldom spend over two or three days in exactly the same place. If they have been here that long they are more apt to be in some other part of the valley, half a mile or a mile away, or perhaps in some adjoining valley.

A few minutes' walk brings us to a branch of the main valley which winds out of sight among the hills, and like the main valley is well filled with bright green brush. And here in the main trail we find two tracks of this morning.

They are either does or young bucks, by the track. As we did not see their tracks above here, it is very likely they turned off into this branch. Examination of the ground shows that they have gone into the side valley, and no tracks are visible coming out.

Now, although it involves more work, we had better swing around to the head of the side valley and come down it; for the wind, you see, blows up it, and the most certain way is to go around.

We soon climb the hill, and taking the table-land follow the course of the little valley, keeping out of sight, however, of the bottom of it; for there is no prospect of the game being on foot now, and it has twenty times the chance of seeing us that we have of seeing it, and if it does see us we should probably not get a fair shot. But here and there the highland that forms the edge breaks into a little short gulch or pocket, filled more or less with brush, and into these we cautiously peep as we wind around their heads. Here's one now that is more brushy than usual, and a deer might lie in it without seeing you. Generally it is not necessary to do more than merely show yourself over the edge, or give a snort or bleat like a deer, or even a low whistle. A middling loud "

Phew!" or " Mah!" is the best, as it is more apt to make a deer get up and look instead of running at once.

Five or six of these side gulches are passed without seeing anything, and we reach the head of the main valley. Now let us wind carefully round the head of it and see if they have gone out, for they may have been going to another valley. A careful inspection shows no tracks. The ground is hard and dry, but in most places a track could be seen. Moreover, they would have been almost sure to travel this well-beaten cattle-trail that leads directly out of the head of the valley. They are probably in the valley; and now look out sharp for tracks when we get into it, but keep a good watch ahead. Make an inspection of the ground at the mouth of every side gulch or valley on the side opposite the one we came up.

About two hundred yards below the head of the valley your eye catches a slight scrape on the dry ground. You notice it only by its shade of color, but it is an unmistakable scrape. Just beyond it are two or three more, and in one of them the points of a hoof have raised a faint rim of dry dirt. And, see, they lead, too, right toward a side gulch of consider- able length which terminates some two hundred yards up in a pocket. Follow them a little further, so as to be sure they lead in there, and then back out and swing around over the hill to the head of it; for you see the wind draws in there too. The valley here is not over a hundred and fifty feet deep, so that climbing the hill is soon over, and in a few minutes you are peering over into the pocket. But all is still. You show a little more of your head and shoulders, but nothing moves. Do you see that thick clump of dark green sumac in the bottom? Give a good " Phew!"

Your " Phew!" is followed by an instant smash-crash, bump, bump, bump, and straight up the opposite side of the pocket go two airy creatures of yellowish brown, not running or even jumping, but me rely glancing from the ground like sunbeams from a mirror. You made your "-Phew!" too loud entirely, and you should have kept out of sight while you did it.

Bang! goes your repeater, and the dirt flies from the ground that one's feet have just left. Bang wang bang slang whang! it goes; the dirt flies in every direction around the glossy pelt, as with a regular bump, bump, bump, and all four feet grouped close together, they seem to merely skim the. ground like birds. But faster than you can send the hissing lead they clear the hill-side, and with a faint bump, bump, bump, and a dissolving view of shining white buttocks, they fade over its crest into the brush beyond.

It is not quite so easy as it would appear to be to hit such vibratory beauty as that. They are a different institution from the deer you have heretofore seen, and are the hardest animal of their size to hit with the rifle when running.

At the water-hole we find a few old-looking cattle- tracks in the edge and a few faint symptoms of old deer-tracks. But be not too hasty. Do you not see that all the ground for yards around has been run over by myriads of quails? A dozen deer could have watered at that spring this morning, yet the ground might now show no sign of them. Let us circle around it fifty or a hundred yards or more away, examining carefully the sides and bottom of this branch valley that leads in here from one side. This branch runs toward another valley nearly parallel with this. That one contains no water, and even if it did deer would be quite likely to travel from one to the other. In so traveling they are quite certain to go up a gulch or cañon like this branch if it leads in that direction.

There is a bright-looking spot of pretty fresh dirt along the water-course at the bottom of the gulch where something has broken down the dirt along its edge. It seems to have been done by a hoof, and done, too, this morning. A few yards farther on, plain as the stamp of a die upon lead, appears the track of a three-year-old buck, the smaller track of a two-year-old or a doe we cannot tell which and the track of a yearling or two. They are marching in Indian file right up the center of the gulch on one side of the dry sandy water-course in the center, occasion- ally crossing it, but generally keeping pretty close to it.

Now you will notice there is little of the heavy bright green sumac or other shady bushes in this gulch. It is also narrow at the bottom, is exceedingly warm, and does not look very inviting as a place for deer to lie down in during the heat of the day. Moreover, deer when at all wild are not apt to lie down very near water, but go half a mile or a mile away. Therefore it is highly probable that they are not in this gulch at all. We can therefore climb up to the top and walk along the level ground to the head of this gulch feeling an almost positive assurance that we shall find the tracks of our deer emerging upon the table-land at the head of it. But on the way let us not forget that the deer delights in abusing the confidence of the hunter. Therefore, since it will be just as easy to take on our way an occasional peep over into the gulch, let us do so. If the deer are still on foot, as they may be, lounging slowly along, it being not yet very warm, we shall be quite apt to see them. And if we find no tracks coming out of the head of the gulch, we shall then know that they have been perverse enough to lie down in there. And we can then go down it with the wind in our faces, and start them in such a way as to get a pretty fair shot.

We reach the head of the gulch, having seen nothing on the way, and there find no tracks. But wait. Do not start into the gulch too soon, on the assumption that the deer are lying in there. I did not tell you that the deer would emerge at the extreme point of it. There are three or four little ravines on each side, and some nice little ridges too, by which they could have walked out. Examine the ground for a hundred yards on each side, going back several yards into the brush; and look with great care, for all may not now be traveling together.

On the other side, some fifty yards below the extreme point of the gulch, you find quite a trail leading out of a little ravine. "Just like a sheep-trail " you will probably report it when you go home, giving an ignorant person to believe there were forty or fifty deer using it. But the whole has been done by these four deer.

And now another question arises. Here are tracks running both ways and both look equally fresh. Have the deer come this way and returned, or have they gone that way first and returned this way?

If there were no water in the question this might perplex you a moment. But as the tracks are evidently made by the same deer whose tracks we saw at the mouth of the gulch, and as one set of tracks leads to- ward the water and the other set leads away from it, there can be little doubt which course is the most likely to be the one they last went. But to be sure follow the trail un- til you find where one has stepped in one of the earlier tracks.

This last way is of course sure where you find such a place. But deer may return by the side of their told tracks. And several may even walk some dis- tance in a trail without stepping on an old track at all, or, at all events, in a place where the dirt is soft enough to plainly show which is the upper track. In such case, if you think it worthwhile to follow the trail and know nothing about the watering or feeding places or anything else likely to determine the matter, observe the following rules:

1st. The tracks leading toward the highest ground are likely to be the fresh- est.

2nd. So are the tracks that wander and straggle the most from the main trail.

3rd. So are the tracks leading toward the most brushy ground if the others lead toward pretty open ground.

4th. So are the tracks leading away from where there is the most travel, noise, or disturbance to a place more quiet and retired.

In nearly all such cases the first set of tracks is made in the night or early in the morning, and the other is the returning track. If you can apply none of these rules, then take the track that gives you the wind in your face. And if there is no wind, take the sun on your back.

At all events, we will follow here the trail that goes away from water. And we may follow it quite fast for some distance; for yonder in its direction are the headlands of another valley; in this dark thin brush through which the trail now leads there is little prospect of the deer stopping at this time of day; besides, it is plain they are making for yonder valley, and if so they will not be apt to stop at all in this stuff.

A quarter of a mile or more the trail leads over the hard dry ground of the table-land, winding through the most open places of the brush, showing that the deer loves good open walking for traveling purposes as well as he does the thickest brush for hiding; and this although the thickest brush is no obsta- cle to him when he is a hurry. The trail is in places almost invisible, but you can still keep its general course.

The bare hard pavement-like stony concrete shows a broad line, of a trifle more bareness, if possible; the little fine hard mossy substance that covers much of the ground shows a broad line a trifle grayer than the rest; and where streaks of softer ground are occasion- ally wet a light scrape or rim of fine dust raised by a sharp-edged hoof meets the eye.

The head of the other valley is reached, and the trail descends into that. This valley is at least three hundred yards wide from edge to edge; the deer are doubtless lying down; the wind blows up the valley; there is no room for doubt as to the best place to walk.

Down into the valley you go, and find the trail winding into another old cattle-trail that leads down the valley. For a quarter of a mile the deer have kept the cattle-trail; the tracking has been easy; your nerves have been on a constant strain. But now comes the tug of war. The deer are leaving the cattle-trail. First one of them wanders off to one side. Then another leaves it; a few yards more one straggles off on the other side. Then that one crosses over the trail, and the last one also leaves it. And now you realize that the decisive hour has arrived.

Probably it has arrived. Possibly it has not. Those deer may in that way wander on for quarter of a mile yet. But still you must prepare to see them at any moment.

And now what is the most important thing to attend to? Obviously to be in the best position to shoot. Out then from behind those thick bushes where you can see nothing. Get on the side toward the sun, so that you will be more likely to get a shot the other way instead of having it flash into your eyes and along your rifle-sight as the deer run up hill perhaps directly toward it. Get on the rising ground along the edge of the hill where you can see something.

Not an instant too soon are you. For as you reach the rising ground and show your head and shoulders a yard or two higher there is a sudden hollow-toned "Phew!" a smash and crash of brush, a' k-bump-bump- bump-bump of hoofs on the hard ground, and about fifty yards ahead you see two shining curves of brown capped by white undulating through the brush.

Bang! goes your rifle, and the bullet hisses clear over one of the curves and, glancing from the ground beyond, goes whizzing away on high. Almost as quickly the curves disappear behind some bush; you catch sight at the same time of two other deer with heads down disappearing on a trot in a brushy gulch on the other side of the valley; the first two reappear with an occasional whirl of glossy brown above the brush down the valley, while your bullets whiz spitefully far above them.

You have already learned the folly of going after a deer when once started. This rule generally, though not always, holds good with these deer. But that place where those two disappeared on a trot looks like a pocket or basin containing thick brush. Those two that went in there acted as if they would skulk if they had a good opportunity. Just for curiosity follow them in there; and do so as fast as you can go.

Arriving there you find it a sort of deep pocket with steep brushy sides about seventy-five yards across, well filled in the bottom with brush five or six feet high such as we saw on the level ground above, but much denser.

You see no motion or anything that looks like a deer, and hear no sound. You snort like a deer, bleat like a deer, whistle, clap your hands, and finally yell. But nothing moves. A liberal shower of stones into different parts of the bush is equally futile. But from the way these two ran off and the fact that you got here so quickly without seeing them go out it is probable that they are standing hidden within fifty yards of you, or else are sneaking out through the heaviest brush that runs through the center. Take that old trail that winds up one side of the basin and go up until you can see down into the brush.

You follow the trail all the way to the top of the basin, and then walk all the way around it on the edge of the high ground. And still you see and hear nothing. But be not too hasty to decide that there is nothing there. If they went out so quickly that you could not see them after running here so fast, then it is certain that they went out on a fast gait, either a run or a trot. In either case the tracks will show plainly anywhere along the edge of the level ground.

Go then around the edge and look for tracks. If you find none, then you know the deer are hiding in that brush. In such case you have an excellent opportunity to try one of the surest ways to outgeneral the skulking deer to get on a commanding point of view and sit him out. He cannot stand it a great while. When all is quiet for half an hour or so often a much less time will suffice the skulking deer gets uneasy. He must move a little. And when you are well above him you can then hardly fail to see him.

But I did not tell you to lose sight of the brush while looking for those tracks. Can you not watch both at once? You must have more ubiquitous eyes than you now exhibit if you expect much success as a still- hunter. Look down there where that little cut at the bottom of the basin branches off from the main gully at the bottom. Do you not see there a yellowish tinge of something in the brush? Explore it at once with a bullet. Why do you hesitate? It cannot be a man or any domestic animal. The loss of a bullet is nothing. The noise will probably not start the skulkers; and even if it should, what could you wish that would be better?

And now it is gone. So it was a deer after all. And the fear of losing a bullet has cost you a deer.

But run quickly to that point that juts out into the basin near its mouth and shoot at the first brown, yellow, white, or gray spot that moves in the brush.

You get there and look long and keenly, but see nothing. Despair begins to settle upon you, when suddenly you catch sight of a small white spot with a small point of black in the center just disappearing in the bush over the other edge of the basin where you were a few moments ago. It must have slipped up that ravine yonder where the brush appears scarce four feet high. And yet you saw it not. A second or two more and you would not have seen it at all. And even now you see no head, no legs, no body; only a small target, and that fast fading in the brush upon the level ground.

How brightly gleams the sun upon the front sight of your rifle as it comes up! And what a thrill of satisfaction you feel as you see it glimmer in bright relief full upon the center of the fading white! You pull the trigger, but no sound of striking bullet comes back. You go and look, but there is no sign of stumbling, plunging, or jumping. The deer has evidently walked on quite unconcerned.

97

You shot toward the sun; that is all. You must be careful how you see your front sight too plainly when the sun is directly in your eyes; a point we will consider again.

But what about the other one? Did it go off with this one?

Perhaps it did. Examine the track and see.

You follow the track a few yards in the course it has taken, but observe no sign of more than one deer. Turning backward toward the basin, you catch sight of a deer some two hundred yards away gayly bounding up the main valley near where you first started the four.

You naturally wonder if that could not possibly be the other deer that was hiding. But you might better wonder if it could possibly be any other one, so close to where you first started them, and in full bound too. I did not tell you to lose sight of the basin while looking for the other one's track. You could have found it just as well by looking down the side of the basin as by following it away into the brush where you could not see what was going on in the basin. There is no use of sitting down now. There is no probability that there is anything left to sit out. But as it lies in your way back and will cost you neither time nor trouble, you may look at the mouth of the pocket. Ten to one, you will now find the tracks of a deer running out of it. In the future be careful how you trifle with the skulking deer.

Chapter Seventeen - Another Kind of Open Ground

The ground now breaks into a range of hills which in the Eastern States would be called " mountains."

There are three or four peaks twelve hundred to fifteen hundred feet high from which the land descends in smaller hills and slopes for three quarters of a mile or so, forming numerous gulche^, little ravines, basins, and a few small plateaus. Scarcely a single tree is in sight, but all the side of the hills is more or less covered with brush. This brush is in most places not over waist-high, and is quite thin enough for comfortable walking. But in some places, as in and around the heads of ravines, the brush is denser and often higher than one's head. Many of the basins and plateaus, as well as some of the lower ridges, are more or less covered with large clumps of scattered bushes, luxuriant and green. On the whole, it is excellent-looking ground for deer to live on, for the hunter to get sight of them and to get a shot at them.

There appears, however, one difficulty; and as it is one we shall frequently meet on open ground, especially in all those States and Territories where there is no rain during a large part of the summer or autumn, we will consider it now.

Although the brush is in most places thin enough for comfortable walking, yet it is too thick to walk through without touching it. Much of it is dry and brittle, and cracks and snaps at the least touch. The ground, too, is more or less carpeted with sun- dried grass and flowers of various kinds that crackle under the lightest tread of the softest moccasins. With the utmost care you can use you still make such a noise that in the woods where we began hunting you would see not a tail the live-long day.

It would indeed be useless to hunt such noisy ground as this in the woods. The best still-hunters of the Eastern woods will almost invariably refuse to hunt when, as they say, " the woods are too noisy." We have already seen one reason why your noise is not so apt to alarm deer on open ground the greater distances, more wind, and the absence of trees. But beyond all these it is evident that these deer do not start from noise as quickly as timber-deer do. That is, all do not. If they did, it would be impossible to get many close shots on such open ground as is brushy enough to contain many deer. The hunter soon finds this out, and hence is apt to conclude that since he cannot go quietly anyhow, and as the deer do not mind noise, there is no use in trying to walk quietly. Once in a while we meet a man foolish enough to think that the more noise he makes the better, as if the deer needed flushing like quail.

All this proceeds from hasty reasoning from carelessly gathered premises. While it is true that many of the deer do not run from a noise that would send a timber-deer flying before you got sight of him at all and here I refer not to the skulkers, but to those that intend .to run but wait a while to see what makes the noise it is equally true that many others do run at the slightest snap of a twig, just as the timber-deer does.

The proper way to hunt here is to avoid noise as much as you can by selecting trails, easing off brush with your hands, going around it, crawling through it, etc., but never to assume that there is nothing just ahead of you because you have just had to make a noise in tearing through some brush that you could not get around. In short, make no noise; but if you must make some, do not be concerned about it, but go on the same as if you had made none at all.

And now another question perplexes you; viz., how high up the side of this range of hills to walk?

A common mistake in hunting such ground is going too high up. Although you will find some tracks and droppings nearly up to the top of those peaks, yet the deer are rarely there in the daytime. Most of those tracks are made by deer crossing the top to the other side, but in no particular haste about getting over. It will rarely be worth while to hunt there, and it is also too far away to command a view of the lower slopes and foot-hills. This applies, however, only to such ranges as are narrow at the top. If they are broad-topped and contain plateaus, basins, etc., on the top, then the top may be the best place.

If deer are not at all disturbed, the lowest foot-hills and ravines of such hills as these will contain about as many deer as any part of them. But if disturbed by hunters, herdsmen, or sheep, etc., they will go higher. As a rule, the middle tier of the hills is the best to hunt; as it is not only apt to contain as many deer as any part, but commands a good view of the upper and lower slopes and ravines. But what means that motion in yonder bush, in that little basin about three hundred yards away and a hundred feet or so lower than we are? There is yet no wind to cause it so to move, and a bird could hardly give it such a jerking motion. A deer nipping twigs from it could, however, give it just such a motion. Move gently over to this side of that next ridge and follow it out to its point. From there you can almost see the other side of the bush. Take an occasional look over the ridge as you go, but be very careful how you do it.

Reaching the point, you discover on the farther side of the bush a little spot of white set in a slight framework of brown, with something like the taper of a brownish-gray leg just below it. In the center of the white is a stubby little black and white tail that gives a highly complacent wiggle. Very much the same kind of a target as that you shot at on our last hunt.

Sit down and keep cool a moment. Then take an inspection of the ground and decide upon the best means to get nearer to the deer. It suspects nothing as yet, and is not going to run. At this time of day about sunrise it will probably stay there several minutes. At all events, your chances of getting within a hundred yards of it are greater than your chances of making a killing shot from here; for both the ground and wind are favorable for a close approach. On such ground as this you must make a mortal shot and not break a leg or lightly cripple such game. Once wounded, a few seconds will carry it into that dense dark chapparal you see beyond there so heavily robing the mountain's breast and shoulders. And once there it is forever lost to you unless you have a very good dog; and even if you have a dog you may still lose the deer or have a heavy task to get it out.

Do you not see a cattle-trail winding up the side of the next ravine? It leads directly to that little basin in which the deer is. Go down this point out of sight, take that trail, on which you can walk quietly, and follow it to the edge of the basin.

You soon reach the trail, and behold! there are tracks in it of four or five deer going both ways. Lose no time, though, in examining them. They are all about equally fresh; there is undoubtedly water in that deep gulch far below; the deer you just saw is undoubtedly one of those that made these tracks; that is the up-hill direction, too; you know the rest.

You speedily conclude that they have been going to water, and that the return trail is the freshest. So going swiftly and silently along the trail you reach the edge of the basin. Peering cautiously over the edge you see nothing.. You take a step or two forward, and suddenly from half a dozen different directions comes a medley of crashing brush and bump, bump, bump, bump of hoofs. A few brown hides glimmer for a moment above the brush in glossy curves surmounted by white rumps, and vanish amid a storm of random shots from your repeater.

The same old mistake you made so often in the woods. How often must I warn you about showing yourself too quickly; about thinking you can see everything because the brush is not very heavy; against deciding too hastily that there is nothing in sight. There were five deer there; you saw only one of them at first; yet all the rest were there browsing also; and yet you see the brush is neither thick nor high. Suppose now you had stood back for a few moments with none of your head in sight lower than your eyes, You could not only have seen anything if it should try to leave the basin, but would undoubtedly have seen in a minute or two more the deer that you saw first. It had only turned a little so as to conceal the white of its buttocks and cast a different shade of color from its side. And you might easily have seen that big buck that stood by a bush a few yards farther on. Remember now that deer are just about as hard to see in such a place as they are in the woods, and do not throw away another such opportunity just by a trifle too much haste to get a better view.

And now we must seek another deer or set of deer. For it would be quite useless to follow these into that chapparal whither they have gone so rapidly bounding. Remember that even here, where there is neither house nor ranch in sight, though you can see many a mile around, deer are not found in every bush. In this whole range of hills, some three miles long, there are probably not over twenty. But that is enough to make fair sport if you are careful and know how to manage them. Move along, but keep as near this elevation as you can. Stop at every good point of observation and after making a thorough search with the naked eye, especially of the ground near to you, take your glass and sweep carefully the lower, higher, and farther ground.

Nearly half a mile beyond where we saw the last deer is a comfortable rock on a high point commanding an extensive view of slopes, ridges, ravines, etc. Let us take a seat and spend ten or fifteen minutes. Yes; call it laziness if you choose, we will not dispute about terms; but we will nevertheless sit. Now search all the hill-sides, slopes, etc., in sight. Give first a general look over the whole with your naked eye; then run over it in detail with the glass. Look especially in the brush of sunny hill-sides; look around all scattering bushes; look in the bottoms of all ravines, etc.; look on the tops of all ridges. Look as if you were looking not for deer but for hares, for rabbits, for rats, even for mice.

Five hundred yards away, and some three hundred feet lower than where you are, you notice a small spot of shiny gray in some bushes. Watch it closely. It may be the sun on a deer's coat, for some of the deer are already laying aside the yellowish-brown coat of summer and putting on the gray of autumn.

Ah ha! It moves a little. And now ahead comes up from behind a bush and takes a long and careful look: and the sun glistens on some polished horns upon the head of a four-year old buck.

Now remember, there is positively no haste, for he does not suspect anything. Show nothing below your head; keep that still; and wait long enough to find out what he intends doing.

He takes a few steps; nibbles a few leaves from 3, bush; then stands a minute or two and wiggles his tail. He then scratches his head with one hind foot; takes another nibble from a bush; and then stands still a moment.

Wait just a moment more before deciding what to do. If he is going to remain there, there is no immediate haste. You may be quite certain he will not descend any lower at this time of day, for it is nearly eight o'clock. And it is highly probable that he intends coming higher up, for there is hardly cover enough where he is to make a good lying-place for as warm a day as to-day will be.

And now he starts. Slowly indeed, but, do you see? upon a long stride, a sort of a stalk of extreme dignity. And now he takes the side of the ravine upon something looking like a trail.

Now is your time for expedition. Out of here by the back way in a twinkling. For do you not see that that ravine runs up to yonder little brushy plateau? He is undoubtedly going there, and will keep the side of the ravine he is on or go up and take the ridge. You must get to the head of the ravine before he does; and keep out of sight while doing it.

Backing out of your present position, you slip along the rear side of the ridge you are on and run along it to where it joins the main body of the mountain. And there, thanks to the old Spanish cattle, is a good trail winding directly toward the plateau toward which the buck is going. With head low down and body bent so as to keep below the brush, you reach the plateau with a short run. Then slowly raising your head you take a look for your game, and in a moment you see it moving deliberately up the side of the ridge some two hundred yards away.

No, no. Do not shoot. A deer walking at that distance, especially on a course both rising and slanting, is entirely too hard a shot for even an old hand to take unless compelled to. Do not even move until you see whether he crosses the ridge, takes the top of it, or keeps on the side he still is on. In any of these events your prospects of a pretty fair shot are far stronger than the probabilities of hitting the deer where it now is. And now see! the deer is going over the ridge. But stop! Do not move an inch until he is out of sight. There he disappears. Now be quick but quiet and get on the neck of that ridge he went over just where it joins the main body of the hills.

You reach the neck of the ridge, and dropping behind a large rock take off your hat and peep cautiously over the rock. And soon you see on your side of the ravine a long low bit of yellowish brown moving through the brush some seventy yards away, with the tips of a pair of horns occasionally surging through the brush in front of it. The brown is moving toward you too, and will pass you some thirty yards down your side of the ridge and near the bottom of the ravine. And you softly ejaculate " Mine."

But beware, dear friend, how you too quickly say " Mine," You know not whether a deer is yours un- til you stand astride of it with your knife. And be a little cautious even then; for sometimes when the point of the knife has pricked the skin of a fallen deer, hunter, rifle, knife, and deer have radiated to the four points of the compass almost as suddenly as if a keg of powder had exploded in their midst.

And now where is your bit of brown? You took your eyes from it to look at the place where you intended to bag it, and when your eyes would return to it, behold! it is gone. Yet none of that brush is over four feet high and not at all thick.

Now do not get excited, worried, or anxious; for if you do you will yield to hurry and flurry, and then it will be a running shot or none. The buck is still there; he probably suspects not your presence; he cannot get out of the ravine without your seeing him; and if you have patience you may still get a good standing shot.

You wait a few seconds and they seem a few minutes; a few minutes and they seem long hours. Surely he has slipped away unseen, you think; that rock would give a so much better view; he may be getting away; no time is to be lost. So Haste reasons with you; and though Patience commands you in thunder-tones to keep still, you will listen to Haste. You put your foot upon the rock and are just raising yourself upon it, when a sudden crash of brush comes from near the place where you last saw the bit of brown. It is followed at once by the well-known bump, bump, bump, and from the bottom of the ravine away goes the buck bouncing on steely legs up the opposite side. He looks now as large as a yearling calf, as with high bounding springs he surges above the brush, with the morning sun glinting on every tine and shining from nearly every hair. Little he cares for the rapid fire of your repeater. He surges away as if it were only play, leaving your bullets all above him as he goes curving downward from the climax of his lofty bound.

He reaches the top of the ridge, stops, wheels half around, and turns his great mulish ears and dark blue eyes full upon you. There again is your artist-deer at last, standing full broadside, bulging with fatness, looming now as large and lustrous as he was before small and dim, as graceful and majestic as he was before ugly and insignificant and only fifty yards away!

Aim at the very lowest point where the shoulder, joins the body; and take a fine sight at that or you will still overshoot him. A tremor runs through all your nerves; the front sight of the rifle wavers all over the target; with a convulsive jerk you pull the trigger. The rifle cracks, and as the smoke clears away, the top of the ridge reveals no trace of your buck.

Did he fall in his tracks? you naturally wonder.

Suppose he did. Will he not stay there a few minutes? Suppose he did not. May you not get another shot before he can cross or get out of the next ravine? Do you not see that with a quick run you can reach the neck of the ridge he was on and may see him if he runs up or across the next ravine, as he probably will do? Why stand here an instant speculating upon the probable result of your shot?

You reach the neck of the next ridge quite out of breath and just in time to discover nothing. But be not too hasty to utilize your discovery. For he may be hiding in the brush. Walk on down to where he stood when you fired and see what has happened. But be not too hasty to get there, and keep a good watch in the brush below while going.

And now hark! a faint crack of brush; then a crash; then another smash of brush, and the old bit of brown is plunging through the brush below. But it is a la- boring, stumbling gait, without any of the bump, bump of hoofs plied by elastic legs.

103

Bang! bang! bang! goes your rifle again, and still the brown goes on. Stop. Save your cartridges. He is wounded, and if you empty your rifle-magazine he may get out of this ravine before you can load again. It is evident that you are now too excited to hit anything; and therefore you had better take a few moments' time to cool down. And in the meanwhile fill up the magazine of your rifle, for you may need all the shots it will hold.

Now make a quick run and get on that large rock that juts out some twenty yards below you. And don't you leave that rock until you see that deer again, even if you have to sit there some time. If he slips out of the ravine unseen which he cannot do if you keep a good watch from that rock you can track him just as well in four hours as you can now, and you would then have much better chances of finding him dead or lying down and so very sick that he would not rise until you got almost upon him.

As you jump upon the rock there is, however, another crash of brush only twenty yards below; the brown again shows itself for a moment; and it sinks at the first crack of your rifle.

On going down to your deer your satisfaction is somewhat marred by finding that your first ball struck the deer high up in the haunch, some two and a half feet from where you aimed.

Chapter Eighteen - The Still-Hunter's Cardinal Virtue

Space forbids the much further continuance of this realistic style of teaching the ways of the woods and hills, as it involves the repetition of too much that is already become familiar from former chapters. There is still another kind of open ground that must be considered, and I shall use it mainly as a text for a sermon upon the greatest of all virtues in still-hunting, viz. Patience.

The frequent necessity of Patience you have already seen. But you have not yet had an opportunity to fully realize its indispensable character in very many cases. There arise many perplexing questions in still- hunting the only key to the solution of which is Patience. It is true that these arise mainly in open ground, more especially open ground of the kind we are about to consider. But there are times in the woods and on all kinds of ground when it is quite as essential.

We are now in a broad open country with few or no hills beyond mere swells. In general appearance it is very much like heavily rolling prairie. But instead of the sloughs filled with long grass so abundant on some rolling prairies, you see here and there long strips of a deep dark green from quarter of a mile to several miles in length, running generally through the lower portions, but sometimes seaming with a verdant scar the very topmost face of quite level ground. These are gullies or barrancas, generally so steep-sided and deep that it is often no trifle to cross one on foot. The greater part of them have numerous arms or side gullies running in on each side every hundred or two hundred yards, varying in length from fifty yards upward. And some of these terminate in pockets or basins, but are generally both deep and steep-sided. These gullies are mostly filled with evergreen brush from six to twelve feet high. Sometimes one of these gullies rises to the dignity of a small canon or valley with water in it, perhaps, and a small line of timber at the lower end. An occasional small tree appears at long intervals scattered over the whole, but from anything that can be called woods or timber we are miles and miles away. The ridges and slopes between these barrancas are more or less covered with grass, weeds, some variety of sage or chemisal or low light brush, the body of which is little over knee-high, though, as in prairie, the flower-stalks may rise much higher. Occasional green bushes are scattered over the whole. This kind of ground in types more or less varied is found in Southern-California, Lower California, and the Spanish- American States and Territories generally. Often the gullies are so sloping at the sides that they are more properly swales than gullies, and sometimes they all contain a few trees or occasional groves of trees. Though it generally goes under the general term of mesa, or table-land, it is often the nearest approach to prairie to be found West of the Rocky Mountains, the gullies having been so deeply cut by cloud-bursts and heavy rains.

Though few would suspect it at first glance, such ground is almost certain to contain game: antelope if not too brushy and if wide enough in extent; deer if the gullies are plenty enough and brushy enough. Such ground is often easily traversed with a wagon, and can always be hunted on horseback, there being always some places where a horse can cross the gullies. There is little ground more pleasant or easy to hunt on foot for one who can endure a long walk, and still less ground upon which success may be so easily had from so small an average of deer to the square mile. The general principles requisite for success on such ground are about the same as those to be applied in hunting prairie of any kind; about the only difference being in the jumping of deer from the gullies.

The high ground is here the best to keep on during the times when the deer are on foot. We will therefore take this long ridge that commands a view of two gullies with their adjacent slopes of several hundred yards each. But while inspecting these slopes do not neglect the top of the ridge ahead of you, and pay strict attention to the edges of every gully and every clump of brush. For while the deer generally lie in the gullies by day and get a large part of their food from the bushes they contain, yet in the morning and at evening they are more apt to be a few yards from the edge, or up the slopes around some bush, or on the tops of the long ridges. And sometimes in hot weather, and generally in cold weather, they will lie during the day in the occasional bushes found over the slopes or on the ridges. And in very cold weather they will generally lie out in the low open brush in the sun.

This morning we will take this particular ridge because it leads on a course of good walking and hunting for two miles or so, with the rising sun on our backs instead of in our faces as we should be obliged to have it if we took advantage of the wind. But the prospects of a deer's being ahead of us on the ridge at all, or, if so, of being near enough to smell us before we could see him on ground so open and with the sun shining on him, are so slight that we will let the wind go and take the advantage of the sun instead.

The extreme care necessary to get first sight of a deer in general is here even more important, if possible, than elsewhere. For upon such ground the deer has every advantage of a wide sweep of vision that you have. Moreover, even in this low open brush that does not reach your waist, and through which the walking is so easy, deer standing still will be almost impossible for you to see at any considerable distance, especially when in the gray coat as we will suppose them now to be unless you can get well above them or have a sky-background, as when a deer is standing on a ridge, or unless the sun makes his back shine. And when you recollect that deer are rarely so numerous upon such ground as in timber, you will see that the importance of seeing one before he sees you is here far greater; especially as on this kind of ground you can rarely get a shot by a sudden dash to some point or ridge, the distances to be run being entirely too long.

On such ground you can scarcely look too far; though the ground for fifty yards around you must not be neglected. You can scarcely have too strong a glass or use it too thoroughly; though you should not use it until you have first given a careful and extensive sweep with the naked eye.

There is scarcely a shade of color from light brown to almost black, not a bit of sheen or a glistening point of any kind on such ground that may not be part of a deer. White spots must also be examined, as the buttocks and legs inside have some white. And if there are antelope .on the range, everything from pure white to brown and dark gray must be inspected; as the head of an antelope lying down will often be a dark spot on the landscape.

We will suppose that you see a deer at last. It is nearly a third of a mile away, but you discover it with your glass browsing from a little bush near the top of another ridge. You decide at once that it is a hopelessly long shot, and that your only hope of a close shot is a detour of half a mile or so to the other side of the crest of the ridge above the deer.

This detour you quickly make; but on peeping carefully over you see no deer. But you do see about two dozen small bushes, and each one of them maybe the bush by which you saw the deer, and it may be behind any one of them. Here arises your first trouble from want of patience. You were so anxious to get a shot that you did not have patience to mark the exact bush at which you saw the deer. You did not even notice that there were any other bushes there. You merely saw a hill-side and a deer and started off.

You look at every bush; they all look small and low; you see no deer at any of them; and you conclude that the deer moved off while you were coming around. You take a few steps and come up on the ridge for a better view. And you get it at once. But it is a rapidly dissolving view of a low-scudding spike-buck, so low that he does not even appear above the low stalks of the white sage. In a moment he disappears without regarding the noise of your rifle.

The buck started from behind the very bush at which you first saw him. Five or ten minutes' patient waiting would have given him time to move around the bush, to shake its top leaves by browsing or to move to another bush. And if you had had patience to back out and go along the ridge some three hundred yards either way, you might have located him precisely, and might then have returned and waited behind the ridge for him to move out in sight.

In this way a large number of shots are lost even by hunters who kill a great deal of game. Too hasty marking of a deer's location, too hasty assumption that the deer has moved away because it cannot at once be seen when the detour is completed, are two of the most irretrievable mistakes that any one but an excellent shot at running game can make in hunting open ground. And even in the woods it is often made, though of course not so often as in open ground, as deer are never seen so far away in the woods as they generally are in the open.

Well, there is another one, and you raise your rifle at once.

Beware! beware! It is indeed only two hundred yards away. But that is a long, long shot for even the best of shots to make at a deer standing breast toward you with more than half his body hidden in that gray sage. You will find that mark extremely dim when seen through the sights of a rifle. Let me tell you right here to beware always how you shoot with the rifle at a mark when bedim med or nearly obscured by brush. Never do it far off if you have any fair prospects of getting closer. Never do it even tolerably close by unless necessary. If you doubt me, try a few shots at the heads of rabbits at only fifteen paces when they are in grass or brush where you can see only the tips of the ears and fancy you see the dim outline of the head below them.

Consider, too, that this deer is headed this way; that it shows no sign of alarm; that there is no gully between in which it may go and get out of sight; that it is headed up hill too; and that there is probably water in that deep ravine beyond where the trees are so green. Reading these facts in the light of your already acquired knowledge, do you not see a strong probability that that deer is lounging away from water to high ground and will come your way? But suppose he does not come your way. Suppose he moves away. Can you not see where he goes, follow him up, and see him again and get as good a shot as you now have? For, remember, he is not alarmed; and whether he goes into a gully, into a bush, or over a ridge, he will go slowly and not be looking much be- hind; for these deer know nothing of watching back until after being started.

The deer stands and stands and stands. And you stand a few minutes and get impatient. The deer's persistence in standing, instead of teaching you that there is little danger of his going far in any direction now, it being nearly time for deer to lie down, only destroys the little patience you have. You fire, and when the smoke clears there is nothing in sight.

Let us suppose it is now the middle of the afternoon. At a distance you see an enormous buck rise up beside a bush, stand a few minutes, nibble a few leaves and lie down again on the shady side of the bush, only changing his bed to get out of the sun as it moves around the bush. You make a detour and get behind a little rise of ground some eighty or a hundred yards away. Looking cautiously over you see just the tip of a horn shining through the weeds. You draw up your rifle-sight about eighteen inches below the horn and fire.

A combination of pirouette, hornpipe, and double shuffle takes place for an instant by the bush, and then just as you think the deer is about to fall he straightens himself out and scuds away in line with the bush. Your ball glanced the base of his horn and stunned him a much better shot than there was any prospect of your making. And if you had crept up behind the bush he would probably have run straight away from it and have left it directly in your line of vision.

And now let us see what patience could have accomplished. The wind was blowing from him to you and he could not smell you. He had not seen or heard you, and you could have remained both quiet and unseen behind that little rise until he rose again. As it is the middle of the afternoon and the day is not very hot, he would probably have risen in less than an hour. And he would then have been in no hurry to go, and would have been as likely to come your way as to go any other. And suppose you had waited until sundown. Would not the game be worth so cheap a candle?

But we must hasten along and suppose our cases fast. You have been tracking some deer and track them to a huddle of gullies, basins, etc., all filled with brush. You fail to see one or jump any of them out of it. You make a circle around and find no tracks leading out. Failing to start anything from the edge you go in and thrash around inside for a few minutes. When tired and perspiring you come out, and about the first thing you find is a series of long jumps on ground you passed directly over when you made your circuit. They were skulking and slipped out of one side while you were tearing around in brush so high and thick that you could not have hit one if you had seen a dozen deer running.

Now only a hundred yards away is a knoll that commands a view of the whole of this place. And after you felt quite certain they were there, and when you know the trick of skulking as well as you do, why in the world could you not go there and sit them out? Want of patience. That is all.

This sitting out a deer and other forms of patience will suggest themselves in many other cases, such as where a fresh trail of several deer divides up and the individual trails begin to wander and straggle on ground suitable for lying down and there is a good point to sit on; especially when it is near evening and the ground is bad for getting a shot at a deer when started.

On such open ground as this it is often necessary to traverse a great deal of ground; and as deer in such open places will not remain on foot so long when

108

the sun is hot as they will in the woods, it may, in warm weather especially, be necessary to move fast. As noise is here of less consequence than elsewhere one may walk quite fast. But the keenness of sight must be doubled in consequence. In cold weather deer will remain on foot a longtime on such ground; longer in the morning than in the afternoon, and will be found mainly along the sunny slopes and hollows.

To jump deer upon such ground is often easy. It is of little use to hunt the ridges or the scattered bushes during the time deer are lying down, as the acreage of such stuff is uncomfortably disproportion- ate to the number of deer. The only way to do is to hunt along the edges of the gullies and around the heads of little side gullies and pockets, etc., and depend upon jumping those that lie down in such stuff. If it be very thick they may skulk or slip away down the bottom of the gully, leaving you amused only with the gay gallopade of their retiring hoofs. But, as a rule, they will spring out on one side and roll away over the open slope to the next ridge, or run down the opposite outside edge of the gully, thus presenting a fine chance for a running shot.

Whether deer are plenty enough on such ground to hunt may be soon determined by inspection of the ground along the edges and around the heads of gullies, also the ground lying between the heads of opposite running gullies and the ridges, points, and gullies leading to springs, if water be scarce. Tracks and droppings will be found on all such ground if deer are plenty enough to bother with.

Patience is no less essential in antelope-stalking than in deer-stalking. A little impatience to know whether antelope are coming to the red flag will often spoil a shot. So when they are feeding along on a certain course and you get around and get ahead of them it will be nearly impossible to resist raising your head too often to see how near they are. And when they come slowly it will be very hard to wait instead of trying to get closer.

Chapter Nineteen - Hunting in The Open and In Timber Combined

There is still another kind of ground, quite common in those countries where the greater number of deer are now to be found. It is a combination of open ground and timber, and when deer and acorns are plenty often affords shooting so easy and abundant that any tyro who has strength enough to stroll a mile or two on gently rolling ground and can hit any- thing at all can often have success enough to make him think he is a wonderful hunter. But, on the other hand, when deer are scarce and wild on such ground, it is in some respects more difficult to hunt than any we have yet seen except the heavy timber. We will, however, consider deer tolerably wild and not so abundant as to make care needless.

It is autumn now, and the acorns are pattering to the ground. Between rugged mountains robed in chapparal of dark, velvet green runs a long low valley which breaks on every side in smaller valleys and gulches into the adjacent mountains, and forms along the sides benches, basins, and pockets of various sizes. These are partly open and partly filled with a low chapparal of brush live-oaks, to the acorns of which the deer are very partial. The bottom and lower sides of the valley are well covered with vast live-oaks that have stood shoulder to shoulder through centuries of time. With their ever-living leaves of dark shining green and broad rugged limbs festooned with hoary moss, they form an almost continuous shade. Along the side valleys, knolls, and benches stand in silent majesty vast old evergreen white-oaks, the acorns of which the deer prefer even to those of the common live-oak.

Is this a hunt or only an evening stroll through a grand old English park? Before us the ground stretches away like a gently undulating carpet; here are soft foot-paths running here and there; on all hands are the massive old trees; here is the cool, delightful shade, and the softest of breezes playing through. And there, too, are the deer, the only thing needed to make the park complete; three standing under yonder tree, and two lying down like cattle beneath it.

Those deer are gone, so we will saunter along farther. Take a look into these little side pockets as you go along, and even up on those benches. Take good long looks down the vistas that open through the timber in various directions, and stoop down occasionally for a longer view. We may not see anything ahead for some time, for those deer have probably stampeded everything on their route. But perhaps they soon turned off into the hills. Go slowly now, and keep a sharp watch on each side, for there are plenty of deer here somewhere, as you can see by the numerous tracks, and ....

Bump- crash-bump-bump-crash comes suddenly from the head of a little side ravine; and just as the rifle comes to your shoulder the heavy green chapparal closes over a fat, glossy rump.

You see it is just as necessary to be careful about showing your head around a corner as about showing it over a ridge. There is absolutely no way in which you can bring head and shoulders in sight of a deer with safety except by being so extremely slow that no motion is apparent. Of course a deer will not always run or even always see you if you bring yourself too quickly in his eye-range. But the greater number of deer will both see you and run. And even where they are exceedingly tame you will be constantly losing shot by it. That last deer was tame enough. He stood on the outer edge of the chapparal in plain view until you walked out several feet in his field of vision.

But let us stroll along. It is all easy walking enough, but if you keep this trail of the wild cattle it will be still more easy and quiet.

A stroll of half a mile or so along the smooth, easy path brings us to a sudden halt. Something far ahead under a tree looks like an inverted V, long, tapering, and dark. Watch it carefully for a minute or two. It suddenly begins to grow gradually wider at the bottom and splits at the top until in a moment there are two V's both inverted and about two feet above the ground. Most marvelous resemblance to a pair of ears.

No. Don't raise your head another inch. What but an animal turning its head a little could have made that motion? The shape alone without any motion should satisfy you.

And now how to get a nearer interview with the owner of those ears? It will not be safe to approach over such level ground as that which lies between you. Nor are the trees plenty enough to stalk behind. And if they were, it would be an unsafe way to approach a deer having his head up. But there is a point projecting into the valley about eighty yards from them. Back out of where you are, slip into this little gulch to the left, cross the neck of the ridge at the head of it, and cross the next little gulch. That will put you on this side of the ridge that terminates in the point you wish to reach.

By the aid of the cattle-trails you reach at last the point quietly and with ease. Peering cautiously over it you see three slim sleek bodies, gray and glossy, lying side by side in domestic peace. There are two fawns lying with their heads over on their sides. The mother lies beside them with head upraised, chewing her cud and watching.

It is a pity to mar such peaceful happiness. But you may not feel so bad about it afterward; so try it.

Bang! goes your rifle; and like steel springs released from pressure the three deer bound in three different directions. There is no rising or getting up. There is only one simultaneous bump of hoofs and all three stand twenty feet apart, all like statues and all looking in different directions.

Bang! goes another shot. Bump go twelve hoofs again, almost at once. And there they all stand again, a little farther apart than before, and all looking.

Bang! goes another shot, and the ball with a chug splinters the bark from a live-oak just above the doe's back. The three deer give a start, trot a few steps, then huddle up all together, and look again.

At the bang! of another shot the three dart from the common center a single bound, stop and look a minute, then run a few yards in an inquiring way here and there, then huddle up again. And so they go on, geting farther and farther away, until the magazine of your rifle is empty. And by the time you can put in another cartridge they are vanishing softly in different directions, each on a soft springy trot,

A few minutes' walk, and your eye catches the billowy roll of a heavy body vanishing among the distant trees. The same old story, you see. You will forget that a deer in timber even when that timber is open like a park without a particle of underbrush is still very hard to see. You were not looking sharp enough or far enough ahead. Keep a keen eye on the edge of the chapparal; for deer, though feeding on acorns, still love to browse, and there are bush-acorns there, too.

Sh! stop! Don't you see those two glistening points in the brush there on the left, some hundred yards ahead? Never let such things escape your eye. Look sharp there where the lower edge of the sunlight breaking through that gorge on the east strikes the chapparal. Do you see two shining points about three inches long and fifteen or eighteen inches apart, just above the brush? Now watch them closely.

See! they move and two or three more points just below them appear in sight for an instant, and then do down. It's a big buck browsing.

Keep down that rifle! Do you want to throw away your only chance? You must make a dead shot on him; for a few yards in that chapparal will put him beyond your reach.

Your only chance now is to possess your soul in perfect patience for five minutes, ten minutes, even twenty or thirty minutes perhaps, until he comes out or shows some spot to shoot at. There is every probability that he will do so as 'he is right in the edge of the brush; it is yet early and cool, and as there is no hunting or other disturbance here, it is much more likely that he will come down here to spend the day in breezy shade than remain in that brush. You can go to that little rise or bench there about fifty yards closer to him; but stay there and wait.

You reach the bench, and the glistening points are still there, surging up and down, and shining more brightly than ever.

You found out yesterday that you were not yet over the buck ague, and you are now getting another lesson in it. You begin to get terribly restless, and fancy you know just where his body is. I might as well tell a drowning man to have patience until I can build a boat to rescue him. Your desire to shoot is worse than the murderer's secret, and kicks and hammers against your per-spiring ribs, until you can no longer resist the temptation.

The rifle cracks, and all is still. The glistening points are gone, but there was no crash of brush or bump of bounding hoofs. Killed, of course, you think, as you hasten to the spot. After a long search you find a few fresh tracks, and see where he has bitten the leaves from the brush. A close inspection shows tracks leading away through the brush, but there is no' blood, no hair, no plunging jumps. Of course you wonder if you hit him. But you will never know. Possibly you did; but probably you did not. Never take such a shot as that but wait patiently for a better one. The chances of a better one are great-er than of hitting by guesswork. He just dropped his head and skulked quietly off.

Sadly pondering the lesson you have just learned, you lounge along for a quarter of a mile or so, when suddenly you see a low dark object some dis-tance ahead. Something peculiar about its shape and color arrests your atten-tion; directly a head with branching antlers rises from the ground in front of it; and in a twinkling the thing is changed into a majestic old buck, the genuine powder-flask buck. Proudly erect he stands for a second, a picture of massive grace and strength, and takes a look around; and then down goes the head again to the ground; the beauty is all gone and he looks as angular and ugly as an old cow. But for an instant only. Again comes up the head, the neck is proudly erect as before, and all the outlines are again those of grace. He is feeding on acorns; and now you can try a task always difficult and often impossible to approach a deer directly within his sight, The ground is too level to allow you to get behind knolls, and he is too far from the hills on either side for a good shot, so your best chance is to crawl directly toward him. Half-cock your rifle and push it ahead of you, leave your hat here, and work ahead with your elbows and toes. The instant you see him raise his head, stop and lie perfectly still until he puts it down again for another acorn. Don't be impatient, and never mind if he does seem to be working away from you. Should he go behind a tree, with head away from you, you may get on your hands and knees and crawl faster; but the instant he raises his head stop at once and remain fixed in whatever position you happen to be. Don't move at all as long as he can see you. And don't try to rise up to shoot.

Fifteen minutes' work brings you within a hundred and fifty yards of him, when all at once he throws his head suddenly up and looks directly at you. Be not at all alarmed; for a deer often looks as if he saw something when he really suspects nothing. But now he looks longer than usual, while you are in a very uncomfortable position, with a very active fire of impatience fast blazing up in your vitals. The only remedy is patience. He surely cannot smell you on account of the wind, and he cannot possibly make out what you are if you only keep still.

Suddenly he turns half around and scratches his neck with his hoof. Now throw your rifle into position for a shot; for he acts as though he were done feeding, and if he starts on a walk he may go some distance before he stops. Again he straightens up and looks around, and through an opening the morning sun shines on his beamy coat and polished horns. And now I guess you had better try him, though it is a long shot for unsteady nerves.

The rifle cracks, and the buck gives a convulsive start, and as a distinct spat of the ball comes back on the air he breaks for the chapparal, no longer on the beautiful ricochet gait we have seen before, but on a regular race-horse gallop. The hissing lead flies be- hind him fast as you can send it from your repeater, and you begin to reflect on the fleeting nature of earthly pleasures, when his gait begins to change to the lumbering gallop of a cow, and in a second he wavers, staggers, and then goes plunging down head first to the ground, shot through the heart.

Such is the hunting in the oak cañons of Southern California, and probably on all similar ground in any part of the Union. If not disturbed, the deer prefer these valleys and shady groves with the side cañons and gulches to the hills on either side. But if hunted or disturbed much they soon go back into the chapparal by day, where it is quite useless to follow them. And sometimes, as in spring and early summer, the majority will keep pretty close in the chapparal all the time, and make few tracks outside.

Chapter Twenty - Subordinate Principles

I have now gone over all the varieties of ground upon which still-hunting proper can be followed to advantage. There are of course many other kinds of ground which abound in deer. But every piece worth still-hunting at all will be included under the heads so far considered.

So, also, I have brought into view all the general principles that lie at the foundation of all still-hunting or stalking of any kind of large game. And all the modifications of those principles that are likely to often arise have been seen. But there still remain some subordinate or special principles to be examined, and some that we have already had a glimpse of must be looked at more closely. A deer when started may generally be halted by any sudden, new, or strange noise in a direction different from that of the noise or thing that alarmed him. But to have this effect he must not see anything to alarm him. Hence if a deer be coming toward you and be not too closely pursued by any-thing, a bleat like that of a sheep, a sharp whistle, yell, or other noise will be very apt to cause him to stop.

But, as a rule, a deer will not stop for any noise in the direction of the cause of his alarm, especially if he has smelt a person. The report of your gun is quite likely to make him stop, if anything will; though I believe that where such is the case there is generally an echo that perplexes the deer so that he knows not whence the sound comes.

Sometimes a strange noise like that of a shot from a rifle will so perplex a deer that he will not run at all until he not only knows what it is but knows its direction. We saw an instance of this in the last chapter. To some this may have appeared a trifle overdrawn. But I know numerous cases of a deer stand-ing while a dozen bullets whizzed around him, at short range too; and have one well-attested case of a gentleman shooting out five cartridges he had in his Winchester, and then refilling and emptying it twice, making thirty-five shots at a single deer only a hundred yards away. He told me this himself; and two of his companions counted the shots.

Such a fool does mere curiosity sometimes make of deer that they will stay to investigate the noise even when they see the shooter plainly. Once, while returning from a hunt that I had to give up because of an attack of sick head-ache, I saw three deer run up a range of low hills quarter of a mile from the wagon. I made a detour and got above and nearly ahead of them; but was so weak and exhausted by running and climbing with the headache that I could scarcely stand. While waiting to catch my breath and let my hand get a little steadiness, they came directly in plain sight of me. Seeing that they would pass out of sight in a minute if I did not shoot, I commenced operations. I had a Sharp's rifle and eighteen cartridges in my belt and one in my rifle. Those deer stopped within sixty yards at the first shot, and one stood there until I fired away the last shot. I tried my very best to miss them entirely; but about the tenth shot one got hit in the kidneys with a ball intended for the shoulder, and about the seventeenth shot a ball intended for the nearest of the two remaining ones hit the other one standing a few steps beyond. After the last cartridge was gone the last one still stood looking, and stayed until I moved several steps toward him with the empty rifle. During nearly all this time I stood in plain sight, making plenty of motion with loading and firing, and after shooting a few times I had to move a few steps to a stone to sit down upon. Yet all the while the deer seemed determined to know what sort of a noise that was, though they saw me plainly.

All such cases are, however, rare exceptions, and generally happen only with deer that have seldom or never seen a man or heard a gun. There is but one sound principle to be drawn from them. And that is this: whenever you see a deer moving, whether merely traveling, or alarmed either by you or someone else, get ahead of him and above him if you can do so.

For this reason it is often advisable to open fire at once upon a running deer, where you have a rifle that can be rapidly loaded. But if you have a single-loading gun or muzzle-loader, and are not a good shot at running game, the chances of the deer stopping anyhow may be greater than your chances of hitting him; and in case he does stop he is almost certain to stop just long enough to let you load and raise the rifle about half way to a level and then he is cantering gayly away. A deer running up hill is very apt to stop once or twice to look back, and even when very wild he is apt to stop at the top of the hill for an instant. Hence it may be best to reserve your fire unless you have a repeater or double breech-loader. But running down hill a deer is not apt to stop. And running on a level he is less likely to stop than when running up hill, but more likely to stop than when running down hill. All these principles will, however, be modified by the question whether the deer knows what he is running from. If he has smelt you or seen you plainly he is far less apt to stop on any kind of ground; but if he has run only from the noise you make he is more likely to stop.

In the last chapter we saw how a deer may be approached in the open field of his vision. In that case, however, he did not see you, or at least noticed nothing suspicious; as, if he saw you at all, he did not know you from a stump.

There is one case, however, in which a deer may be approached while looking directly at you and perhaps suspecting what you are. There are some deer so tame that you may do this even on open ground for a short distance; but I do not refer to such, and no conclusions should be drawn from such cases. I refer to deer pretty wild; though, as a rule, it can be done only with tame ones.

Here, for instance, is a big buck a hundred and fifty yards or more away. He is standing in brush nearly shoulder-high; you can see only his horns and ears, and they are turned directly toward you. It is plain that he has seen you first and is ready to go at any instant.

You know the difficulty of hitting the head at that distance; you know the folly of trying to hit his body by guesswork; and you also know he will not tarry long. Now the same brush that conceals his body also conceals the greater part of yours this being supposed to be brushy open ground, the only place where this kind of approaching can be done with any fair chance of success and by taking advantage of that fact you may with quickness cut down the distance to seventy-five yards before he starts. Down, then, with your head if you can, and run directly toward him. If you cannot hide your head drop your hat, or you might as well drop it in either case. But run, run, run as fast as you can, and never mind necessary noise, but make none needlessly. You will often lose a shot this way, but you will more often get a better one than you could have had from where you first saw the head. In the same way you may charge on deer with a horse.

You have already seen that if you walk too fast you will make too much noise, will not have time to look as closely and carefully as you should do, and that your quick motions will catch a deer's sight more quickly than if moving slowly. But there are other cases besides that above given where it may be expedient to walk very fast. Suppose, for instance, the ground is in such condition from crusty snow or dry leaves or other cause that you must make a noise in walking, or when it is in good condition generally you come to a place that you cannot get through without making enough noise to alarm every deer within it. Then, as a rule, the faster you go the better. For a deer does not always start the instant he hears a noise, and even very wild ones will often wait a moment to see what it is, to see if it is coming closer, etc. Moreover, they may on a windy day or on ground of peculiar formation be deceived in the distance or direction of it though this is rare and wait a minute or two to hide or look. In such case every yard that can be gained upon a deer is important. And as a deer cares little for the mere amount of noise, the quality and nearness being the main things that determine his action, you lose much less by your extra noise than you gain by the extra speed. So, too, when you must go down wind, the faster you can go the greater your chances of getting close enough for a running shot before your scent reaches a deer's nose. In all such cases it is not advisable to run as you did on the deer in the brush; though you had better do so in every case in which you attempt to approach a deer that is alarmed and looking at you, as he will only stand about so long anyhow, and the mere rapidity of your motion will not hurry him much.

But, in general, you cannot commit a worse error than walking too fast. And if deer are moderately plenty, the wind favorable, the walking soft and still, you can scarcely go too slowly in all those places where you are likely to see a deer at any moment.

Many good hunters say, "Never follow a deer that has run away, but look for another." This advice is substantially sound, but like nearly all good hunter's advice is so carelessly stated that it is bad advice. To follow directly on the track of a started deer is generally useless unless the deer are exceedingly tame and the ground very rolling; and even then it is often use-less except upon snow. Yet there are times when you had better follow a deer.

A deer when started will go from a quarter of a mile to two or three miles. This will depend upon his wildness, the nature of the ground over which he has to run, and the cause of his alarm. During this run he will stop from one to a dozen times and look back a few minutes or seconds only. He will then walk a few hundred yards, stopping several times to look back. Then he will feed or browse a little and do plenty of looking back. Then he will wander about and stand-around for a while, still looking back. And finally he will lie down and think nothing more of the back track unless he be one of the learned ones that always watch the back track. But some deer such as a very fat buck on a warm day are decidedly lazy. I have known such a one run only out of sight over a ridge, stop in the, comfortable shade of a big bush, watch there a few minutes, and then lie down. So I have known a band of deer run over two or three ridges and there stop and begin feeding in five minutes, keeping then no more watch in the direction from which they came than in any other. These and many others I have known were cases in which the deer ran only from noise and did not know what caused it. But deer when very tame will often do it when they have seen or smelled you. But even in such cases do not follow directly upon the trail if you can possibly avoid it. And be twenty times more careful than ever before how you peep over a ridge.

Although this will generally fail with deer at all wild, yet it by no means follows that it is necessary to follow them at once. Suppose you start a handsome buck or a band of deer this morning. It may be worth while to take the trail in the afternoon and follow it up as you would the trail of any deer. And though it might not reward you to keep directly on the trail all the time, it may be best to follow it up to the point where the deer begin to straggle and browse; then back out and make a detour; and then either sit them out if it be open ground and you can get a commanding view, or else hunt as you would for any deer. But deer of any kind either wild or tame may often be followed and overhauled by a dashing runner. And a very ordinary runner can often get ahead of a started deer or flank him so as to get a good shot. This will generally fail. But success attends the effort so often that I do not hesitate to say, always follow a deer under these circumstances:

1st. Where the deer runs around a hill and you can cut across it or run around the other way, or where he runs over it and you can run around it quickly.

2nd. Where the deer runs into a basin, pocket, or valley and you can make a short-cut to one side or the head of it. If such basin or pocket be up a hill some distance the deer will be quite apt to stop awhile in it.

3rd. Where the deer runs into a long valley with a broad bottom or a narrow one with a good trail at the bottom. In such case run parallel with the ravine, but on the dividing ridge, and keep out of sight except when you peep over. A deer is apt to be in little haste in traversing such valleys.

4th. In all cases where the ground will allow you to, make a circuit and get ahead of the deer or even abreast with him, but on one side.

While doing this you must never forget that the deer even when walking moves quite fast, and when he is running you have not a second to spare. Your only hope lies in cutting off distance, and that in the shortest possible time.

Hence there are kinds of ground, such as across a wide valley or up a long hill, where you will see at a glance that running would be folly.

Deer will sometimes stand and let a man at a distance pass by, especially along a road where they know people travel; for a deer knows about as well as a man what a road means. But even when there is no road deer will sometimes stand. And then they will be apt to trot off and walk, trot or run for a mile or two, and look back just as if pursued. Therefore, when some one comes rushing in and tells you about an "awful big buck" he just saw along the road or near a spring, instead of rushing frantically out on a wild-goose chase, just coolly inquire what the deer was doing, whether he saw your informant or not, and whether he moved away, and whether he went off on a walk, trot, or run. And remember that a deer started by some one else is no better to follow than one you have started yourself.

When you start a deer that you cannot see, but only hear or get a glimpse of, spring at once to the highest bit of ground at hand. And if you do not see the game at once do not get uneasy, for it may have stopped a moment in brush or somewhere where you cannot at once see it. You will generally lose nothing by such patience, for if your deer has passed on out of sight you will be too late to head him off. And if you are going to track him there is no haste. But if you see him again at all shoot at once, for it is likely to be your last chance for that time.

Antelope rarely stop to look back much until at a pretty safe distance. They are generally sufficiently amused with the first crack of a rifle, and have little more curiosity about its nature or direction. And though they may stop and take a long look at you, and look very large and close as they loom up against the sky, yet that stopping-point is far away, and the moment you move they are apt to move also. There is little or no chance for you to head off or flank these slippery beauties, though a companion may sometimes get behind them by a long detour if you keep still and let them watch you.

Antelope are also such wide travelers that unless exceedingly tame or upon very advantageous ground it will rarely be worth while to follow up any that you have once started. But there are kinds of ground upon which with a good horse it will be worth while. And in such case and in fact with deer also it is always best to give them plenty of time to get quieted down. And even then approach them from behind or one side if possible, and not on the back trail.

Chapter Twenty-One - Two Or More Persons Hunting in Company, Hunting on Horseback

Thus far the beginner has been supposed to be entirely alone; for the most necessary knowledge is how to manage a deer when alone. But two or more good hunters may often assist one another very much; on some kinds of ground it is quite essential to have a companion; in some places it may be unpleasant or unsafe to hunt alone.

After what you have already seen of the habits of deer very little information is needed about hunting with a companion. By your side, ahead of you, or behind you he should seldom be. Two persons are much more apt to be heard than one; each one is in haste to get the first look over a ridge; each one hurries and flurries the other, just as two pointers or setters working together on a warm trail of birds are apt to excite and more or less demoralize each other even beneath the very whip of the trainer. Consequently there is four or five times the danger of alarming a deer, and of missing one if shot at. Two persons unless very steady shots should never try to shoot at once at the same deer, or even into a band. Let one have the first shot even though a second chance be lost. And it is poor policy for two to try and creep together even on a band of deer or antelope. If one cannot get around and lie in the course the game is likely to take when it runs, he had better stay back and leave all the fun to his comrade. Men who have hunted for market or for skins for a long time may of course acquire the stolidity of butchers and not excite each other. But the mere amateur had better heed the above advice.

In moving over pretty level ground two persons should keep abreast: in the woods just far enough apart to keep in sight of each other; in open ground still farther apart. Then if either start a deer it may run across the course of the other one. On rolling ground you may generally keep closer together than on level ground. In going up a valley take opposite sides of the bottom, if the bottom be a hundred or two hundred yards or so in width. But if narrow at the bottom, with high sides, it may be better for one to take the bottom and the other the high ground above or walk pretty well up along the side. Should the bottom of a valley narrow and deep contain trees or brush in which deer are apt to be lying this should always be done, as they will not be apt to start unless some one be in the bottom, and then the one in the bottom may either get no shot at all or a very poor one. Should the valley be both narrow and shallow so as to be a mere gully from which deer will start at sight of a person along the edge, then you should take opposite edges. In going around a hill take opposite sides, whether you go around at the base or at the top. When going along a ridge toward the point each person should take one side of the top just below the level of the top, so that he can see anything running along the sides or top either. In traversing a ridge the other way one had better make a circuit and get upon the back of the ridge far away from the point, and then let the other ascend the point. The same plan is often advisable in traversing a short gulch or ravine, instead of each one taking one edge. But it is not always worth while to take this trouble unless you have reason to believe you will start something. You will of course divide at all windfalls, brush-patches, etc., where there is any probability of a deer, and either keep abreast in going around or let one take a wide circuit first and get on the opposite side while you go through. Movements of this sort become quite obvious after you once thoroughly know the habits of deer. It is scarcely necessary now to tell you where to post a third or fourth companion if you should have one with you.

Good deer-driving may often be done by a single person. One man can generally start a deer from a piece of ground, especially if he goes down wind, quite as effectually as a dozen dogs. There is a partial exception to this in the case of the skulking deer; but, if they are at all plenty, enough of them will run to give your companions a shot. This is often the only way that a piece of noisy or very brushy ground can be hunted without dogs.

This driving may be done by letting one or more persons go through the ground where the deer are likely to be, cracking plenty of brush on the way, while the rest are posted at probable points of escape for the game. But this is not worth while unless you already know about where the game is, or you are driving a basin or gulch or hill almost certain to contain something. A better way when you are uncertain of the game and are skirmishing about at random to find it is to form a line, and move abreast about a hundred yards apart in the woods and two hundred to three hundred or even more in open ground. But if the open*be very rolling or brushy, keep the same distance as in the woods. This line should be curved by the ends going forward and the center lagging a little when approaching a likely looking place. This, however, requires good know- ledge of the ground and a previous understanding among the party. I have seen Indians do it to great advantage in very dense woods, making a perfect drag-net of the line.

A large number of persons may be used in such a way. But first-rate work can be often done by four or five and without bending the line. It requires only a general knowledge of the places where deer are likely to be, and of the directions they are likely to take when started. Here, for instance, is a set of short ravines running into a main valley. These little ravines lie nearly parallel with each other, are quite numerous, brushy, and good places for deer. Now instead of going down one and up another, etc., as a single person should often do if he is to hunt them at all, the line should sweep across them all; one person being at the head, another at the mouth, the rest between. This is because it can be done in one quarter of the time the other way would require, and because the deer are more apt to run up or down the ravines than across them.

When hunting with companions always shoot when a deer runs toward any of them, even if you have no good shot. For if a person be not expecting it, a deer may be out of shot before he knows it, or may slip past him quite unseen and unheard. A shot is the surest warning that can be given.

When you hear a comrade shoot, run at once to a rock, piece of high ground, or other commanding position. Remain there some time keeping a sharp outlook, for a deer may not be running away from your friend fast. Or he may be wounded and only walking away. And if the ground be brushy it will take both patient and keen watching to keep a slowly traveling deer from passing you unseen and unheard. But never go at once to your companion unless he calls you, for he may not be done shooting, or may have wounded, one and be trying to get another shot at it, etc. etc.

In hunting antelope with companions in the ways above shown, the distances you should be from one another must generally be vastly greater than when hunting deer. They should be at least doubled for the very tamest antelope, unless upon very rolling ground. And for wild ones on ground that is but a little rolling the distances should be five or six and sometimes nearly ten times as great. When antelope get once started upon a certain course they are often hard to turn from it by anything approaching from the side; especially if the leading buck get ahead before he sees the danger. Hence a horseman can dash in quite close to a long-strung-out band of antelope by running in well behind the leader. They can be turned, however, and driven back and forth by being headed off by outposts placed far enough out ahead of them. Deer could probably be managed the same way upon the same kind of ground, though they are ready enough to swerve from their chosen course when they see danger on either side of it. And they care but little for leaders. All such hunting on the plains must, however be done upon horseback.

The use of a horse in general still-hunting is a point upon which hunters differ. The truth of the matter I take to be this: Wherever a saddle-horse can be used to carry you to and from your hunting- ground, to carry you from one point of it to another and at the same time carry your game out, by all means use one. For even then you will have all the walking necessary for exercise, etc. And in general, the more you can ride the more you can walk.

But whether it will be worth while to remain in the saddle while hunting is a vastly different matter. In hunting antelope so much ground has often to be traversed that a horse is almost a necessity. So sometimes with deer upon prairie and other open ground of that nature. In such cases most hunters remain in the saddle until they catch first sight of the game. Then they dismount and proceed as is usual when hunting upon foot.

But others remain on horseback all the time and shoot from the saddle or jump off and shoot quickly. And this is what is really meant by hunting on horse- back. Whether it is ever expedient to hunt antelope in this way may be doubted. The shots are generally so long that a horse would have to actually hold his breath to allow you to take a fine enough aim. And even by jumping off to shoot you would gain but little if antelope were very wild, as a long running shot would be about all you would get.

It is now as hard to find antelope that do not know exactly what a man on horseback means as it is to find wild-geese that do not know what a man in a boat means. Consequently the main reliance must be in approaching them without their knowing it, or by true still-hunting or stalking. But this can hardly ever be done with a horse, which they are very sure to see or hear. All the success with a horse depends upon the assumption that the game is not so afraid of a mounted man as of one afoot. And this is now rarely the case with antelope.

121

There are, however, many places where deer are not so afraid of a mounted man as of one on foot. This may result from two causes, both directly opposite. First, because they rarely or never see a mounted man. Secondly, because they never see a man in any other way and are not disturbed by horsemen.

And first: Where deer seldom see a man on horseback there are many that will have little fear of one, and will let one ride up within easy shot, either standing up or lying down, and looking at the combination with some curiosity, but with little concern. Consequently if the ground be noisy from any cause, "or the ground be too level or brushy for still-hunting, you may do far better to both hunt and shoot on horse-back. So where a country is quite open and level enough, like prairie, you may often do better with a horse, wagon, or sleigh than you can on foot. Deer know the tread of heavy animals perfectly, and will often stand quite unconcerned about the tramp of hoofs when they would fly from a light crack of a twig.

Secondly: Where deer are used to mounted men, but are not much disturbed by them (as in Lower California, where no one hunts, and only once in a long while a dash is made with the lasso at a deer on open ground, but where scarcely any one is ever seen on foot), this may be the best way to hunt, as you may not only get closer to deer than you could do on foot, but can traverse far more ground in a day. Deer vary, however, about this, and I have seen plenty that, though used to horsemen and not disturbed by them, were easier to approach on foot. And where they are hunted much on horseback they learn perfectly what a horse means, and will often run at the sound of hoofs without stopping to see whether there be a man on the horse or not, and this, too, when wild mustangs and cattle are ranging the hills and the deer feed among them without fear. They seem to know the different sound of the hoofs of a horse with a man on him just as well as a man can generally tell it. The only sure way to test the question whether hunting on a horse is better than on foot is to try it. And often the advantage of traversing more ground overbalances all else. If one is to go stumbling with heavy boots over noisy ground he had much better be on a horse and go as fast as he can. But if he will wear moccasins and use thorough care he can approach almost any deer or antelope much closer than he can on a horse, provided the deer has not seen him at a distance. If you cannot keep them from seeing you, as when you are on level ground, etc., then your chances will be better on a horse, unless the deer are too much hunted on horseback. When a deer sees you, you can often get closer by a dash on horseback than if on foot.

A good hunting-horse is not the easiest thing in the world to get. It is commonly supposed that some phlegmatic old hack whose sensibilities have been blunted by a thorough course of work, starvation, and thrashing is best for this purpose. But such a horse is rarely sure of foot and is sure to be slow. When you start out hunting you naturally desire to get somewhere before dark. Such a horse is also quite as apt to be a fool as any horse is. There are plenty of old horses that never exhibit any symptoms of sensibility until you come around them with a gun.

Far better than any such stock is a good active young horse. But he must have " horse sense;" and so must his rider. The hunting-horse needs kind and rational treatment, and above all quiet, cool, easy handling. He must not be jerked or kicked for being uneasy under fire. By such treatment, as well as by firing over his head, you can completely ruin a horse that is already quite well trained. And whipping and scolding will never make him allow a dead deer to be put on his back. He may allow it that time, but an- other time he is liable to object most seriously about the time you get it on and begin to tie it fast. He should be allowed to smell of the deer as long as he wishes, being patted meanwhile instead of scolded. Then if he does not yield, quietly blindfold him until it is firmly lashed on. If you put it on so carelessly at first that it slips and hangs on his side or under his belly, especially if he succeeds in kicking or " bucking" himself free from it, you will be apt to have trouble with him in the future.

Sometimes a very good horse cannot resist a trifling nervousness when you raise the rifle; a nervousness not born of fear, but only of expectation. In such case you will have to dismount to make any sort of a fine shot. And you will have to do so nearly al- ways to make a very good long shot. If your horse will not stay where you leave him, have a rope thirty or forty feet long knotted into several large loops at one end, with the other end tied around his neck and then looped around his nose with a noose that cannot slip off. Carry over the horn of the saddle the set of loops, which should be so arranged as to take up nearly all the rope and come under the horse's feet when cast off. Cast them off when you jump, and you may leave your horse a long time with the certainty of finding him firmly anchored somewhere very near by, no matter how well he may understand getting away with a picket-rope. This is much better than a bayonet or other sharp picket-pin, as it takes no time to cast off the rope, is not so liable to come loose, especially in soft ground, and needs no pounding on hard ground. Holding the rope while you shoot is very unreliable as well as a little unsafe if your horse be too fearful.

Chapter Twenty-Two - Special Modes of Hunting, The Cow Bell and Tiring Down Deer

As before stated, the art of still-hunting consists not in the use of tricks or artifices, but in the ready and skillful application of sound common-sense principles.

There are, however, a few modes in which deer and antelope may be hunt- ed that are special and approach the nature of tricks. Some of these, such as luring antelope within shot by a red flag or kicking up the foot behind one occasionally when stretched upon the ground, thus taking advantage of their curiosity, etc., have already been so fully and frequently described by other writers that for the sake of brevity I will omit them and confine myself to two modes which, so far as I can remember, have never been written about before. Though both are in fact noisy hunting, yet, being the outgeneraling of a deer by a single person, properly belong to still-hunting. The first is the use of the cow-bell.

In many parts of our country the deer are used to the sound of the cow-bell during the spring, summer, and autumn, and wherever belled cattle run those deer that have been accustomed to seeing the cattle and hearing the bell at the same time, so as to associate the two, will be little afraid of the bell, provided they are not hunted in this way, Therefore, when the autumn leaves are dry and crackly, or the snow is stiff and noisy, or the brush is thick and high, it is well to try the cow-bell.

Hang the bell over your shoulder so that it will sound as if on a cow, and walk along fast, never minding the noise of your feet, but keeping a very keen eye ahead. Two companions, one on each side, about one hundred to three hundred yards from you and forty to a hundred and fifty yards ahead, may often work well in brush or on snow, but on snow they must be farther out from you than on bare ground, unless it is very brushy. It is well to have a set of signals with the bell so as to tell them if you see a deer, or, if on a trail, which way it turns, etc. Deer act very differently before the bell, and it is always liable to fail, though it will often give you great success. In thick brush deer that are accustomed to belled cattle will be apt to play along before the bell about a hundred yards or so ahead, stopping to look back at it, and watching its direction so closely that they do not notice your companions on the sides. Sometimes they will stand quite unconcerned, looking at you until you get in plain open sight, so that you can get a good shot. And sometimes they will run at the first sound of it, and not let you even get sight of them. I have seen an old buck so bothered by the bell that it seemed impossible to make him run, although for five minutes I did my very best to miss him; and my fingers were so numb with cold that I could hardly load the rifle, while he stood looking at me in the utmost amazement, at only fifty yards. Every time he started to run a single jingle of the bell would make him halt and look all around. This buck was celebrated for his wildness, but no one had thought of trying a bell on him, although belled cattle had been ranging with him all summer. But with some deer this will not work at all. I was staying once at a logging- camp when a light sleet suddenly made the hunting very bad for a few days. Having noticed that many of the logging-teams wore small bells, and that deer stood around, browsed, and even lay down within sound of these, I got a bell and went after the deer. Deer were quite plenty, and the first day I jumped over a dozen single ones whose tracks I saw, and doubtless more whose tracks I did not see. But every one of these jumped out of sight. The next day I muffled the clapper of the bell so that it would sound as if very far off, and the result was the same as the day before. I afterward tried it on soft snow with no better success. The reason probably was because I went away from the road. Had I kept in it at early morning and late in the evening I might have done better, though the main trouble undoubtedly was that the moment they heard it they got up and looked, and the difference between me and a logging- team was too striking. The difference in the tread had also something to do with it. They had not been hunted with a bell before, but were exceedingly wild from being still-hunted by Indians and market-shooters. I never tried the bell on California deer, but should think it would be of little use, except where cattle wear bells; though if the ground is such that you must make a noise anyhow, it would be well to try it anywhere. And it is sometimes a good plan to put it on a horse in hunting very bushy or very rough ground,- where deer cannot see far. Some deer know the step of a man so perfectly, however, that they cannot be deceived by anything, and nothing but the utmost strategy and caution will avail. And whenever the ground will allow still walking you had better depend only upon strategy and caution in hunting all deer, and let horses, cow-bells, etc., alone.

The other mode is tiring down a deer so that he loses his wildness so far as to allow you to get close enough for a shot. This can generally be done only upon snow so light as not to impede your walking, while it enables you to follow the trail without delay in looking for tracks. It may, however, with a very fat deer be done on some kinds of bare ground where rapid tracking is easy. I am aware that deer may be run down on a deep crusty snow by a man on snowshoes. But this is mere brutal butchery. Whenever the snow is deep enough and hard enough to do that the deer are so poor as to be almost worthless either for venison or for their hides. I refer only to tiring a deer when in good condition and when he has some chance for his life.

Probably every one who has been much among old hunters has heard of that illustrious individual who can "run down a deer and whip him into camp with his ramrod." Like the man who "shoots from the hip as well as anybody else can from the shoulder," he is a little hard to find. You can find his cousin, his nephew, or his uncle without much difficulty, and you can find plenty of men who have seen him; but you cannot find him yourself. This admixture of what is probably sheer nonsense with what is real truth has caused many persons to disbelieve the real facts of the case.

If a deer be chased all day by a man upon a dog- trot, or even upon a rapid walk, the deer toward evening will tire down, not so that the man can catch or strike him, or even get within a stone's throw of him; but the deer will get more and more careless, and stand longer and longer at each stopping-place, and even begin to feed, until finally the pursuer gets a pretty fair shot at him.

I am here compelled to go outside of my own experience. I never would pay so high a price for a deer as such hunting involves, and consequently never tried it. But I have time and again met Indians in the woods following a trail on a dog-trot, and talked with them about it. And I have known friends of mine stopping at the same camp at which I was stopping try the same thing. There was always a pretty general agreement about two things:

1.st That a deer may often be shot in this way, but that in general it will take nearly an all-day tramp of at least three miles an hour, and for anything like certainty it should be at least five miles.

125

2.nd. That some deer cannot be overtaken in this way in one day; but the pursuer must camp on the track and take it again in the morning, or must return to it if he goes off to camp. The second day, it is said, is quite sure to end the chase; but often the first day will not. I once knew two men who were most tireless trampers try it for three successive days on only an inch of snow that had been stiffened by a thaw, and give it up. They had to take different deer every day, as they left the trail each night so far from camp that they thought their chances better with a new one.

On the whole, this is a mode of hunting suitable only for a man of great endurance who cares not how soon he works out the mine of youth and health; and even such a one had better let it alone unless the ground be too noisy to still-hunt and he must have a deer.

How far this plan would work with antelope if followed on horseback I cannot say. All the antelope it has been my lot to meet were very wild, made nearly half a day's journey at the first run, and would probably have completed the day with another run if I had been foolish enough to follow them. They have far more endurance than a deer.

All such modes of hunting as watching water-holes, salt-licks, turnip-patches, pine-choppings, etc., although literally still-hunting, I pass over as involving neither knowledge nor skill, except to keep still, hide in a tree or in a hole in the ground, or lie flat on the leeward side to see the deer when it comes, and avoid overshooting it; a thing we will consider under the head of shooting.

Chapter Twenty-Three - Deer in Bands. General Hints, etc.

At all times of the year and in all countries deer are found often in companies. Two yearlings running together, a doe and fawns, two or three does and a buck, or sometimes two or three bucks together are quite as often met with as is a single deer. At certain times of the year, however, deer often gather into bands of from six to fifteen or twenty-five, and in some parts of the country into much larger bands. When this occurs and where it is most apt to occur is of no consequence even if it were possible to give any general rule upon the subject. You will know a band quickly enough by the tracks, and one or two days' hunting will tell you far better than any rule could do it whether they are in bands or not.

Hunting a band of deer requires, however, some special care. When banded, deer range farther than when single or in small companies, and shift oftener from place to place. They will have perhaps eight or ten points of radiation from the general center of their range, a basin here, a valley there, in another place a meadow, surrounded with brush perhaps, here another basin, there a rocky ridge, etc. Each one of these may be half a mile or even much more from the next one, and from half a mile to two or three miles from the general center. All are certain to contain food and probably water. Each one of these places will be connected with the others by trails, upon which the deer will be almost sure to travel in passing from one to another. In any one of these places they may pass several days, and may also pass only one day even when undisturbed. The general center may be some unusually choice feeding-ground, or the only spring for many miles, or may be one of those peculiar spots that deer often take a special fancy to with-out any apparent reason. A band of antelope act about the same way, but upon a vastly larger scale.

To this general center a band of deer may come every night for several nights, or may come for two or three successive nights; and then stay away for several nights, especially if scared away from it.

Deer acting thus are in many respects harder to hunt than when single or in small companies. The prospects of making a good bag when you do find them are much better than when they are scattered, especially when on ground where you can get above them or ahead of them. But the prospects of any one day being a blank day are also much stronger than when hunting scattered deer. Unless you take a whole day to it and find out just where they are in time to get "the evening hunt" on them, you will often discover only where they are not. And this discovery you may make just too late to go where they are. For unless you find fresh tracks at the general center which you can follow back, it will often use up the best hunting-hours of the whole morning to find where they were last night. And this will sometimes be the case when you find the tracks at once in the morning. For you cannot safely follow such tracks back rapidly, but must be keeping a constant watch for the game. And if you once start the band it is quite apt to make a long run; and it will be several days before it returns to that part of its beat. There are also so many more ears to hear you, so many more eyes to see you and noses to smell you, and some are always watching. They may be scattered about over one acre, or over ten or more and if one starts he generally carries the rest along in a general stampede. To stalk a band requires in fact more caution than to stalk a single deer, although your chances of catching sight of game are much greater in case of a band.

A troublesome question often arises what to do when in tracking a band you see a deer. It may be only a single deer not belonging to the band. It may be one of the band, and the nearest one to you. Or it may be the farthest one off, and a dozen more may be standing around in brush or lying down be-tween you and it. If it is within fair shot you should make sure of it unless it is too small or poor, etc. For nowhere is the maxim " A bird in the hand is worth two in the bush" more true than in hunting deer or antelope. There may be more near by, and the attempt to see them may alarm the whole. Even ante-lope can lie on quite level ground between you and one standing up without your suspecting it, and if you raise your head an inch more to look for them you may alarm the one you can easily make sure of. But if the one you see is too far off for a certain shot it may be bad policy to shoot at it at once without waiting to see what is closer by. What to do then must depend upon many considerations. If the ground will allow closer approach without getting in sight or wind of game or making too much noise, it is better to get nearer. If it is at the time of day when the game is moving about and the nearer ones will be likely to move in sight it may be best to lie still for a while and watch. If at a time when they are likely to be lying down it may be better to shoot at the one you see, as the others may not move again for hours; the one you see may be the only one on foot; and even that one may lie down at any minute. If early in the afternoon, the ground bad for a running shot, and the one you see too far away, it may be best to sit down and wait for them to rise toward evening. And all this may be changed by the fact that they are moving from place to place and the brush prevents you seeing the rest of the band. For deer can feed along through brush quite low and thin without your seeing them unless you are well above them.

Banded deer may deceive you very much in your estimate of the number of deer about. They then do so much more moving than when single that they will track up an immense amount of ground in such a way that you would fully believe there were at least twenty deer where there were not over six or eight. And even two miles square of ground may be so tracked up by a restless band that one would declare deer very plenty, when in fact they may be scarce, the next band being two or three miles away and the whole average being only two to the square mile. A band will occasionally keep quite still for several days or weeks. But the rule is the other way.

In shooting into a band in rough or brushy ground you are very apt to get demoralized. You should shoot just as deliberately as at any time, not hurrying in the least because you see other deer than the one you are shooting at. And, above all, you should keep account of every deer struck, whether it fell or ran off and which way it ran, etc. Otherwise you will be very apt to lose them. Do not show yourself until through shooting, and do not allow yourself to be tempted to do so by seeing them move off. Even if they go off running you had better not show yourself unless you can make a cut-off.

There are some general hints that apply equally to single deer and banded ones which may as well be considered here.

In going after a particular deer or band of deer you need not listen to any gabble of settlers, herdsmen, teamsters, and others who tell you they always see them at such a place, see them there every day, etc. etc. etc. The fact generally is that they see them about once in four or five days or a week, which is probably as often as the man goes there, and which he calls "every day." This is just about the time it takes them to return to that part of the range when once driven away. A man going to that place once in five or six days will generally stand the same chance of seeing the deer that a man does who goes there every day. You should generally go to the place toward which they ran if you go within two or three days after they were seen.

When deer run into a high brushy hill-side and disappear, wait and watch for several minutes. Even a single deer is liable to come to an opening and stand a minute for a look, and some one of a band is very apt to do so.

If you are near a water-hole or bit of choice feeding-ground and see a deer's head and neck come peering over an adjacent ridge, unless you are sure he sees you or he is close enough for a sure shot, keep perfectly still. This is very apt to be a survey for danger before coming in to water or feed. And if he backs off instead of coming ahead don't be in too much haste to go after him, for he may be coming around by a trail or down the next ravine.

Though deer can go without water, especially when the browse is wet with dews or fogs or rain, yet in hot weather, especially in the dry countries, they are very fond of it. Hence if you can find the only water-hole for a long distance, and camp so close to it as to keep the deer away from it for a night or two, you will be very apt to find them hanging about in the close vicinity in the morning waiting for a chance to come in. This is vastly better than watching the water all night and crippling one or two with an uncertain shot, or pot-shooting them with a shot-gun. I have never tried it, but a friend of mine, who is otherwise an excellent hunter, does it with great success, and considers it almost sure.

Antelope generally, if not always, water by day, and cannot, when on dry feed or sun-cured grass, go with-out water as long as deer can. But much more care must be used in watching for them. You must be better hid and be in such position that no motion is necessary before shooting. If you cannot hide, the best way to wait for either deer or antelope to come close enough after they once come in sight is to lie flat on your face or back and not move a muscle until you are ready to shoot. Then if they are certain to see you any-how, jump as quickly as you can. But otherwise move slowly and make no noise, as you may in this way get standing shots instead of only running ones, as may be the case where they see you or you have to move quickly.

When game has once seen you it is of little use to drop or back out of sight and try to sneak around after it. It is quite apt to leave as soon as you get out of sight. Even the little cotton-tail rabbit, when at all wild, has an idea that this proceeding means mischief, and both deer and antelope are generally so deeply impressed with that idea that in such case you should risk a much longer shot than when the game does not see you. If too far off and you have a companion at hand, leave him for the game to watch while you go around.

When you see game at a long distance, before you start off to make a detour for it wait long enough to find out what it is doing. It may see you and leave as above shown, and if it is to leave it had better leave while you can see it and know where it is going, etc. Or it may be feeding on a course, in which case it may be best to first learn its course. Or it may be standing around preliminary to lying down, in which case you have plenty of time and will be quite certain of a shot. Or it may be merely stopping an instant on a long walk, in which case you do not want to sneak on the vacant place, but want to know where it is going.

Of the many idle theories among hunters about deer there is one that demands some attention because there is really some truth in it, or, rather, it is truth wrongly stated. This is what is called the "moon theory." It is stated in various ways, but the substance of it is that when the moon is above the horizon during the day and when it is directly opposite the zenith deer are on foot feeding, etc. When the moon is above the horizon during most of the day it is not much above it during the night. If in the last quarter or in the first quarter, it is above the horizon more during the day than at night. Consequently so much of the night is dark that the deer do much less roaming then than about the full moon, when it is light all night. The more roaming they do at night the less they do by day or, rather, in the first half of the day. But deer are generally on foot about as early in the afternoon during full moon as at any other time, and often earlier, because they lie down so much earlier in the morning. Now if the moon is in the first or second quarter it will be above the horizon only in the early part of the night. The latter half of the night being dark the deer will feed more after daylight, at which time the moon will generally be somewhere about our antipodes or opposite the zenith. So when the moon is in the last quarter it will be still above the western horizon about the time the deer, having lain down early in the morning, rise again to feed in the afternoon. The whole of which amounts to this, that the lighter the night the longer the deer will roam at night, and the more they move at night the less they will move in the first half of the day.

Beware of selling out future chances too cheap. Suppose you are camped at a certain place and toward evening find fresh tracks leading into a nice little brushy basin or valley or some place that you cannot hunt to advantage before dark or on account of the wind or other cause. Should you go after the game and start it the chances may be all against your getting even a running shot. And it may run a mile or more, so that it would take you all next day to find it. It may in such case be better to leave the game alone that night and be there at daylight in the morning. The same may be the case with a band or a single deer that you actually see. If it is too far off or too dark to shoot to bettered by leaving the game undisturbed until daylight.

When hunting you may often be puzzled in high mountains by finding on top of the ridges plenty of tracks and trails running in all directions, with plenty of beds, droppings, etc. Yet with your utmost care you will not discover a deer. This is quite apt to be the case where the ridge is much less than five hundred yards or so in width, and often so when it is even wider than that. The reason is that the deer are on the ridge only at night, using it mainly to cross from side to side, spending nearly all the daylight down the slopes and ravines far below the top. Where these slopes and the sides of the ravines are very steep such ground is hardly worth hunting, as it is too much work to get a dead deer out of them. The best mountain-hunting is in the valleys or basins or along gentle slopes and ridges.

The noises made by a deer are of little importance. The bleat is much like that of a sheep, but generally shorter. The snort is a hollow whistling "phew" often long drawn. You will quickly enough know either one the first time you hear it. The cry of the fawns and their mothers' call the hunter has no business to know anything about.

Of slight importance are the distinctive colors of the deer's coat, "the red coat," "the blue," "the gray," etc. You must watch all colors at all times, for a deer may show any one of these shades at almost any time according to the part you see of him and the way the light strikes it, etc. etc. The blue and gray coat are always the same as far as hunting is concerned; for nothing from light gray to black can be neglected. Red is the summer coat; the others the fall and winter coats. In the mule-deer of California the red is often a dirty yellow or ocher color.

When in timber, especially timber with low-hanging branches, do not forget that a deer can see your legs and leave before you can see anything of him. You must stoop frequently in such ground. The same is the case in descending a tree-covered hill into a valley or basin. If you have any reason to believe there is game in it, enter it if possible from the lowest point you can find. And in general, when hunting a valley with sloping sides clad with timber, keep in the lowest part of it (a creek-bed or other depression if possible) that will give you the best view beneath the trees.

It may sometimes be best to purposely give deer your wind; as where they are lying in a basin or windfall and will have to run up hill, and it would be too long a shot for you if you should keep on one hill-side and try to start them by sight of you or by noise, in which case they would be certain to run up the opposite side. And even when deer are on foot the formation of the ground may be such that your chances of hitting one running up the side while you are in the center would be better than the chances of getting a good standing shot from either side.

Should you see cattle or horses on your hunting- ground be careful not to alarm them, as they will be apt to stampede all game within hearing of their hoofs. No other animals, nor even birds, should be unnecessarily alarmed when game is near. Both deer and antelope know what alarm of other animals means.

Chapter Twenty-Four - To Manage A Deer When Hit

The popular idea of the effect of a bullet upon a deer or antelope is about like a woman's idea of the effect of shooting in general; viz., instantaneous death of the thing shot at. Few persons who have not tried it would ever dream that after hours of patient toil, and a shot fired with perfect coolness and accuracy, the glossy prize that you just now so fondly imagined yours beyond a doubt may be suddenly resolved into the most slippery intangibility on earth, and that the hunt instead of ending has in reality only commenced.

Yet such with wild deer is the case about one third of the time, and on open ground, where longer shots must be taken than in the woods, it may be so quite as often even with pretty tame deer.

This provoking feature is, moreover, becoming more and more common. Time was in all the States of the Union when a good cool shot armed with a rifle shooting a bullet scarcely larger than a pea could shoot a hundred deer in succession without ten of them running over two hundred yards before falling dead. And these ten would not go over four hundred or five hundred yards. And the greater number would fall either in their tracks or in sight of the hunter. The reason of this is as simple as anything in the world. Deer were then so tame that the great majority would either stand and look at the hunter without running at all, or if they did run would go only a few yards and stop. The greater number would stand broadside to the hunter inside of seventy yards' distance; the hunter was a cool deliberate shot; the rifle was perfect in its accuracy to that distance; and therefore the ball was always, like the stock of the Credit Mobilier, " placed where it would do the most good." And deer were then so plenty that the hunter was sure of one or more such shots in a very short time. So easy was it then to pick such shots that the old-time hunter rarely thought of such a thing as shooting at a deer much beyond a hundred yards, or at one running, or at one that showed only the rear half of his body. He nearly always waited for a sure shot at the point of the shoulder or just behind it, reaching the heart almost invariably; though he often shot deer in the head.

But it is scarcely necessary to say that that day is past. There are yet a few places where deer are still tame. But the deer of the period is not an animal in which a ball can be placed where you wish to place it. And the antelope of the period is still less so, as he must be shot at longer distances, and on more or less windy plains that affect the aim of the hunter and the flight of the ball. Not only are the wildest regions of our country now penetrated by hunters, but since the general use of breech-loading rifles many of them poor ones, many of the best ones being kept so dirty and rusty that they will hit nothing, all of them tending by their rapidity of fire to make careless shooting the rule there is five times the amount of shooting at and scaring game that there used to be from an equal number of hunters carrying rifles that never threw " a wild ball," and that were so slow to load that every shot was fired as if it were the last ball within fifty miles.

For these reasons the deer and antelope of the period are vastly different animals from those that used to pose in sculpturesque attitudes about fifty yards away from Daniel Boone, David Crockett, and others.

One third of them must be shot at, at distances that the old-time hunter would have considered too far. And here I refer not to what are considered long-range distances, such as three hundred to six hundred yards, but to one hundred and fifty to two hundred yards; distances at which the old-time hunter passed scornfully by the biggest old buck with the feeling of full confidence of soon seeing another at less than half that distance. Another third of them must be now shot while running; a shot that the old-time hunter with his long heavy rifle, with its long-horned nuisance of a crescent-shaped scoop in the butt, with its hammer invariably upon the cap, and its trigger th'at could not be pulled without setting it unset, rarely thought of even attempting. The other third still present good shots and may be nearly always killed in their tracks or within a hundred yards of the place where struck.

When we come to analyze rifle-shooting you will conclude that I tell the exact truth when I assert, as I do most positively, that the man who talks of placing a ball where he wishes to place it in a running deer or antelope at any distance, or at one standing beyond a hundred and fifty yards, is either an ignoramus or a braggart who takes his listener for a bigger fool than he is himself. I draw the following principles not from my own experience only, but from that of the very best shots I have ever seen, men whom I believe it almost impossible to excel; and when we come to analyze shooting I will try to prove them from indisputable principles:

1. To hit a running deer in any part of the body at any distance is a first-class shot.
2. To hit at a hundred and fifty yards anywhere within ten inches of the center of the shoulder of a standing deer or antelope, or strike the body any-where at two hundred yards, is a first-class shot.
3. To hit a deer at all at a hundred yards when you can see only part of it in brush or among trees is a first-class shot.
4. To hit one in the vitals at only sixty yards when it shows only a small spot of dull color in dark heavy timber is a first-class shot.
5. It being now impossible to hit the majority of deer or antelope where you wish, let us consider the effect of bullets upon different parts of the body, and the vitality of the animals after being struck. I speak now only of the ball in common use, a solid ball of about forty-five hundredths of an inch in diameter, quite long and generally hardened with tin.

A shot in the head or spinal column will drop a deer in his tracks. A shot through the kidneys or in the rectum will nearly always do the same. A shot anywhere in a circle of six inches around the point of the shoulder will often drop a deer at once, but is much more likely to let him run from fifty to two hundred yards, and sometimes half a mile or more. Shot above the center of the shoulders or in the brisket only a deer may run for miles. Shot anywhere between five inches back of the shoulder and the hams the deer may run all day, depending upon the veins, bones, etc., that are touched by the ball. A deer with a hind-leg broken can with ease keep clear of a man all day, and with only a fore-leg broken can often run away from a dog, unless the dog be a pretty good one. The worst of all shots and the most common one in all shooting at long standing shots and at game running crosswise is what is called the "paunch-shot." Every shot from the fifth rib to the hip-joint nearly half the body of the animal may be practically regarded as a "paunch-shot." A deer or antelope can run for miles when thus shot, and I have seen a yearling buck shot through the center with an ounce round ball (solid) run away from a common dog, and escape on a fair race of over half a mile. And this, too, on quite open ground where the dog had a full view of the deer and lost no time in hunting the scent. An antelope is quite as tough as, if not often tougher than, a deer, and the expedition of either animal in getting away when half shot to pieces is often amazing.

It is common to hear people talk as if it were only necessary to let a wounded deer alone and it will lie down and either die or get sick. This is true enough if it be badly wounded and time enough be allowed it. But when will it be so sick that it will cease to watch upon its back track and either run away before you get within shot at all or go plunging through brush at your approach and give you a poor running shot? Of course "it is only a question of time;" but you will find that sweetly delusive formula very poor consolation when night closes in upon you and you wish to go somewhere else in the morning, when falling snow covers the bloody trail, when it leads into heavy windfalls or brush, and on bare ground when the blood ceases to flow and the cripple settles to a walk on ground where tracking is hard. For the tracking of a wounded deer is very different from that of a well one. You can tell very nearly where a well one will go, and without this knowledge tracking on bare ground is often impracticable. But you cannot count upon the movements of a wounded deer, except that generally he will run to the roughest and most brushy ground there is within reach. The number of deer lost on bare ground by the best of trackers and good shots is almost incredible to those who have not hunted and associated much with them. And even on snow many are lost.

One means of remedying this loss of game the use of a rifle-ball that will effectually stop anything struck anywhere in the body I shall point out in a subsequent chapter. But no rifle will kill a deer at once by hitting a leg unless very high up; and therefore every hunter who can should have a good dog at his heels.

A really good dog to overtake and stop a wounded deer is hard to get, and harder still to keep. There are enough that can do it, but they will spoil more shots for you than they save deer. Little or no training is required, as a dog that is at all fit for the purpose will take to it naturally. But he should be trained and kept in absolute obedience about remaining behind until sent out, even though a wounded deer be escaping before his eyes. As such dogs have generally more or less of some headstrong and intractable blood in their composition this is no easy matter to do; and as the average hunter is always in agony when he sees anything toothsome escaping, and is always blind to the fact that a dog can follow a trail in one or two minutes just as well as instantly, the average deer-dog of the period, like the retriever of the average hunter with the shot-gun, always starts like a rocket at the report of the gun. And having learned this, the next step in his education quite naturally follows; namely, running in without waiting for you to shoot.

The first thing to do when a deer is wounded is generally to do nothing. If he runs in a direction where you can head him off and get another shot, it is generally advisable to do so; but if he has not seen you, and you have to run so that he will see you, you had better not show yourself at all unless he is making for thick brush and you can get another shot at him before he reaches it. It is generally far better to drop quietly out of sight and watch him.

The action of a deer when wounded depends largely upon where he is hit, but mainly upon whether he has seen you or not, and also upon his wildness. If not very wild, and he has not yet seen you, he will generally take a few jumps, perhaps not more than one or two, then walk a few yards, stand still a while and look around, and then lie down. If he has seen you, or knows pretty well what the crack of a gun means, he may run several hundred yards before stopping, and then, after taking several backward looks and walking a little, will lie down. If jumped and shot on the run, he will probably run much farther than if shot when standing and suspecting no danger. If near brush or rough ground, a deer will be quite apt to make for it if he sees you, and so certain to if pursued that if you cannot make a good cut-off your only chance of keeping him from the brush is to let him entirely alone; he may then lie down before he reaches it. A deer only leg-broken will travel much farther before lying down than if hit in the body, and will generally stand up longer under a paunch-shot than under any other shot in the body, though, if let alone, will soon lie down with this. Sometimes deer will start off on a walk and go a mile or so to brush without stopping, and sometimes will plunge ahead on a full run until they fall either stone dead or from sheer exhaustion.

It would be of no use to waste further space in detailing specifically the various maneuvers of a wounded deer, for those above given include nearly all kinds, and the same general plan of handling must be followed in all cases. And this is…

1. No matter how sick the deer may appear to be, no matter how he staggers, bleeds, or looks like dropping immediately, shoot at him just as long as he stands up.
2. Do not be afraid of spoiling meat or hide, for as long as he can keep afoot you are in danger of losing both, or having a troublesome time to get them. Do the same when he is down, if he can hold up his head or his eyes are bright, unless his back is broken.
3. If he goes off, let him go (unless, as before stated, you can head off or flank him), and for several hours do nothing to disturb him. If it is near night you had better let him go until next morning. If he is badly hurt he will probably never rise after lying down a while, and at all events is likely to get so sick and stiff as to be quite easy of approach. But if followed up at once he will be watching, and unless very much hurt will be too keen and too lively for you.
4. On taking his track to follow him up, proceed just as you would on a well deer, and don't go blundering and thrashing carelessly along because you see blood or signs of stumbling or staggering. If you find

the blood increasing on the trail you may expect to find him dead, or very nearly so. But if it is decreasing it may need all your care to secure him.

Most of this caution is often needless, especially on snow and with a rifle of large caliber. But I have given it on the plan I have, followed throughout giving best and surest methods. You will rarely lose one by following too closely these rules, though they may of course sometimes cause you unnecessary delay. Where falling snow will hide the track, your only chance is often to follow at once.

Excited by the sight of blood and signs of stumbling, burning with anxiety to retrieve the game, and impatient of any delay, one is almost certain at first to rush ahead after a crippled deer. But you must remember that (except heading, etc.) all means of pursuit, the trail, the blood, etc., if any, will generally be just as available in four or six hours, perhaps even the next day, as they are right after shooting. By waiting you generally lose nothing. By not waiting you may lose all.

Nor is it always advisable to slip a dog at once, if you have one by you. For the sake of keeping him in good habits, he should never be allowed to start from your side for a moment or two, or until you give the word. And even then it is not always best to let him go until you get some idea of how the deer is wounded, and how far he will run. If he is likely to lie down soon it may be folly to slip your dog; for a deer that would lie down in two minutes and never get up if left alone may run for miles if kept going, and even if your dog be swift and sure he may run the deer into thick brush or some bad ground where it will bother you to get him out. Moreover, the flesh may be badly bloodshot or the contents of the intestines worked all through the interior by a chase. But if a deer is only leg-broken, as a rule the sooner you let out your dog the better, for it is likely to be a long chase, and the deer should have as little start as possible.

On falling snow when you have no dog, and there is danger of the track getting covered or confused with other tracks, you may perhaps overtake and get another shot at a deer by a stern-chase yourself. This is a job, however, which I would recommend you to sublet before you commence, as it is very exhausting and vexatious. A wounded deer, if not too badly hurt, will watch back, and will be quite sure to see.

It is far better, even in falling snow, to wait a little while, and when you get in sight of a place where the cripple is likely to stop go around and come in from one side or behind, as in tracking a wild well one.

I once saw a big strong man who was hunting quails beside me drop like a sledge-struck ox at the report of a comrade's gun some ninety yards behind us in the brush, clap his hand to his head, and exclaim in agony, "O my God!" He still lives, in Monmouth County, New Jersey; for the only wound we could find on him was a grain of No. 8 shot in the lobe of one ear, which our comrade who did the mischief, now a prominent lawyer in Jersey City, picked out with the point of his pen-knife. Other men shot half to pieces have fought like tigers or run like deer a long while before they fairly knew they were hit. Individuals among deer and antelope differ about the same way in vitality. I have seen a big buck drop in his tracks and lie there with the same bullet-hole in the same place that another and smaller deer has carried for miles without falling.

And I have seen an old buck antelope run ninety yards on as beautiful and almost as swift a trot as St. Julien ever made on the race-track, with both heart and lungs cut into perfect pulp by a .65 expansive ball with two hundred grains of powder behind it, and which would probably make the next one wilt like a wet rag in its tracks. Therefore if you happen to kill your first half-dozen or even dozen deer in their tracks or in your sight, do not delude yourself with the idea that there is no danger of deer escaping your rifle, but always use the same care above advised.

If a deer runs any distance and then falls he is pretty sure to be dead. But be sure that he falls, for if he runs and lies down it may need all your care to get him. If he falls at the report of the gun and then gets up and runs it generally means hard work and care to bag him. Therefore it is best always when a deer drops at once to run directly to him if there are no other deer at hand. Especially do you need to run if he struggles to get up, even though he fails; for a deer often recovers himself for a while, even when mortally wounded, being badly stunned at first, then getting over that and getting away to die afterward. But do not let a deer see you running to him if you can help it, and if near enough always give a struggling one another shot without going up to it, as the sight of you often revives one wonderfully.

How to manage a deer when killed is a matter in which your natural tact, as well as information from any woodsman, hunter, or settler, will serve you sufficiently well that for brevity I shall omit the most of what I could say about it, and by the time you have killed a few deer you will readily pardon me for spending most of my time in telling you how to shoot one instead of what to do with it after being shot.

Nevertheless there are just a few points that I will mention by way of saving you needless work.

It is considered style to charge on a fallen deer with a "hunting-knife" and " cut its throat." All the hunting-knife you need is a common round-pointed jack-knife. Everything else is a nuisance except as a butcher-knife or cleaver at camp. If the deer is not dead, finish him with a ball in the head, and let his throat alone or you may get in sudden trouble. If he is dead his throat needs no cutting, as a dead animal bleeds only a trifle from the throat. If you mean to open him at once you can give him no better bleeding than opening. If you wish to run on for another deer, stick the dead one in the chest and turn him with head down hill.

Covering up a deer with brush, snow, etc., especially if you leave some article of clothing upon it, will protect it from all animals and birds about as well as hanging up, unless you hang it very high. And this latter is no easy thing for one person to do, unless he packs a hatchet to cut forked sticks with large enough to prop up a good sapling. But with two such sticks, one being longer than the other, a bent sapling with a deer fastened to it can, by working them alternately, be run up quite high. Hanging by the head protects from birds but exposes the hams to animals, and vice versa. The inner bark of the basswood makes good rope, but the skin of the lower part of the deer's legs cut in strips is better and easier to get. This is also good to tie a deer to the rings of the saddle-girth.

The best way to get one home if you cannot reach it with a wagon is on a horse. Lay it behind the saddle and lash firmly to the girth rings or buckles; or it may be tied to his tail and dragged. A deer may be dragged very easily on snow, dead leaves, or dry grass by being pulled head first; and by throwing away neck and head, skinning and cutting up the forequarters and packing them in their skin, fastening the edges of the skin together by running a string through holes in each, the whole thing may be made into quite a nice sledge. But in very bad ground the best way to get a deer out is to let him take himself out. I have let many a one go unshot at in such places. It is a far greater thing to boast of than to bring out the saddles or a hind-quarter, leaving the rest to waste.

Chapter Twenty-Five - The Rifle on Game at Rest

The great difficulty in killing any sort of game with a single ball is that a miss is as good as a mile. To remedy this the scattering principle of the shotgun was introduced. And the success of this depends upon a principle directly opposite to the fundamental principle of the rifle; to wit, that a miss is as good as a hit. That is, the true center of the charge never need exactly cover the game. And as a matter of fact it probably does not once in a hundred times, even when the gun is the hands of the very best shots. .

The consequence of this is that the same aim that with a shot-gun would suffice to kill a thousand successive pigeons at twenty yards would not suffice to even touch one out of a thousand at twenty yards with a rifle-ball.

This fact is soon learned by a little target-practice with the rifle. The beginner finds that mere approximation, however near, will not do. Absolute accuracy only will suffice. But the beginner when he becomes a skilled target-shot finds when he first tries his rifle on game that the difference between shooting at game and at a target is as antipodal as the poles of the universe. The confidence with which he sets out to hunt is soon engulfed in amazement at the almost unappeasable appetite that lead exhibits for empty space. And this is the case upon any game. I have seen a friend who could cut the spots of a playing-card at twenty yards almost without fail for a long series of shots miss almost every shot at the heads of squirrels in trees not twenty yards high. And this was not because of excitement, but from causes I shall hereafter mention, such as overshooting, varying play of light on sights, dimness of marks, etc.

The insatiable appetite of lead for circumambient space becomes still more marvelous when it is fired at large game. Fire twenty shots at a target as carelessly as you please with a shot-gun, and you will find about every load scattered quite evenly around the bull's-eye. You may of course notice that the bull's-eye is not exactly in the center; but it is so nearly so that if the charge of shot had been a solid mass it would have hit every time within two or three inches of the center. This is, however, more apparent than real. Now what could be more reasonable than to suppose that the same aim with a rifle at a deer at fifty or sixty yards would surely hit him somewhere?

The rifle is far more accurately sighted than a shot-gun; it shoots far more accurately; you look at the sights and see them plainly on the body of the animal; there is a margin of ten or twelve inches for possible error; a clear miss seems impossible. Yet a person shooting a rifle as he would a shot-gun can miss twenty successive deer standing broadside at only forty yards with about the same ease and certainty that he could hit them with a shot-gun. For a whole year the very best target-shots will at seventy-five yards probably miss more deer than they hit; and at a hundred and fifty yards the very best gameshots will always do the same: and all this without any "buck-ague" or nervousness entering into the question. This of course would not be so if the game were always in the same position, light, etc., and always standing full broadside. But as deer are generally seen it would be so.

You have already seen how a deer can be "too close." And now you can understand why overconfidence producing a little lack of care in aiming can make you miss a deer within a stone's throw. And beware that you do not forget this, for even old and good shots are often deceived by a deer being "too close." Think it over and sing it over every time you start for the woods. And I recommend as a very suitable line for this purpose,

"Thou art so near and yet so far."

In almost every miss you make for the first season or so, and in nearly all cases where the game is missed because of being "too close," your bullet goes above the game. This tendency to overshoot is the most universal and ineradicable error that exists in the whole range of hunting with the rifle. As I shall recur to it again, I will now merely sum up the cases in which it is likely to be done, discussing only a few of them in detail. And most of them will suggest their own remedy.

• All cases of the least carelessness in aiming, whether from haste, over confidence, or nervousness. This results from catching with the eye too much of the front sight.

• Having the rifle sighted to a point beyond what is commonly called its natural point blank, thus carrying the ball above intermediate points.

• Over-estimating distance of game and purposely shooting higher than is really necessary.

• Having a dull front sight not easily seen.

139

• Shooting toward the sun.

• The sun lighting up the base of the front sight instead of the tip, so that you take too coarse a sight by mistaking the base for the tip.

• Shooting in insufficient light, especially at night.

• Shooting at a dim mark.

• Too much reflection of light from the back sight, thus blurring your view of the front sight.

• The varying play of light and shade upon open sights, making it almost impossible under constantly changing amounts and direction of light to always catch precisely the same amount of the front sight.

• Ocular aberration upon the front sight, or the impossibility of measuring with the eye always the same exact amount of the front sight, even where the light, etc., is always the same.

• Shooting downhill. This may be partly from having the light strike more directly upon the back of the front sight so that the base is mistaken for the tip. But it is more because the apparent center-line of the animal's body is thus raised above the real center-line by the line of sight striking obliquely. In this way a shot four inches too high, that if fired on a level may still hit a deer, error is very hard to avoid.

• Up-hill shots when very long and you attempt to allow for distance. When short there is little or no trouble.

Besides overshooting there are errors enough that you can make. As soon as you begin to correct that error you will be troubled some with under-shooting.

This will be caused by

• Fear of overshooting causing you to take too fine a sight at distance you have learned that it is unsafe to attempt to allow for the drop of your bullet, because of the liability to overestimate distance. This you can never entirely overcome. There is a certain point at which the ball if fired on a level will certainly drop below the game. And yet the only safe rule for shooting at that point in cases of doubt whether to shoot higher or not is to resolve the doubt always and instantly in favor of the level sights. This will insure the most hits, but will necessarily cause some misses.

• Not understanding how far your rifle shoots on a line practically level, and holding a fine level sight on game that is plainly too far beyond the point blank.

• Very long shots down a steep hill. This is partly from underestimating the distance of the object aimed at from the foot of a line dropped perpendicular-ly from the rifle to center of earth, a thing we are very apt to do on a long steep hill. It may also be that the coincidence of gravitation with the downward motion of the ball increases the ratio of its fall.

• Underestimating distance over water, over clear snow, and across a deep valley with a broad bottom. These three with the long down-hill shot which is analogous to the shot across the deep broad-bottomed valley are about the only cases in which you will underestimate distance. And you will be troubled little with them until after the beginning of a reaction from overestimating.

You will also be apt at first to shoot at the middle of your game. Should you hit it there you will then have a long and perhaps futile hunt for it unless shot with a very large or expansive ball. You should aim either directly at the shoulder or just behind it; and in either case low down. About one third of the distance up the body is the right point. In the shoulder is the better place to shoot your game with a small ball, provided it has enough penetration. Just behind the shoulder is the better place for a ball that lacks penetration. Behind the shoulder a ball damages less meat by settling of blood. On the other hand, a trifling error in placing a small ball too far back or too high may allow your game to run a mile or more and even escape you entirely. The same might be the case with a shoulder-shot, but the same amount of variation would not be so apt to let the game escape as in case of a shot back of the shoulder.

Beware how you shoot unnecessarily through thick brush and twigs at any considerable distance. A pointed ball is especially bad for such shooting, as a small twig may set it wabbling and thus deflect it, whereas a round or flat-headed ball would cut it off without turning. This often spoils long shots in the woods.

But after all, the most important point is never to be in a hurry. Fire as you would at a target; that is, as coolly and deliberately. Never hasten a second because the game shows signs of starting or because you think it is going to move, or because there is more than one deer or antelope waiting for your bullet. Place no dependence upon speed of fire. No matter how many shots you can fire or how fast you can fire them, shoot every ball just as if it were your last one.

After you acquire some experience in shooting at game you will learn to shoot quicker and in a way that to a bystander would appear as if you took a careless aim. But the carelessness is apparent only and not real. It is quick carefulness. But it will not do for anyone to begin with.

Many persons who are good off-hand shots scout the idea of resting the rifle on anything when shooting. This is partly right and partly wrong. On a long shot there is no one whose shooting cannot be improved by a dead rest; especially if there be any considerable cross-wind blowing. For a short distance a rest is entirely unnecessary for one of any experience in shooting game, unless his nerves be unsettled by climbing, running, etc. But the beginner had better take a rest even for close shots whenever he can get it without making any movement that may alarm the game.

There are different ways of holding the rifle in target-shooting. But I think there is but one true way of holding it in shooting at game.

• The butt should be against the shoulder and not against the muscle of the arm. And where there is much recoil it should be firmly pressed to the shoulder.

• The head should be held well back and not with the nose against the right thumb. If there is much recoil to your rifle you will be apt to flinch under fire if your nose comes in the way of your thumb. Many rifles are, however, so artistically made in the stock that the eye can be brought down to the level of the sights only by crowding the nose against the thumb. Another advantage of holding the head back is that the farther the eye is removed from the back sight on the barrel the less you will be troubled with any reflection of light from its edges and the clearer will be its outlines.

• The left arm should be well extended along the barrel so that the elbow makes a very obtuse angle. The advantage of this is that the rifle may be thus turned more quickly upon the mark; quite an important matter when the mark is moving. But when game is standing or you are shooting at a target the advantages of this position are not apparent. But as it is quicker and better for some kinds of shooting, and just as good as any for all kinds, the habit of so holding the arm had better be cultivated.

There are two ways of shooting.

• Shooting with a steady arm. Here the rifle lies in the hands almost like a log in mud. It is held fairly on the mark and kept there until fired.

• Shooting with an unsteady arm. Here the rifle cannot be held still. The front sight will wander around, over, under, and across the mark. All the shooter can do is to fire when the front sight touches the mark in crossing it; generally when coming up from below.

The first way, or shooting with a steady hand, is the only way in which first-class shooting can be done; for no other mode can be relied upon for a long continuance or series of good shots. This is the method of all the best, or rather most reliable, shots at game.

But it must not be supposed that this implies any slowness. The rifle need not lie at rest for over half a second, and generally does not do so. A good shot using this method will appear to shoot even quicker than one using the second method. Yet there is a short time when the rifle does lie, practically at least, at perfect rest. And during that time, short though it be, the trigger is pulled.

The second way is about the only method available to nervous persons. Since being broken down by ill- health several years ago I am unable to shoot in any other way. It is utterly impossible for me to hold the sight at rest on the mark as I once could. By this method many shots can be made as well as by the first way. But one is liable at any time to send a ball flying wild when firing at the easiest kind of a mark. And on days when an unusual degree of nervousness is present this liability becomes provokingly frequent, and is often attended by the still more provoking trick, also the result of nervousness, of balking or flinching at the trigger, giving it a nervous twitch either without firing at all or else firing it a yard or two off the mark. But whenever the hand of the hunter is made unsteady from any cause this is the only way to shoot, as it is generally useless to wait for the hand to reach its complete natural steadiness.

A hard trigger may be drawn in three ways.

• By a slow steady pull. This is the best way when shooting a very hard trigger with a rest. But when shooting off-hand a better way is

• Resting the finger upon the trigger with about two thirds or three quarters of the pressure needed for release and then suddenly applying, when the exact instant arrives, the rest of the necessary pressure.

• Pulling trigger with a jerk, the finger being kept off of the trigger until the instant of pulling. This is the same as is done with the shot-gun at flying game, and is worthless for: the rifle except for snap-shots.

There are two ways of pulling a set trigger.

• Keeping the finger free of it until the exact instant arrives and then just touching it. This is the only way a very light set can be fired. But a better way is to have the set so that it can be just touched without releasing it and then

• Allow the finger to merely touch it until the exact instant comes and then increase the weight of the touch.

Both the set and the hard trigger have their advantages and disadvantages for a hunting-rifle. Finer off-hand shooting can undoubtedly be done with a set trigger. But it is too easy for good running shooting, especially when there is little time to spare. And it is too unsafe with a trigger set to carry the rifle cocked even when expecting game to jump.

The real truth is that hard triggers are generally made absurdly hard. For such a promiscuous conglomeration of numbskulls as generally constitutes an army a six-pound pull is well enough. With an easy pull soldiers would decimate their own ranks more than those of the enemy. But for hunting, a pull of two pounds or even a pound and a half at the outside is safe enough. And in hunting, whatever is unnecessary is a nuisance.

For target-shooting, where the trigger is not set until the rifle is raised, a trigger that will not bear touching is well enough. Even there I think it unnecessary; but it can do no harm. But for hunting it should bear a touch of at least three ounces in weight.

The best of all is a combination of both; the hard trigger being not over one and a half or two pounds' pull, and the set bearing a touch of three ounces before going off. Then use the hard trigger for all close shots, quick shots, and running shots, and the set for all fine shots and long shots.

There are different ways of bringing the sight on the mark. But for hunting there is but one true way to raise the rifle from underneath. The experienced shot will often apparently fire as it comes to a level. And often he will actually do so. But this is because long practice has made him automatic in regard to care and precision. The beginner must never be be- guiled into doing this because it looks smart and dashing. The heroes you read of in novels, etc., did not. begin in that way. Nor do they ever shoot so

On all close shots it is better not to raise the sights upon the spot you wish to hit. It is better to see the whole above the front sight. Or aim so that you will hit the lower edge of the bull's-eye on a target. This plan is best because of the danger of overshooting, already so great, being increased if the front sight should cover the bull's-eye. On a long shot you may cover the bull's-eye with the front sight. But on long shots as well as short ones the beginner had better hold the sight both fine and low, not trusting himself to decide what is a long shot until he has seen a good many balls fall short of his game.

Chapter Twenty-Six - The Rifle on Moving Game

So vast is the difference between hitting even with the shot-gun an object at rest and an object in motion that it was many a year after the introduction of the shot-scattering system before any one attempted much to kill game when in motion. Many men are still living who can plainly remember when wing-shooting was almost an unknown art, practiced only by a few city sportsmen, while the country sportsman always waited for the rabbit or quail to stop. Even now this art is confined to those who can afford to waste plenty of ammunition and have the time and opportunity to practice. Even now it is conceded that even a moderate proficiency is no easy thing for anyone to acquire, and for a large number of people is a hard thing to acquire.

If such be the case with a gun that covers with its missiles a space of thirty inches, how much greater must be the difficulty of doing the same thing with a gun whose missile covers only half an inch or even less! We have already seen the immense difference between the shot-gun and rifle on game at rest. And at least the same degree of difference must exist between shooting with them game in motion. Such has always been believed to be the case, almost all riflemen conceding the difficulties of using the rifle upon anything in motion; only a very few of them being able to hit even so large an object as a deer or antelope when running; and all who talked of shooting on the wing with the rifle being classed as braggarts who knew nothing at all of shooting.

The world turned out to be wrong in its opinion of what could not be done with the shot-gun. Is it wrong in the opinion it has so long held about the capabilities of the rifle? Some advanced people think that it is.

In the winter of 1877-78 there appeared a gentleman whose sudden bound from obscurity to worldwide fame, from comparative poverty to comparative wealth, merits attention. Probably no man ever before won such applause, such notoriety, and so much money in so short a time from any exhibition of skill. It is safe to say that with either rifle or shot-gun no man ever again will do it.

This gentleman sprang upon the stage with a challenge that was at first received with a universal laugh of sneering contempt. Those who knew him knew, however, what he could do, and he lacked no backers in San Francisco. He at once began giving exhibitions in California, and demolished glass balls and even ten-cent pieces and bits of lead-pencil tossed in the air, and did it with an approach to certainty that silenced the laugher and turned the scoffer into an admirer.

He made his way East and from thence to England, France, and Germany, amid a storm of applause and "gate-money," winning the hearts even of princes and dignified old emperors by the rapidity and accuracy of his shooting.

It is not impossible that his success was partly due to the romantic story of his life as an Indian captive from childhood. This there seems no reason to doubt; and, aided by a fine physique and the tremendous power of long hair, flop-hat, buckskins, and badges, it possibly went far toward storming the susceptibilities of our foreign friends as well as the softer sex and softer members of the harder sex at home. But he certainly did such shooting as would before have been by many deemed impossible.

From his first appearance upon the stage Dr. Carver has had an enormous amount of practice with the rifle. And this he still keeps up. Like all other "professional" shots he plays with ammunition by the barrelful where an amateur or ordinary hunter uses less than a handful. He has all the advantages of powerful strength and perfect health, is in the prime of life with perfect sight, and was undoubtedly one of the best of field-shots before he appeared in public; nearly all his life having been passed in the field. The rifle has now reached about as high a state of perfection as can be expected from it, so far as its accuracy at short range and convenience of aiming are concerned. We are therefore justified in assuming that Dr. Carver can now do with the rifle at short range about all that can ever be done with it; certainly all that can ever be done with it by any ordinary amount of practice.

In 1878, about the time the loudest thunders of applause were rolling heavenward; when the words "marvelous," "miraculous," "wonderful," "astonishing," "witchcraft," "sorcery," "jugglery," "sleight of hand," etc. etc., echoed from half a million tongues; when Eastern editors were vying with each other in the effort to determine whether Carver's shooting were " instinctive," " intuitive," " innate," or " natural;" when Eastern reporters were filling columns with his romantic history, and telling how he could kill more birds on the wing with a bullet than most sportsmen could with shot, and then winding up with the affecting tale of how he "accidentally discovered" his wondrous God-given power in trying to bag a bluejay's tail for the pretty daughter of an Indian chief, an obscure individual in the mountains of San Diego County, California, who had never seen a glass ball, had the audacity to think that the crowd was a little too enthusiastic.

In the columns of the Chicago Field he then took the ground that Carver's shooting was neither marvelous nor extraordinary, but simply new, and hazarded the prediction that if there were any profit in it there would in a very few months be plenty of successful imitators. Carver honored the rural impertinence with his most crushing challenge, to which the rustic succumbed at once. His prediction was, however, quickly verified. Imitators by the score arose, most of whom have excelled the best records made by Carver during his first six months of glory. And before long we began to hear of wonderful boys and even wonderful girls that hit glass balls and pennies in the air with a rifle. These prodigies are on the increase. The other day I read of two new cases in one paper, neither over ten years of age.

During all this time it seems not to have occurred to the editorial or "scissoring" world that these wonderful boys and girls may prove two things instead of only one thing. According to them the hitting of glass balls in air by a child of ten years old proves only that the child is a wonderful performer. Is it not just possible that it may also prove that the performance is child's play?

The almost universal opinion of Carver's shooting was that it settled the long insoluble problem of shooting on the wing with the rifle. The majority thought that the ability to do this was restricted to Carver himself. Others thought that it could be acquired by imitating his methods, especially that of keeping both eyes open while aiming.

A few now think that the whole thing was a delusion; that the performance is a very easy one, and instead of being marvelous was simply novel; that, the novelty being now worn off, the shooting amounts to nothing for any practical purpose. But the opinion of the great majority is the other way. Thousands even, of men who use the rifle still believe and long will believe that Carver solved the question and discovered or invented the art of wing-shooting with the rifle. Already we have the "champion wing-shot with the rifle" by dozens. Already "wing-shooting with the rifle" is talked of as a thing of course. And it may be safely said that the world in general now believes and long will believe that the ability to break glass balls in air and blow nickels skyward with the rifle as Carver did carries with it of course the ability to shoot game on the wing with the rifle. And if such small things may be hit, the tripping of the heels of such a large object as a deer or antelope follows as a mere matter of course.

It will therefore be worthwhile to analyze this shooting and see just what can and what cannot be done by it. We shall then be in a position to understand the question of shooting running deer.

At the outset one very significant fact stares us in the face, a fact that no one yet seems to have taken the slightest notice of. That fact is this: Dr. Carver and all the imitators who have followed him have in all their public exhibitions been careful to shoot at no pigeons or other birds on the wing, to shoot at no balls tossed across the line of fire or at any angle to it, and to shoot at nothing in motion when at any distance where it would require the most ordinary amount of skill to hit the same object if at rest.

In order to understand clearly let us consider skill as of three degrees:
• That skill necessary to hit a three-inch ball at rest at ten paces, offhand with open sights.
• That skill necessary to hit at forty paces.
• That skill necessary to hit at seventy paces.

The first is the very lowest skill necessary for rifle-shooting. This may be cultivated in a single day by any person male or female of over ten years old, and many a boy of eight or nine can hit balls at rest all day at that distance upon the first trial. With a little practice the ball may be hit at ten paces by almost any one without any sights upon the rifle, and with a little more practice without even raising the rifle to the shoulder. But everyone who has ever shot at game with the rifle will readily admit that this degree of skill is absolutely worthless in the field. This degree of skill is attainable by mere sense of direction aided by practice. A baseball pitcher with his ball, a teamster with his whip, a boy with the " nigger-shooter" or blow-gun can soon learn to hit such a mark nearly every time.

The second degree of skill, or hitting a three-inch mark at forty paces, used to be very ordinary in the days of muzzle-loaders. Since the breech-loader has so generally come into fashion it has, for reasons we shall point out hereafter, become a very respectable degree of skill. This degree is absolutely necessary for anything like successful shooting on any kind of game however large or close. But it is far from being sufficient, and he who can do no better will miss in the long-run fully one half of the game he shoots at unless he confines himself to very close shots.

The third degree, or hitting a three-inch mark at seventy yards, is about the highest skill attainable with the average breech-loader with hunting-sights and offhand. There has long been an idea that much better shooting was possible. Of course better shots may be made. But he who takes the same pains to count his misses that he does to count his hits, and takes the average of a long series of shots, will speedily conclude that to hit a three-inch mark four times out of five at seventy yards is about as well as there is any hope of doing without very fine sights.

The first of these degrees of skill is that used in all the shooting at glass balls that Carver and his imitators do. A ball is occasionally shot at twenty yards, but the experiment is rarely repeated and is not half the time successful at the first shot. All the shooting is done inside of ten paces, generally at eight paces, and where mere sense of direction will almost suffice to hit it every time.

The ball is therefore at a distance where almost no skill at all would be required to hit it if it were at rest. Now is it not practically at rest?

The ball may be taken just as it hangs in air, just after it turns to descend, or even some time after beginning to fall. Anyone who has ever practiced any with a shot-gun at such marks knows that it makes little difference which way it is done so long as you continue to catch it always at that point. Just after it turns is, however, the best, the sight being taken at the lower edge. The ball, too, is always tossed to about the same height, is always at the same distance and in the same direction, and is always descending at the same rate of speed. No one who has ever handled a gun needs to be told how quickly the gun begins to return to the same place when often tossed up to it. And in the same way the rifle-sights soon begin to align themselves almost automatically with anything always in the same position. How easy this becomes with a little practice is shown by the fact that with a month's practice men who had never before handled a rifle almost equaled Carver's best scores on balls. How easy it is to do naturally is well shown by the feat of Mr. Maurice Thompson, the well-known archer. At the very first trial he broke with bow and arrow thirty-five out of fifty balls tossed in air at ten paces, shooting, too, as fast as the arrows could be placed on the string. This was indeed a feat, since it takes considerable skill to hit with an arrow a ball at ten paces even at rest. This would be fully equal to the same with the rifle at twenty-five yards; a little feat that neither Carver nor his followers have ever cared to attempt in public.

The whole secret of the matter is this: that a body descending inside of ten paces, descending straight and always at the same speed, becomes with a little practice practically in a state of rest at any point along the line at which one accustoms one's self to shoot at it. It is practically a body always in the same position and at the same distance, and the most careless aim if only low enough will hit it. A grazing ball that would not count on a bull's-eye will also break a glass ball. The case is not very much altered where pennies are substituted. It is far easier to hit a one-inch mark at ten yards than to hit a three-inch mark at thirty yards.

This is owing to the greater clearness of the mark and other causes we shall see hereafter, such as trajectory motion of object, etc. Still, pennies are harder to hit than balls, and with remarkable unanimity the "champion rifle wing-shots" always prefer balls to pennies, though more than twice as expensive and far more troublesome to handle. They also take care to have the pitcher a little closer, shoot at a very few of the pennies, and never attempt a long score. And the full score of those they do shoot at is generally suppressed.

The man who first tossed up two pennies and hit both with a double shot-gun before they touched ground was considered at first a very wonderful shot. Such a one will even now raise a stare of wonder among folks who know nothing of shooting. But everyone who has ever tried it a few times will admit that it is quite an easy matter, requiring only a little practice, and that it by no means implies the ability to send two woodcock whirling right and left to earth. The ball and penny shooting with the rifle stands upon the same footing. The performance was something new. To those who knew nothing of rifle shooting it was naturally surprising. The only real wonder is that anyone knowing anything about shooting should have been deceived by it or thought there was any sleight-of-hand about it. And it no more implies the ability to kill game in motion than hitting pennies with the shot-gun does. To waste no further time on this point, let us see what Carver has done in the field with the rifle.

He is credited with having killed at Logansport, Ind., four woodpeckers out of six at about fifty yards; all crossing shots. This would be indeed marvelous shooting. But as Carver never alluded to it himself, and never has ventured to shoot at birds in his exhibitions, we may well consider it, what it really was, pure good fortune. Success of that sort runs in streaks. I have made runs of shots with the rifle on running rabbits that I know I could not repeat in fifty trials. When Dr. Carver was getting a thousand dollars a week for pulverizing balls at the Minnesota State Fair he was invited out to shoot grouse. It was early in September, when grouse lie well to the dog, are full grown, and generally rise at less than six paces. There flies no bird that presents a fairer or much larger target. The Doctor had shot thousands before; he was not out for meat, but only for sport. He knew that killing grouse at that season with a gun is child's play. He shot sixty-five in all; and he took precious good care to do it with the shotgun. Why did he not take a rifle? Perhaps he can tell us better himself. Here is an extract from a letter of his describing a chamois-hunt in Austria on the preserves of Count Wilzek. It is from the Chicago Field of Nov. 20, 1880. Here is a record of three days' shooting, in his own language too, by the man who was being wined and dined by princes and potentates for his "marvelous," "natural," "instinctive," "intuitive" shooting. Yet the reader must not suppose this is bad shooting. It is first-class work under the circumstances. I cite it only to show the enormous difference between ball-shooting and game-shooting. Probably no living shot could excel it. But just count the misses and the shots let go for want of time to shoot. Remember, too, that Carver is the quickest of living shots with the rifle, and that if anything can be done by snap-shooting with it he can do it.

"Monday morning found me up bright and early, dressed as a mighty hunter, armed with a Winchester rifle, model 1876, and a six-foot pole with a spike in it. All eyes turned toward me, the Yankee hunter; as I stepped forth, dressed in an English hunting-costume, my long hair carefully combed, many an expression either of contempt or admiration went up from the crowd of beaters, but all in German, so I could not understand. I learned afterward that I was looked upon as a good subject for many purposes, but 'nix good' for chamois. We started at the foot of an immense mountain and climbed toward the summit for three hours. At last we reached an impassable barrier; the Count motioned me to sit down by a little tree. I took my seat, and for the first time looked down the mountain. I came very near falling; turning my eyes toward the summit I dare not look again; everything was still as death, and thus it remained for perhaps twenty minutes, when bang! went a rifle on our right. The next instant there was a rush of stones down the sides of the mountain. The Count sang out, "Here he comes" and sure enough he came rushing down the side of the mountain like lightning. He made a great bound and stopped on the side of the mountain, but only for an instant; he cast one wild look in our direction, and jumped out of sight. He ran on our right and soon disappeared, and the next we saw of him he crossed the mountain far out of reach below us. How sorry I was not to get him; it was the first one I ever saw. We sat still for a few minutes, when directly under us, not more than ten yards, stood another chamois. I raised my gun. The Count says, 'Nix, das ist eine frau;' and so it proved, for in another instant out stepped a little kid. They stood still for nearly a minute, then ran along the side of the mountain without observing us. In chamois shooting none but the bucks are shot; there is but slight difference in the horns, but a hunter can tell a buck at a long distance. At first I could not see the slightest difference. The sound of the beaters now reached our ears, the rattle of stones above us. I looked just in time to see three young chamois bound away. Soon comes another with a kid, dreadfully frightened at the beaters. She ran within ten feet of us and stopped. She was looking behind her and did not discover us until I laughed. She was so frightened she turned around and knocked her little one over, and away she went down the mountain. We sat still for a long time until beaters reached us, without seeing any more; then we prepared to go down.

"Bread and honey, how is that for breakfast, to climb mountains on? But once more I shouldered that old Winchester, and followed, all smiles, far in the rear. A distance of five miles, then we commenced to climb another mountain. At last I reached my position, the lowest one of all, thanks to the kindness of the Count. I watched the other shooters until out of sight, then sitting clown with a beater left to look after me, the Count taking a chance himself. He excused himself from me by saying he never had any luck; and so it proved, the females all paying him their respects, much to his disgust. I had not sat long in my position when I saw the horns of a stag through the trees directly on my right. The beater said, 'Shoot.' I was not in any hurry, I felt so sure of him; he stepped out exposing his shoulder to me. I said to myself, ' I have got you, old man,' and took a careful aim; bang! went the Winchester, away went the stag up the side of the mountain. I shot three hundred feet too high and ruined a top of a big pine; it did not take me long to get the old Winchester leveled once more. I shut my eyes, pulled and jerked until it went off; good shot, just back of the shoulder, but a downright fluke. The stag gave one bound and then came end over end down the mountain for more than two hundred yards, a grand sight for a hunter. All was still for more than half an hour, when bang! went the guns all along the line above me, and down the mountain came a fine buck chamois. He stopped two hundred yards; bang! went my gun, but still he came on; bang! bang! went the Winchester, but still he came on until he was within fifty yards. I still kept shooting; seven shots had missed. He tried to run along on the side of the mountains; this was the last chance, and I stood up and fired. Now or never; hit, by Jove! He clung to the side of the mountain for one minute, then rolled down to the bottom. He, my first chamois, was killed. Hurrah for Carver! We did not have long to wait until down the mountain came another; bang! went the old gun. Hit, but where? Through the haunch, by that great Yankee too. One stag and two chamois, when down came another. I turned my battery loose as soon as he hove in sight, and the chamois was so frightened that he ran within ten feet of where I was sitting. I still pumped away at him. He never stopped, although we could see four holes in him, he came so near. He followed a little path for a short distance, and quietly laid down and ' passed in his chips.' What fun I was having, to be sure! when down came another. This fellow was undoubtedly engaged on some newspaper, and was going to press; he went. The shooting for the day was over three chamois and one stag; one chamois had five bullets in him. The Count gave me the skin, and I will always keep it in remembrance of my astounding luck. To say I was proud is just what I mean. We went home, my lameness all gone.

"The next morning, bright and early, away we went again. This time we did not have so far to climb, and were soon in position. The first objects I saw after taking my seat were seven deer; but before I could think they were gone. I had just time to get my gun in readiness when three chamois crossed in front of me, going undoubtedly on pressing business. They went. My banging at them did not even attract their attention. Dear reader, if you are ever asked the question, 'Can chamois run?' say 'yes,' for my sake; but with all their speed, they are sometimes foolish, and will stop every few jumps, and give the hunter a good opportunity to shoot. All was quiet for a few minutes, when bang! went Dr. Cup's gun. A fine young buck stopped far up the mountain-side. I took deliberate aim, the bullet crashing through his shoulder. Almost at the same instant I heard a noise on my right; I looked, and within fifty yards was the finest stag I ever saw. Bang! bang! went the gun in quick successive shots, and the noble stag commenced rolling, end over end, down the mountain, the chamois coming down the other. This I will say is the best shot I ever made. With four shots I killed two chamois and one stag, two bullets in the stag's neck within two inches of each other. The shooting over, Dr. Cup came down, and said I ought to thank him for the stag, as he missed him twice."

I consider it safe to say that no improvement or discovery has been made in the art of rifle-shooting on moving game; that snap-shooting with it will always be worthless beyond the very shortest distances; that no way of making a rifle can obviate the natural difficulties of shooting with it; and that the use of two eyes, though just as good as the use of only one, will not help us a particle.

Practice at balls is, however, by no means to be despised. Practice at anything is better than no practice at all. But do not deceive yourself with the idea that hitting balls implies hitting game.

Chapter Twenty-Seven - The Rifle on Moving Game (Continued)

The great hindrances to successful shooting with the rifle at running deer and antelope are precisely the same that prevent successful wing-shooting with it. Shooting at the two first is the more easy only because of the greater size of the mark. But this size, great though it be, does not even at quite short distances permit the least carelessness in aiming. For, as we have seen, such carelessness is bad enough even when the game is at rest. The hindrances are:

• The limited amount of time causes one to raise the rifle too hastily and run his eye too hastily along the sights. By which means one is almost certain to take too full a front sight and thereby overshoot, unless the rifle be held very low.

• The fact that in three shots out of four the game is moving at some angle to the line of fire, thus requiring the aim to be taken ahead of the mark. From this flows
• The difficulty of determining how much to allow for the motion of the game; and
• To measure off that amount of space even if you do know how much is needed; and
• While doing all this and firing at the point of blank space in which the game will be when the ball reaches it, to preserve the proper elevation; a matter difficult enough where there is no allowance to be made for motion. All the conditions, too, are constantly varying.

The best way to obviate the first difficulty is to raise the rifle slowly, or rather deliberately, running your eye along it and catching a full clear view of the sights as it comes up, concentrating your attention upon the sights instead of upon the game. When shooting a shot-gun the game is the principal object of vision. One scarcely sees even the gun-barrel, and almost never sees the sight upon it. The tendency to do the same with the rifle is very strong, and in one who is a good wing-shot with the shot-gun is at first almost irresistible. But nothing is more certain to cause a miss at any considerable distance. Suppose a man with a shot-gun can average nine rabbits out of ten shots, all running, and all pure snap-shots. Suppose the same man can fire a Winchester at the rate of two shots a second at a standing mark, shooting close enough to place nine balls out of ten in an eight-inch ring at twenty yards pure snap-shooting with the rifle. How many times would the same man hit rabbits inside of twenty yards, the rabbits all running and the rifle being fired in the same manner as at the eight-inch ring, or fired in the same manner as the shot-gun was fired to hit nine rabbits out of ten? The answer to this problem as given by actual experiment is amazing even to one who knows the vast difference between shot and a bullet at a sitting mark. I believe I understate rather than overstate it when I say he would not touch one rabbit in ten, on an average of one hundred shots or more. When at a hundred yards or over, or when at only fifty yards and running fast, the same aim that with a shot-gun would kill fifty successive quail on the wing will not suffice to even scratch one running deer out of fifty except by accident.

The sights must therefore be seen as plainly and taken with the same degree of fineness as in a fine shot at game standing. A certain amount of time must be lost in doing this. It might better be lost while raising the rifle than at any other time. For it must be lost anyhow, and during that time the game is getting farther away. Now if you jerk the rifle hastily to the mark you will find the temptation to fire when the sight first glimmers on the mark almost irresistible; and if you do fire it will almost certainly be with too coarse or vague a sight. But if you raise the rifle deliberately, looking for the sights as it comes up and holding your eye firmly upon them, this danger will not be half so great. You will have no trouble in keeping sight of the game all this time, whereas if you make the game the first object of vision you will find it very hard to catch a clear sight. And if you toss up the rifle as you would a shot-gun, it will actually take longer to find the sight afterward than when raising it slowly and running your eye along it as it comes up. Moreover, when raising it slowly you are much more apt to raise it directly into the spot at which it is to be fired, so as to require no adjustment or shifting afterward; a thing which is the very essence of all good shooting with either shot-gun or rifle.

In the next place, if the game is running across the line of fire even at a very acute angle the rifle should be raised ahead of the point you wish to hit. In accordance with the principle above stated (if the ball is to be fired ahead of the mark at all) it is much better to raise the rifle at once to the point at which it is to be discharged than to raise it upon some other point and then shift it. For if you raise it upon the game the temptation to fire then will be too strong; and if you raise it behind the game and attempt to shift it forward you will be tempted to fire when the sight first touches the animal's outline. In both cases you will be liable to shoot too high because you will be quite certain to be too hasty.

The necessity of firing ahead of moving game has been so strongly disputed by some who are unquestionably good field-shots, and the principle is so es-sential in shooting moving game with the rifle, that it merits some attention. The question is one susceptible of positive proof by the plainest principles of philosophy; so I will omit all boasting of " experience," etc., and call upon an impartial arbiter.

If two railroad trains were running parallel at a hundred yards apart and at the rate of thirty miles an hour, a ball fired from one at a mark upon the other would strike the mark the same as if both trains were at rest. (We are suppos-ing, of course, that the wind will make no difference.) But if one were moving at only one mile an hour, a ball fired from that would strike the other train at a point distant from the mark aimed at just twenty-nine thirtieths of the dis-tance the train fired at moved while the ball was passing a hundred yards.

In other words, the ball moves sidewise with the lateral motion of the train from which it is fired at only one thirtieth of the speed it had when the train moved thirty miles an hour instead of one mile. The ball in both cases takes the diagonal of a parallelogram built upon the line of fire a hundred yards, and the line of space the train from which it was fired moved while the ball was moving from train to train. The parallelogram in the second case is only one thirtieth of the width of the one in the first case.

Suppose now the train containing the rifle were at rest, but the rifle were a hundred yards long, or long enough to follow the mark and keep its muzzle against it while the ball was passing up the barrel. The ball would in such case hit the mark although the breech of the rifle were at rest. Because in such case the ball is carried along sidewise by the constantly increasing motion of the long extended barrel. And now suppose the barrel to be only three feet long instead of three hundred feet, but following the mark with the line of sights. What will then become of the ball? If those be correct who insist that the lat-eral motion of the gun in following game is sufficient, the ball will follow the same sidewise course as if it were still acted upon by the constantly increasing lateral swing of the three-hundred-foot barrel. In other words, if one half of the long barrel were slit off for two hundred and ninety-seven feet on the side opposite the direction the mark is moving, so that the ball can escape from the side of the barrel at any point beyond three feet from the breech, the ball will nevertheless decline to escape and hug the other half of the barrel as closely as it did when the barrel was whole. There is no possible escape from this conclusion. The ball must take the same course in the half-open barrel that it does in the whole one, or it cannot get far enough to one side to reach the mark. Whether the ball will leave the opening or not is an experiment any one can easily try by whirling a ball up a tin tube slit off in the same way as the barrel.

For those who like more imposing philosophy I add the following principles, which are as firmly established as the law of gravity:

• Nobody can describe a curve unless constantly acted upon by two forces one of which must be a constantly increasing force.

• Whenever a ball is released from the increasing force which curves its course, its path will at once change to a straight line.

• This line will be a tangent to the curve that constituted the path of the ball before its release from the force that curved its course.

• No tangent to a curve can reach the same place that the curve itself would arrive at.

When a gun-barrel is held at the shoulder and moved sidewise in following crossing game the muzzle moves much faster than the breech. And the ball is therefore subjected to a constantly increasing force from one side. This increasing force combining with the forward motion imparted by the powder must produce a curve, although it is apparently a straight line. If any one doubts this let him take a string, double it and loop it over a nail on a board, then holding the two ends together and moving them sidewise like the pendulum of a clock run a lead-pencil down between the strings. He will find that, though the strings be straight and the path of the pencil apparently a straight line, it is actually a curve. Now how can this curve continue after the sidewise action of the barrel ceases? And how can the ball reach the game unless that curve does continue? There is no escape from it; the lateral-motion advocates have solved the problem of shooting around the corner without even bending the gun-barrel; we have only to whirl the gun fast enough and around goes the ball; a little faster and it will turn the next corner; faster yet and it will almost return to " plague the inventor" in the rear.

You can now calculate for yourself about how far a deer running at a hundred yards will leave behind him a ball fired at a certain speed. The swing of the barrel does of course carry the ball sidewise, but it is like the motion of the train going at one mile an hour. It is only about one thirtieth or one twentieth of what is necessary. All calculations by figures of the amount of margin to be allowed are, however, of little use in the field. A wheel rolled down a hill where you can see the balls strike, and swallows skimming along water, etc., make good targets from which to get some idea of the distance necessary to hold ahead of moving game. Those who deny the necessity of holding ahead are pleased to stigmatize as theorists those who prefer an appeal to philosophy instead of talking about their own experience and sneering at the experience of all others. To those "practical men" who feel hard toward "theorists" the rolling-wheel target and the swallow on water are most respectfully recommended.

There is, however, another element that prevents the ball's reaching the mark in time. From the instant your brain decides to pull the trigger until the ball escapes the rifle some time is lost. The passage of nerve-force from the brain to the finger, over four feet; the fall of the hammer; the explosion of cap; the evolution of the gas from the powder, all these take time. It is indeed but a short time, but it is time nevertheless. Take a muzzle-loading rifle with globe-sights and set trigger, load with a round ball and so small a charge that you can see every ball strike. Then let someone with a long string pull a small mark across in front of you at different distances and rates of speed. You will be surprised to find at how short a distance you will shoot behind it if you hold the sights directly on it.

The effect of these two causes combined is much greater than one would suppose who has never shot at running game on ground where missing balls can be seen to strike. It is so great that there seems to be no point, however close, at which holding ahead of crossing game can be entirely neglected if the game is moving fast. And there seems to be no motion, however slow, which will permit such neglect if the animal be at any considerable distance. I do not mean that holding ahead is always necessary to insure hitting the animal, but it is almost always necessary if you wish to hit the animal in the best place. Nor is it always necessary to hold the sights clear of the animal's outline, but only ahead of the point you wish to strike. But when the game is at any distance or speed even the whole body will be missed, and this even when the course of the animal is only quartering, unless the aim be taken ahead. Hence holding ahead is always safe; is generally expedient; is often indispensable to success.

There is, however, another way by which the same result may be attained. If the rifle be raised behind the game, whirled rapidly past it, and fired as it is passing, the muzzle of the rifle may move sidewise as much as an inch or two from the time your brain gives the order to pull the trigger which to you appears to be the actual time of firing, though it is not until the escape of the ball. If one fifteenth of a second a space imperceptible to the senses were lost in this way and the motion of your gun-barrel were at the rate of thirty inches a second, it would move two inches sidewise without your knowing it at all. Now an inch at the gun-muzzle may equal three or four feet where the game is. Consequently at the time the ball gets its final direction from the muzzle the line of the sights may be several feet ahead of the game without your suspecting it and while you firmly believe you held on the body.

155

This is a very effective way of using the shot-gun, especially on birds curling backward on either side of you. This, with the fact that the scattering of shot often renders holding ahead unnecessary at short distances, accounts for the reasoning of many who insist that holding on moving game is sufficient "if the gun be kept moving."

But this is a bad method for shooting running deer, because

• It is just as necessary to regulate the speed with which the line of sight overtakes the animal and to fire at the right time as it is to select the proper distance to hold ahead; and it is quite as hard to do so.

• In doing so you cannot retain so well as by the other method that clear and perfect view of the sights that is indispensable to avoid overshooting.

• And, worst of all, you cannot in this way allow so well for the rise and fall of the deer and the intervention of trees, etc., in the path of your bullet.

A running antelope is a gently gliding movement, soft, swift, and spirituelle. But little allowance need ever be made for its up-and-down motion, and often none at all is needful. But a running deer is generally a bounding deer, often a bouncing deer. The mule-deer when running generally throws himself aloft at least two feet, and often three feet or more, at every blow of his springy legs upon the ground. The Virginia or white-tailed deer runs indeed with a graceful canter, but still rises fully the width of his body at every spring. And here arises the great source of misses on deer running straight away. If the deer is at any distance over thirty or forty yards, allowance must be made for this motion. But the tendency is to hold the sights upon the body and fire when it shows the most conspicuously; to wit, when it is in the air. The consequence is that the ball whizzes through the space the deer has just left in its descent. Sometimes, however, one will fire when the deer is on the ground, in which case the ball gets there as the deer is rising, and either misses it entirely or hits a leg.

The ball should be fired at the point of space the deer will occupy when the ball reaches him. This will always involve some guesswork, because it is impossible always to calculate the right distance to fire ahead, and it is also impossible to hit with certainty a blank point of space, even if you do know its exact distance from the mark. Try shooting a yard to one side of a bull's-eye at a hundred yards on clean snow, and see what kind of a score you will make as compared with what you could make at the mark, and you will at once see another reason why wing-shooting with the rifle will always be quite a puzzle.

The best point at which to fire is the point at which the deer will reach the ground in his descent. And this can be calculated with much more precision than would at first be supposed possible, although it certainly involves much guesswork. The way it can be done most successfully I believe to be the following:

• Raise the rifle ahead of the game, remembering it is a rifle and not a shotgun.

• Raise it deliberately, getting the same fine clear view of the sights that you would take at a deer standing at a hundred yards; or if you cannot do that, then hold low.

• Keeping your eye on the sights, carry the rifle along ahead of the deer until you catch the motion of the body enough to see where it will be when the hoofs touch ground.

• Fire at that point, but fire when the deer is in the air,

The great point is not to be in haste. Be not at all be alarmed by the fact that the deer is getting farther off. Your chances of hitting at a hundred yards with a well calculated and directed shot are better than the chances of hitting with three or four careless ones at fifty yards. Place no dependence on speed of fire. Even from a repeater, fire every shot as though it were a single muzzle-loader. Speed of fire is a splendid servant but a wretched master.

Of course there will be times when a pure snap-shot is necessary. At very short distances snap-shots will of course often hit. But never take one even at a short distance unless another bound or two will take the deer out of sight.

When in timber you may be edified by the whack of your bullet into a tree-trunk. Watching for an open place in timber is quite as essential as any other part of the operation of shooting running deer. And this can be done better if the rifle be raised ahead in the first instance.

It seems to be supposed by some that shooting moving game is much easier if both eyes be kept open.

If you will experiment with your finger raised in line with some object you will find, by opening and shutting each eye alternately, that only one eye is used in thus aligning your finger. This will generally be the right one. But you will find by further experiment that you can soon train the left one to do the same thing. And you will find the proof conclusive that the brain can attend to the report or nerve of one eye as well as the report of both. It can concentrate its attention upon the picture produced upon the retina of one eye alone and be quite blind to the picture upon the retina of the other.

This it will readily do in case of the eye we are most accustomed to use, but it can be trained to do the same thing with the other. The consequence may be that when the gun is raised the eye that is in line with the sights may receive the most attention from the brain, and the other one may be pretty much ig-nored. If you will fire a rifle alternately from each shoulder a few times, sight-ing always with both eyes open, you will be apt to conclude that such is the case, and that binocular or two-eyed shooting is a delusion. Such, I think, is the case after a thorough trial of it. It is just as good as one-eyed shooting, but no better, and nothing can be accomplished by it with the rifle that cannot be done with one eye. For shot-gun shooting it has a few slight advantages, but for the rifle it has none; and I cannot, on crossing shots, estimate so well the distance to hold ahead of game as when using one eye. Sufficient practice would probably make two eyes just as good for this purpose as one eye.

There are some other rules given by many good hunters for shooting a running deer, two of which are maintained by so respectable a number of good shots as to be worthy of notice. They are in fact the same as I have given, but owing to bad observation and carelessness of language are so mangled in sense and distorted in expression as to be misleading.

The first is, " Hold the rifle ahead of the deer, and, when you see him through the sights, pull."

This would of course do for a short distance, though even there it would probably place the ball back of the center of the body; but for any considerable distance it will not do. A swinging target with a blind so arranged that you can only see the bull's-eye when it passes an opening in the blind will soon dispel this illusion. But the best refutation lies in the rule itself. This is holding on the mark and not ahead of it. Why, then, resort to such a bungling way when it is so much easier to raise the sights directly upon the deer? Who would think of shooting at a bird in such a way? The fact is that those who shoot in this way pull the trigger before the animal comes into the line of the sights. A little practice at the swinging target and blind will show you that you must shoot before. But you will at once see how it can easily appear otherwise to a careless observer.

The other rule is, "Hold on the shoulder low down." This will of course do if the deer is close and is descending. This rule undoubtedly originated, as did the last one, among hunters in the woods only. No one who ever shot much in the open would so express it. But the fact here probably is that, as in the other case, the trigger is pulled a trifle quicker than the shooter thinks it is.

If a deer is trotting or running very low you may disregard the up-and-down motion, though it is better to allow for it when you can. A deer even on a trot often rises considerably. A deer at full speed generally hugs the ground like a hare. In such case the up-and-down motion must be disregarded. After we have examined the question of the flight of bullets, long-range shooting, etc., you will understand the monstrous nonsense of talking about shooting deer on the run at two hundred and fifty and three hundred yards as a matter of course. It is of very little use to shoot beyond a hundred and fifty yards; and there is no man who, taking all shots, can hit a deer running at that distance more than once in three shots, and it is doubtful if anyone can do that. All the talk to the contrary is based upon guessed instead of measured distance.

Chapter Twenty-Eight - Long Range Shooting at Game

There is probably no subject connected with shooting about which so much nonsense has been written and spoken as the distance at which game can be killed with the rifle. This was bad enough in the days of muzzle-loaders. It has become doubly bad in these days of long-range and mid-range breech loaders. We now know that such shooting as Cooper and a host of novelists have ascribed to their heroes, such shooting as we have all in our early days read about as being common among the backwoods hunters, was impossible with any rifle, and especially with the small-bored rifle and round ball then almost universally in use among hunters in the woods. But now that rifles are found in every shop that will shoot into a two-foot ring at five hundred yards (under target-shooting conditions and care), it is quite natural to suppose that game can be killed as a matter of course at three or four times the distance at which it could once be done.

More game is now killed at two hundred yards and over than was formerly killed at that point. But this is not because of any improvement or discovery in distant shooting, but because game is scarcer and wilder, and more chances must be taken, and because the ease of loading the breech-loader and procuring its ammunition makes people more liberal in expending ammunition. I do not hesitate to assert that no advance whatever has been made in the art of killing game at long ranges, except in so far as the breech- loader allows one to fire more shots before the game gets too far away. I say this notwithstanding the fact that the popular opinion is quite the other way.

The old muzzle-loader by the use of a lengthened ball and more powder could with globe-sights be given a great accuracy at quite long ranges. This was perfectly understood by most of the old-time hunters, who often went to the annual "turkey-shoot" equipped with a weapon that at two hundred and three hundred yards can hardly be beaten today by any of the boasted breech-loaders. Many of those who hunted on open ground used the "slug" or long ball, and some used it even in the woods. Many long shots were made with it, and probably more game was killed at long range out of the same number of shots than is now killed with the best of modern rifles at the same distance. They all did plenty of boasting of their long shooting. But from long-range shooting proper, such as we are now considering, they nearly always abstained. This was not because they could not do it, but because they soon learned that, whatever their skill at the target or turkey, at measured distances, it was far easier to get closer to game than to hit it at long unmeasured distances.

There are several reasons for the extravagant ideas afloat about the distance at which game may now be killed.

• The incurable mania for gilding the gold of simple truth. This afflicts hunters as badly as it does fishermen.

• The love of "scissors" on a newspaper for copying everything that savors of a good fat "whopper," such as the stuff that has gone the rounds of the United States this year about the Boers of South Africa knocking over spring-bucks at eight hundred and nine hundred yards as a matter of course.

• Sincere and natural mistake in overestimating distance, a thing that scarcely any of us can learn to avoid, and that causes the oldest hunter many a miss. The beginner sees a deer at a long distance, looking more like a small fawn than a full-grown deer. He shoots, and perhaps the deer falls at the first shot.

" Ge-ra-shus! What a shot! Four hundred yards!" exclaims the delighted novice. He hastens to his game without stopping to measure the ground. He pants and puffs in getting over it as I have seen older hunters do in lifting a hundred-and-twenty- pound buck on a horse, trying to make themselves be- lieve it weighs two hundred and fifty pounds. When he reaches home the ground, still plainly seen by Fancy's eye, has expanded to four hundred and fifty yards. When he comes to tell of his wonderful shot he very naturally wants to do himself full justice, and so he leaves himself a little margin of fifty yards more for possible error. And to the day of his death he will sincerely believe that he killed that deer at almost five hundred yards. And to the day of his death this idea will be a mental whirlpool that will suck in and whirl out of sight all the driftwood of contradictory facts that years of later experience can throw in his way.

Now the novice was perfectly right in one point that he made a very long and very fine shot. The deer was only two hundred yards away, but he was still right in calling it a long shot; for notwithstanding the popular impression to the contrary, two hundred yards is a long distance to hit a deer even in the most favorable position.

The very swiftest ball or the most speed-sustaining ball you can fire from a rifle falls fast enough in two hundred and fifty yards to miss every deer or antelope at which it is fired with the sights set for a distance twenty-five yards on either side the animal; either undershooting or overshooting it. You will find that at three hundred yards a mistake of twenty yards in your esti- mate of distance will cause a miss, at four hundred yards a mistake of fifteen yards, etc. These figures are of course not exact, and will vary with the rifle. But they are not over three or four yards out of the way for the best long- range rifles.

If you doubt figures or anything that savors of "theory," put up a target at two hundred yards with your rifle sighted to that point. Fire a few shots, re- ceding from the target twenty-five yards each time and firing with the same sight. But do not try to hit the bull's-eye, but only to discover the fall of the bullet.

Having satisfied yourself what the rifle will do, find out what you can do in estimating distance. Try it first in timber, making an estimate of the longest distances and then pacing them. Then try it on quite open and level ground, estimating and pacing up to four hundred yards only. There will be a startling shrinkage of conceit somewhere.

But perhaps you think the faculty of judging distance can be cultivated. Of course it can be improved. By doing nothing else it might even be cultivated to a high enough state of perfection to make five bull's-eyes out of six up to four hundred yards with the target shifted at every shot. But with such time as one can generally devote to that business he will be more apt to miss the bull's-eye five times out of six.

But suppose you are quite an accurate judge of distance under the above conditions. Recollect there is no antelope there just ready to leave; no rifle in your hand, with your finger itching for the trigger. The difference that this alone makes is almost in- conceivable. There is also another tremendous difficulty, the ever-shifting conditions of ground, light, etc., which occur in hunting. Now up hill, now down hill, here through timber, there over timber, through brush or over brush, up canons and across canons, over ridges and over flats, often with scarce a second to spare, judging distance in hunting is a vastly different matter from what it is on always the same kind of ground with plenty of time and no game in sight.

Moreover, whatever your skill may be, your gauge unconsciously shifts with the ground. The standard you use on the plains today will not do for the foothills tomorrow; the one you use in the foothills is too small when you get upon the mountain's breast; this fails you again when you get among the higher peaks; and when you return to the lowlands you are again "all at sea" for a few days.

Speaking of the inside of St. Peter's at Rome, Byron says :

"Its grandeur overwhelms thee not; And why? It is not lessened, but thy mind, Expanded by the genius of the spot, Has grown colossal."

Who has not felt this when among the mountains, and wondered at the ever-changing deceptiveness of heights and distances?

Traveling once with a friend who was boasting of his ability to roll deer right and left at five hundred yards running or standing, and whom this poetry failed to touch (as it will the reader, being the only poetry in the book), I asked an old surveyor at whose camp we stopped how he could estimate distance.

"Well," said he, "when I stay several days on one kind of ground I can make a tolerably fair guess on short distances. But as soon as I get on a different kind of ground I don't know anything."

Considerable practical skill may, however, be cultivated up to two hundred and fifty or even three hundred yards on the plains, and there are hunters who can judge distance well enough to hit an antelope at two hundred yards three times out of five at the first shot, all other conditions being of course complied with. It is doubtful, however, if anyone can do this anywhere but on such open ground as antelope frequent.

If you think I underestimate what is good shooting at two hundred yards, look over the two-hundred-yard scores made at matches by our best target-shots. Recollect, too, that these scores are generally better than can be made by any mere hunter, the difference being that the hunter can generally shoot as well at game as he can at a target, which the mere target-shot cannot do. Remember, too that the bull's-eye is clear white or black on a black or white ground, is eight inches in diameter, is always in the same light, position, etc., and that its distance is known to a foot and the sights set exactly to it. The target-shot has every advantage, the hunter every disadvantage. These scores are nearly all made, too, with globe sights. Take the best of these scores, and bear in mind that it takes a five shot to hit an antelope with certainty, and even that when near the edge may represent only a crippling shot; that a four shot will hit only about half the time, and then probably cripple him; and that all the rest will be quite sure to miss the animal entirely or only break a leg.

" Shall I shoot from where I am or try to get closer?" is therefore a very important question. Except upon quite level plains the chances of getting within two hundred yards are always greater than the chances of hitting beyond that. The chances of getting within a hundred and fifty yards are generally greater than the chances of hitting beyond that. The chances of getting within a hundred yards are often greater than the chances of hitting beyond it. I have had a pretty high degree of skill in guessing distances, adjusting sights, and hitting natural marks up to four hundred yards or more. But I am perfectly satisfied that if I had never seen a long-range or mid-range rifle, if I had hunted always with a rifle that would not shoot an inch beyond a hundred and twenty-five yards, I should have killed much more game than I have. For that very skill has beguiled me too often into opening a cannonade when I could easily have gotten closer. And this even with wild antelope on quite open ground.

For the last three years my rule has been to shoot at nothing beyond a hundred and fifty yards if there is an even chance of getting closer to it, and not to shoot even that far if there is a fair prospect of shortening the distance. I fully believe I have gotten more deer by it. I certainly know that there have been fewer broken-legged cripples. For deer and antelope on the plains fifty yards might be added to this distance, for elk another fifty yards, and for buffalo another fifty. Beyond this point you had better make it a rule to get closer.

All this is of course on the assumption that the game does not see you. If it sees you, longer shots must often be taken. But I have seen deer so tame that your chances of running or even walking sixty or seventy-five yards closer were much greater than the chance of hitting at two hundred yards. And this, too, when they were looking directly at one. But where the game is not alarmed it is a safer rule to treat the best long-range gun as if it were a short-range muzzle-loader, and turn every point to make a sure shot.

I know that some will disagree with this. I know all the stories about how So-and-so killed an antelope at eight hundred yards, and how What's-his-name hit a goose at half a mile, and how the other man hit a deer in the heart running at five hundred yards, etc. etc. etc., ad infinitum. I know, too, how it all is done. Nearly everyone who has played much with a long-range rifle has made remarkable shots at long distances. I have made my full share of them. So long as these are classed where they belong, as accidental shots, it is well enough to tell of them. But when any one attempts to draw conclusions from them, then, in the name of philosophy, I protest. Until one can make them at least once in ten trials at unmeasured distances they are utterly worthless to reason from, even though considerable skill entered into them.

One way in which game is often killed at long distances is by it standing for "sighting shots" until you finally get its range. But it is quite as apt to jump at every shot or two just enough to derange your calculations. And in either case the shooter is very apt to forget all about the number of shots that did not hit. Still, where it is evident that game cannot be more closely approached, this is sometimes an effective way of getting it; though the chances of hitting it at all are always largely against you.

The delusion of long-range shooting is fostered by the ease with which with a long-range rifle the dirt can be made to fly just over or under a distant object. We shall see in another place the worthlessness for hunting of what is generally known as the " line-shot," by which is meant a shot on a line running up and down through the mark, and that the only" line-shot" worth anything for hunting is on the horizontal line, the hardest of all to make. But it takes bull's-eyes instead of line-shots to kill game. Moreover, what appears to be only a few inches' deviation from the distant mark is really a few feet. And to reduce those feet to inches without measuring the distance will be found a little problem the solution of which will generally puzzle you until the game gets weary of awaiting the answer.

The main difficulty of accurate long-range shooting cannot be obviated by telescopic or any other kind of sights or arrangement of sights. The estimate of distance remains the same whatever sight be used.

Whenever it is necessary to shoot beyond the point blank of your rifle, discount your estimate of distance about twenty per cent on two hundred yards, twenty- five on three hundred, thirty on four hundred yards, etc. And whenever in doubt between two estimates of distance, decide at once in favor of the shorter one. By letting long shots go where there is a prospect of getting closer you will of course lose some game. But you will get more in the end.

Chapter Twenty-Nine - The Effect of Recoil Upon Shooting

In the days of heavy long barrels with light bullets and moderate charges of powder, the days of muzzle-loaders, the recoil, or "kick," of the rifle was so slight as to have little or no effect upon the direction of the ball. But in these days of short light barrels with long heavy balls and often heavy charges of powder, the effect of recoil upon the direction of the ball is so decided that scarcely any point about shooting is more important than this sometimes is.

The true theory of the recoil of a gun I believe to be this: The backward pressure of the gas upon the breech of the gun begins at the same instant with the forward pressure upon the ball. In each case the powder is acting against inertia or weight. But the inertia or weight of the gun, being one hundred or more times the inertia of the bullet, will resist the pressure much longer before yielding to it than the vastly lighter bullet can resist. So that the inertia of the ball is overcome and changed into motion in a trifling fraction of the time in which the inertia or weight of the gun is overcome and changed into motion. And this great difference in the time of yielding, or in the conversion of force into motion, makes an immense difference in the relative speed of the two motions.

Suppose a fifty-pound anvil hung in air by a cord with a hole bored in one side that will admit a bolt of lead of the same weight as the anvil itself. If the bolt were fired from that hole with a fuse, the anvil and bolt would both move in opposite directions at the same rate of speed. This would be the case whatever amount of powder were used, the increase in charge only increasing the speed of both. If now the hole and bolt were both gradually reduced in size, the motion of the bolt would increase and the motion of the anvil decrease in the same ratio, until with a small enough buckshot and a few grains of powder fired from a short hole there would be no motion in the anvil perceptible to the eye without instruments. And even this small amount of motion would not begin until after the escape of the ball.

Recoil, therefore, depends:

• Upon the relative weights of gun and projectile. This is the most important condition.

• Upon the time allowed for continuance of the backward pressure. Length of barrel may, however, by its additional weight cancel this effect.

• Upon the quantity of gas evolved and quick- ness of evolution.

Many brains have been badly racked over the effect of "air-pack" in the barrel, the "backward rush of air into the barrel," etc. etc. Even if there be anything in these ideas, they are of no use for us to consider, for they cannot be obviated or allowed for; and we therefore might as well confine ourselves to considering those conditions that we can control or make allowance for.

It is probable that in every case where a respectable load is fired the gun yields slightly while the bullet is passing along the barrel, and actually moves back-ward before it escapes. But unless the charge of powder be excessive, or the ball be very heavy in proportion to its caliber, this backward motion will be so directly in line with the axis of the bore of the rifle that the ball will go as true to the line of the axis as if the rifle had been solid as the eternal hills. On the other hand, if the charge is excessive, or the ball very heavy in proportion to the gun, and especially if both these causes conjoin, two very different effects may result.

• The barrel may be thrown up or down, or to one side, before the ball leaves it, so that the ball starts into the air on a different line from that in which the axis of the bore was held when the trigger was pulled; but still always so exactly in the same direction, and so exactly to the same extent, that the effect is precisely the same as if the gun had not moved a particle, it being only necessary to arrange the sights so that the axis of the bore will point the proper distance away from the mark.

• The recoil may be so violent that the barrel is thrown off irregularly, or not to exactly the same place every time, so that the rifle will shoot wildly.

The first of these effects is seen in many of our very best rifles, and does not seem to interfere in the least with their accuracy. The second is seen in many light rifles that are overloaded, and especially in many of the light pocket-pistols made with large caliber, heavy ball, and heavy-charged cartridge. With some of these last-mentioned rifles you cannot hit a deer at a hundred yards more than once in five or six shots, and with the pistols cannot hit a mule, much less a man, at fifty yards in half a day. At the same time, either of these may shoot perfectly true if loaded with small charges and lighter balls.

The first kind, or the regular jump of the barrel to the same position, may be either downward, upward, or to one side, but in most all cases is apparently upward. In a nine-and-a-half-pound Maynard, seventy grains powder, thirty-two-inch barrel, .44 caliber, ounce long ball, that I once owned, the recoil invariably threw the barrel downward. A Sharps .44 caliber, seventy-seven grains, eight and one half pounds, round barrel, twenty-eight inches long, did precisely the same thing. Both these rifles at twenty-five yards threw the ball four inches lower with the full charge than they would with half a charge, or than they would throw a round ball even with full charge. On sighting the empty barrel with the level sight, and then looking through it, the axis of the bore was plainly seen to point four inches above the center, and on the exact spot where the balls fired with half a charge were massed.

So interesting was this question that I once spent a long time in trying to make these rifles kick in some other direction, or to vary in some manner the perfect regularity of their downward motion. I tried hanging the muzzle in a scale, hanging breech in a scale, strapping them to heavy cross-pieces under the muzzle and breech, hanging very heavy weights on the breech while the muzzle rested on a solid beam, and having the weight just touch the surface of a pan of water, with an attendant to watch it; in short, everything I could think of except a vise. In no case, however, could I make them vary a particle. The full charges sent the bullets invariably into the same hole both these, especially the Maynard, were very accurate rifles just about four inches below the bullets with the half charge and the round balls with full charge, all of which also cut the same hole. And the strangest part of it all was that both to me and my attendant the rifles in every case appeared to jump upward; and certainly did so, though they must have first jumped downward before the ball escaped the muzzle, for of course the barrel could not bend. These results were always the same whether the rifles were fired offhand or from rest, no matter in what direction or whether solidly backed or fired from a suspended sling. Yet this Maynard was so accurate that I once fired with it five successive balls into a four-inch circle at two hundred yards.

On the other hand, a light barrel when overloaded is more likely to jump up than down. A very light carbine generally does; so does a shot-gun, especially a double one, if both barrels be fired simultaneously when heavily loaded. So do most all pistols. A Russian model .45 navy at only seven paces with its common cartridge shot two and one half inches higher than it did with the heavy ball and some of the powder taken out and a round bullet put in the cartridge; yet this pistol was very accurate. Most all pistol-cartridges are overloaded, it being necessary with most of them to aim at a man's toes at twenty yards to touch him at all; and it is no wonder that when "the finest police in the world" shoot at a man across the street, the servant-girl looking out of the attic of the house behind him is more apt to suffer than the bifur-

165

cated target. So much do some of these pistols jump up that even after building an extra story on the front sight and cutting down the back one it is almost impossible to prevent overshooting with them. Sometimes a pistol will also spring to one side as well as up. A Wesson's .32 short-barrel pistol springs to the side where there is the least pressure of the hand on the stock shooting to the left when fired from the right hand, and to the right when fired from the left hand, and also jumping upward in each case.

A double gun will throw outward with each barrel, or away from the direction of the other barrel. I have a double rifle of which the axes of the barrels converge at about twenty yards, and on looking through them they can be plainly seen to cross. With a moderate load a rifle so built will throw out just about enough to carry the two balls on parallel lines, so that only one sight is needed. But where a heavy charge is used this convergence is not always enough, and the rifle will require double sights. With one sight my rifle will throw each ball outward six inches at thirty yards, and the two sets of sights diverge so as to converge the axes of the barrels still more than they are set. When one barrel is sighted it points across the line of the bore of the other at about only five paces. And yet each barrel is perfectly accurate with its own sight. This gun also throws down a little as well as outward. It shoots a round ball with great accuracy, but it will go higher and inside of the other ball, which is about one third heavier. It will shoot round balls with a single sight, and also the heavy ones with a small charge. It is probable that any double rifle would, for perfect accuracy, require double sights when large charges were used with heavy balls, though the barrels may be set sufficiently converging for light balls or heavy ones with light charges of powder. Double sights are not such a nuisance as one would suppose, for after a little practice the eye shifts at the same time the finger does, and with as little danger of mistake, so that the quickest kind of running shots may be made with them.

From all these facts important consequences flow:
• A rifle or pistol may kick so as to be worthless unless lightly loaded.
• It may be perfectly accurate and yet require different sighting for different balls or charges.
• Bullets and charges should not be changed in any rifle without testing carefully to see the effect.
• A double gun may need double sights for heavy charges.
• The force of a ball may be affected by the yielding of the gun. The heavier the ball, in proportion to the caliber, the longer it will take it to pass along the barrel, and consequently the longer the time the gas will have to overcome the gun's inertia, and the greater will be the loss of force in recoil if the gun yields. This becomes of some importance in long shooting, especially with a long heavy ball; and if the gun be loosely or carelessly held, instead of well backed by a solid shoulder, the ball may drop enough below where it should go to miss a deer at three hundred yards and even less.
• A gun may also throw irregularly, to one side or other, by being carelessly held or not always held alike, such as the pistol above mentioned. I have not

noticed this, however, in any rifle I have owned, and should pronounce one that would do it as either over- loaded or worthless.

In buying a rifle this should always be looked after. and before going into the field with any rifle it should be well tested. If its recoil is irregular, do not take it; if regular, it is just as good as if it did not recoil, but the extent and effect of its recoil must still be perfectly understood.

Chapter Thirty - The Killing Power of Bullets, Explosive, Expansive, and Other Bullets, Slit Bullets, Buckshot, etc.

Your success in bagging your game without much exertion and labor, and often in bagging it at all, will depend largely upon the mere shape of the bullet you use.

The effect of a bullet depends of course upon the derangement of some of the vital organs of the body or upon loss of blood. But this is the ultimate effect the one that too often benefits only the wolf and the raven. The immediate effect, or that which most benefits the hunter, is often as much the result of the accompanying shock to the nervous system as of the mere derangement of vital organs. In the brain or spinal cord one ball is about as good as another. But not so in any other part of the body; not even in the heart.

The first requisite of a killing ball is of course penetration. But after a certain amount of that is attained excess is superfluous. All rifles of .40 caliber or over, even the small Winchester, have sufficient penetration with a solid ball to kill a deer or antelope stone dead in nine tenths of the positions in which they are generally found. And even a much smaller rifle has penetration enough for nearly all broadside shots. Nearly everyone who has tried increasing the quantity of powder to increase the killing effect of a solid ball has been disappointed, especially if the ball be very hard or sharp-pointed. And many a one has yet to learn that a hundred grains of powder behind a long, tapering, hardened ball is no better than seventy or sixty unless for raking shots on bears or buffalo. And already many a man who has laid aside the Winchester '73 model (forty grains of powder and two hundred of lead to .44 caliber) and bought a new "Centennial" model or the model of '79 (both with longer ball and more powder) has discovered that, except for raking shots or where the ball strikes bones and turns or flattens, he has gained little by the change; the hundredth part of an increase of caliber amounting to about nothing. And if he should buy a .44 rifle, shooting a rod of lead a foot long with half a pound of powder behind it, he would still find no difference upon alt the soft parts of an animal, especially just behind the shoulder. It is often said that a small ball penetrates better than a big one, "cuts sharper," etc. This seems unworthy of notice. It overlooks entirely the question of momentum or crushing force. But, like the idea that "fine shot has better penetration," it is believed by many.

Essential as is penetration, something more is needed. And that is striking surface.

Striking surface is given of course by diameter of the bullet. And this diameter may be given in two ways.

• Normal diameter given by the molds.

• Abnormal diameter given by the ball expanding upon striking.

Either of these is sufficient. But the first requires a rifle of very large caliber. The second gives the same killing power to rifles of smaller caliber. Thus a flat-headed .44 bullet will have as much killing power where excessive penetration is not required as a sharp-pointed ball of .50 caliber. The sharp ball will not spread at all upon mere flesh, while the flat-headed one on striking will spread at once to more than the diameter of the other. Flat-headed balls cannot, however, be shot accurately for any distance. The head must be only half flat or rounded or merely blunt, and this is rarely made blunt enough to flatten a ball traveling at the low velocity of nearly all the long balls, especially when hardened as they generally are. For a very little tin makes a great difference in preventing the flattening of a ball.

Of all solid balls none flattens like the round ball When made of soft lead and driven at a high velocity this is the most killing solid form in which any given amount of lead can be cast, unless great penetration, is needed. And when large enough its penetration is sufficient for all game. And this can be much increased by hardening it.

The flattening power of any ball may be vastly increased by making a hole in the front. This is commonly called the " express ball." An express ball is, however, more properly a short swift ball fired with an enormous charge of powder, and may be hollow or not.

The killing effect of a ball is largely influenced by its velocity. And this entirely aside from the question of penetration. Velocity increases the flattening and also the rotation of the ball; which latter has a decided tearing effect A .44 round ball with ten grains of powder will make in a rabbit a hole but a trifle larger than itself, and if through the "paunch" the rabbit can often run away with the wound. But seventy grains behind the same ball will cut the rabbit half in two. A Winchester '73 model will decapitate a rabbit with its two hundred grains of lead and forty grains of powder almost as completely as an ax would do it. Open a cartridge and take out five sixths of the powder and the ball will barely get through the rabbit's head, leaving it almost uninjured outside of a hole of its own diameter. This difference is probably due to the difference in the spinning motion of the ball as much as to the difference in flattening.

It is said that at too high a velocity a ball will not flatten as much as at a low one, as a tallow candle at a high velocity will pass through a board without flattening. This is true only where the ball is fired through a thin resisting medium. At a high velocity the candle will cut a smaller hole through a half-inch board than when at a low velocity. But if fired at high velocity through something thick, like a beam or several boards, the hole will be not only deeper but larger at the bottom than when the velocity is low. It is the same with the bullet. A ball grazing a deer an inch or two deep will perhaps, aside from the cutting power of increased rotation of ball, cut a smaller hole at a high velocity than it would at a moderate speed. But where the body has any considerable thickness, so that the ball has more time to expand, the higher velocity will tell.

I have heard good hunters maintain just the reverse of this; to wit, that too much powder would make the ball flatten so as to stop its penetration. There is nothing in this. The penetration of a ball that will flatten at all to any useful extent depends upon its momentum; that is, its weight and velocity. Its penetration is more of a crushing force than a piercing force like that of the sharp-pointed balls. And the higher its velocity the farther in it gets; provided it be solid or have' not too large an expansion-hole in front.

It is thought by many that a ball that lodges in an animal is more effective than if it passes through; as the nervous system then receives the whole shock of the ball. This is often a mistake of effect for cause. The ball does not kill better because it stops. It stops generally because it has greater killing power; to wit, its expansive power. A ball having enough extra force to tear its way entirely through an animal and continue its flight must leave about the same amount of force in the animal as if it had only force enough to get just through.

As a rule, it is best to have balls pass through, especially solid balls. From the entrance-hole of a small bullet the animal bleeds little or none, and the flesh on the side where the ball stops will be badly bloodshot. If it goes through you will be more apt to have the aid of blood to help you track the animal if wounded; it will also bleed out much quicker and be much less injured by settling of blood.

Where great penetration is needed it had better be given by hardening a ball with tin than by sharpening its point. As much as twenty-five or thirty percent of tin may be used without injuring the rifle-grooves by an ordinary amount of use. A ball of terrific penetrating power may, however, be made as follows: Take a long bullet and cut it in two just below the point where it rides the grooves by rolling it under a sharp knife-blade. Then drill or bore a large hole through the butt-piece, replace it in the molds, and pour through the hole a hot mixture of equal parts of Babbitt-metal and tin. A mold for casting points like this may be easily made by half-filling the upper part of common molds with two pieces of brass or iron brazed in. The points may then be put in another mold and lead poured around them. But you can easily make all you need by the other method. From a .40-caliber rifle with sixty grains of powder I once shot one of these through two cast-iron stove-griddles and two jawbones of an ox all wedged together in a box, and the ball got through the other side of the box. Such balls are, however, of no use for ordinary hunting.

It is not many years since the English sportsmen in India commenced using a short cylindrical ball with a hole or well in the front, instead of the ponderous round balls and solid bolts they had before used for tigers and other dangerous game. These were sometimes made explosive by the insertion of a cartridge of some kind in the hole. Others were fired without any explosive filling, leaving the ball to fly open with its own force upon striking.

Some of the British sportsmen brought their rifles to this country on hunting-trips, and it was not long before some of our own countrymen tried these bullets.

As about every other great improvement, extravagant nonsense was soon told about them. "Blowing open the head of a grizzly-bear" with a .22-caliber pistol-cartridge inserted in the ball, as if the head were a snuff-box, "pulverizing" heads as if they were puff-balls, were among the least marvelous of the effects attributed to them. Some discoursed of "express shock" as if the ball were a condensed thunderbolt suddenly released in an animal's body; others talked of the velocity being so terrific as to "drive the ball into perfect dust." Still others, with that marvelous love the human mind has for paradox, discovered that the smaller these bullets were the more terrific and killing was "the express shock."

This improvement soon suffered the fate of every good thing that is overrated, and detractors arose. Many old hunters on the plains and in the mountains denounced them as worthless for game of any considerable size. Even foreigners gave the same verdict; one Scotch gentleman, returning from a Rocky Mountain tour, comparing in the Forest and Stream their effect on a grizzly-bear's shoulder to " so many humblebees." Men like Col. Judson and J. H. Batty, who had seen them tried and tried them themselves, men who certainly cannot be accused of ignorance, pronounced them inferior for general use to the solid ball.

For years a voice within which I took for the voice of humanity, but which, judging from the fashion of the day, must have been the voice of folly, had said in thunder-tones: "If you are going to kill an animal at all, kill it. Don't torture it." No sooner did I hear of this improvement than I adopted it. I have shot about three hundred deer with balls so made, have experimented with it in various ways, and must say most decidedly that while it is absurdly overrated it is still the most valuable improvement, next to the breech-loading principle, that has been made in rifles within the century.

I first made them explosive by inserting in the hole a .22 long pistol-cartridge with the bullet either cut off or taken out and replaced with more powder.

The same thing may be done by dropping a very small nail into the hole head first, filling it around with powder, and putting a tight-fitting cap on the nail and covering with wax, etc. These will explode on the softest flesh and even on water. An eight-pound jack-rabbit standing on his hind-legs and struck in the middle was distributed in a hundred pieces for thirty feet around, not a piece big enough to fry being left. Firing into the water just below a mud-hen a .22 cartridge in the ball raised it five feet out of water and broke its back, one wing, and one leg, though none of the ball touched it. From such a ball I very naturally expected tremendous results.

One of the first things I observed was that upon deer, coyotes, wildcats, and foxes the explosion produced no such effect as it did upon hares. Though the balls could be distinctly heard to explode and the flesh found blackened with the powder, there was no blowing or rending effect whatever. The hole was precisely the same as that made by the same ball left with the hole unfilled by anything. The killing effect appeared upon deer to be even a trifle less, and the penetration of the non-explosive ones was perceptibly the best. Determined to thoroughly probe the subject, I bored out some long-range .44 balls so as to admit a .32 long cartridge. Two of these I tried on an ancient Thomas-cat that had outlived his usefulness. Neither upon the shoulders nor upon the head could I discover any blowing or rending whatever, though the hole was blackened by powder. The hole was large and constantly expanding; but was merely cut the same as the empty balls would do it. Blocks of dry cottonwood, straight-grained, one foot long and about eight inches in diameter, that one blow of an ax would split in two, I utterly failed to split or even crack. With eighty grains of powder the balls penetrated only some four inches and were torn in splinters, while the hole was blackened with powder.

The reason of this will be readily seen. A Winchester '73 ball two hundred grains of lead and forty of powder, caliber .44 ball quite flat-headed, will split a rabbit completely in two with a raking shot, or cut it half in two with a broadside shot. But through a deer, a wildcat, coyote, or other tough animal it will make a hole but a trifle larger than itself. A firecracker fired in a glass vial left uncorked will split the vial in a hundred pieces if it be very thin, but will not even crack it if it be tolerably thick like a small ink-bottle. The difference in the first case is of course in the toughness of the flesh, in the second in the toughness of the glass. The tough bottle resists the gas long enough to allow its excess of pressure to escape at the mouth. In the same manner tough flesh resists the pressure long enough to allow the gas to escape around and behind the bullet. And in the case of the bullet the pressure of gas is also relieved by the ball cutting a large and increasing hole in front about as fast as the gas can fill it. Continued experiment and observation convinced me at last that, unless filled with some violently detonating powder that would be too dangerous to use, a ball is actually better to be left merely hollow.

The reason of this is the lack of penetration of explosive balls. In an average of over fifty shots at game, as shots must now be taken, penetration is about as essential as anything. To contain enough of any explosive that could be safely used the hole in the front of the ball must be both large and deep. In any ball of moderate caliber this would leave the rest of the ball so thin that when it explodes there is nothing but splinters from the sides and a light butt. If fired empty it will fly into flinders upon striking, and upon such solid parts as the haunch of a deer will tear a bad flesh-wound and often let the deer get away on three legs. When made explosive, the explosion, which begins at the depth of about half an inch, retards it much more, not only by backward pressure, but by opening the ball faster than it otherwise would open. By exploding around the feet, explosive balls are also much more certain to alarm game that might stand until you get its range by seeing the balls strike.

Much better in the long-run is the ball made simply expansive by a hole in front. It is common to place in this hole a hollow copper tube, filled with tallow or wax. All of which is idle toil. The effect is precisely the same with nothing in them. The accuracy is the same up to all ranges at which it is worthwhile to shoot at game at all. Beyond those ranges they will all turn over butt foremost. No difference is perceptible between the accuracy of balls cast hollow and solid ones, except of course at long range. The extent to which a ball shall expand is a very important question. A ball may be made to fly into pieces so small that you can scarcely find one in an animal. Or it may be made to break up into six or eight or ten pieces. Or it may be made to simply spread out like a mushroom without breaking. Or it may be cast so as to merely increase its diameter about one half, etc.

By many the expansion of a ball is supposed to depend upon its velocity. Up to a certain point this is of course true. But beyond that point it depends almost entirely upon the diameter, depth, and shape of the hole in its front. If a ball be made with a wide deep hole as wide at the bottom as at the top, so that the wall of lead around the hole is thin, stands only on a thin butt and has only a thin attachment to that butt, it will fly into flinders the instant it strikes the softest flesh, even if the velocity be quite moderate. On the other hand, if the hole be small, shallow, and tapering to a point at the bottom, the ball cannot be driven into splinters by any velocity that can be given it. It will merely fold back over its base like a mushroom. Bone of course would splinter it somewhat, as it would a solid ball. But upon soft flesh it would not splinter.

The effect of these different balls can be almost predicted. Suppose you have a fair shot at an animal, and hit it behind the shoulder, in the chest, or in the kidneys with the first bullet. The effect of a ball thus dashed into a hundred splinters upon the most vital organs must be terrific. We can readily see how persons can talk of the terrific effect of "express shock" upon even such an animal as the tiger. It is practically a charge of small shot fired directly into the seat of life.

But suppose you do not have a fair shot, and you strike your animal where penetration is necessary. Suppose your little hollow ball hits a bone heavy enough to tear a solid ball in two. What then? As there is a limit to the penetration of fine shot beyond which no powder can drive it, so is there a limit to the penetration of ball-splinters to pass which no "express" power will avail. If the ball is to penetrate or crush very far, it must have momentum. To have momentum it must have weight. To have weight it must hold together.

Here is, I think, the whole ground of disagreement about these bullets: A thing once highly praised is soon fancied good for everything. Found not good for everything, the natural conclusion often is that it is good for nothing.

I very soon found that the killing power of such balls upon an animal struck in or very near the right place was immensely greater than that of solid balls, that they were but a trifle better upon "paunch-shots" and not as good upon "haunch" and "stern shots" as the same ball solid. I lost deer struck in both places, and even a half-grown fawn I followed for over two miles, though a ball had exploded exactly in the center of its body. As one may shoot twenty successive deer with a .35-caliber solid ball and drop them all inside of a hundred yards, so one may shoot as many with one of these balls and see most all of them wilt like wet rags almost in their tracks. From such data the reflective hunter reasons not. He well knows that two hundred shots might tell a very different tale, and that, year in and year out, penetration is just as essential as striking surface.

The ball made with a small tapering hole will not produce such instantaneous death upon striking the vitals as does the ball that flies to pieces. But as it nearly doubles its diameter, its effect is about four times what it would otherwise be. And this is quick enough upon all the vitals of ordinary animals. Such a ball can also be given all the penetration that is necessary for ordinary animals. For unusually large animals they must be vastly superior to the more hollow ones.

Making a ball expansive does not, however, completely compensate for smallness of caliber. For penetration and crushing force it must positively have actual weight. A pound of powder could not drive a ten-dollar gold piece much over two or three inches into solid flesh, striking of course with its flat surface. And lead is only about half the weight of gold. There must be weight behind to force the widening front of an expansive ball through solid flesh, or even through the contents of the stomach. Now if the ball be made long so as to give this weight to a small-calibered rifle, you lose much of the velocity which is so essential to a good trajectory as well as to the rotatory and cutting power of the ball, etc.

The killing power of all long bullets is, however, vastly improved by making a hole in them. But the quantity of powder must be increased where it is small, as expansion checks the penetration immensely. To increase much the efficiency of such a bullet as the Winchester '73 model, the hole should be small and tapering and hardly half way through the ball; but then it should shoot at least a hundred grains of powder instead of forty grains. The Winchester "Centennial" would be improved in the same way without any increase of powder, because it has a much longer ball. All the rifles on the market shooting long or mid-range balls with seventy or eighty grains or more of powder can be much improved in this way, though all would be much better to have more powder and a shorter ball with smaller hole.

The hole in the ball is generally made by a plug inserted in the molds. A hole equally good can, however, be made with a gimlet or awl, unless you want a large deep hole. The ball can be replaced in the mold and bored through a hole at the front end. Or it can be bored more true by having a guide-hole bored in the "loader," into which you can run a gimlet and bore into the ball after it is loaded in the shell.

A round ball, if large enough, makes a splendid expansive ball, being most truly "express" up to a hundred and fifty or two hundred yards. For the reasons before given it must, however, be large so as to have penetration enough. The hole must also be made more flaring at the entrance than in the other balls, or it may slip through without expanding at all.

I have tried very large and very small holes in both long and round balls, and am satisfied that there is no way in which a ball can be made to first penetrate well and then fly to pieces. Its flying into splinters depends so entirely upon its shape that it will fly at an inch or two of depth no matter what its velocity. And if it be made with a very small hole it cannot be driven into "splash" upon mere flesh.

I have tried and am still trying to so shape a ball that it will expand upon the stomach and soft parts of an animal, yet penetrate the solid muscle, etc., without expansion. The results are not wholly satisfactory. Hollow balls can be so made as to penetrate wood without expansion, yet expand upon water. But they all tend to expand upon flesh if the hole be of any size; and if too small, to slip through without spreading.

A ball well hardened with tin is much less likely to break up than one of soft lead. But if the hole be too large the very hardest ones will splinter at once.

Deer are occasionally still-hunted with buckshot in shot-guns. It is a wretched apology for the rifle, and the distance at which deer can be killed with buckshot is vastly overrated. Even at forty yards, with ordinary guns, two are crippled to one that is killed. Neither Ely's wire cartridges nor any mode of loading buck-shot can remedy this very much. Of the cartridges over one half will either go like a solid ball and miss generally entirely, or they will go like loose buckshot. Not one half will go as they are intended to go; and when they do, they do not add much over twenty-five yards to the range of the gun. The killing effect of a single buckshot is not to be compared to the effect of a rifle-ball of the same size. It lacks both the velocity and flattening quality and the cutting power of the rotation. Buckshot kill only by their number or by the accidental striking of a vital part; generally both conditions are necessary. The temptation to shoot with them at deer too far off is almost irresistible. And the certainty of crippling is about in inverse proportion to the probability of killing with them. Before a pack of hounds or for close night-shooting the gun may be tolerated. For still-hunting its use is an outrage and a sin.

I have never tried bullets slit or sawed into pieces half way to the center. Where great penetration was not needed they would doubtless be better than the solid ball. But they would be hard to make well, and could not give the same striking surface as if made with the proper-shaped hole in front. Neither could one made with an expansion-hole in the rear. Such a one would doubtless expand upon bone or a solid mass of muscle like the haunch. But almost any ball will expand enough on such parts. And they are precisely the parts where much expansion is rather undesirable.

Chapter Thirty-One - The Hunting-Rifle, and Flight of Balls

So much space has already been and still must be devoted to more important matters matters, too, upon which you will find little or no information elsewhere that the subject of the best hunting-rifle must, like the care and management of the rifle, in next chapter, be passed by with the briefest mention of a few important points. To properly discuss such subjects requires almost a volume of itself; and as they are already somewhat discussed in works now extant, we must subordinate them to the principles of field hunting and field-shooting.

In the first place, then, the action of your rifle, as is also the question of repeater, single-loader, or double barrel, is largely a matter of taste. All actions are strong enough and durable enough. The quickness and ease of the action you can yourself decide as well as any one. All hunters have their preferences, and all have a peculiar weakness for their favorites that makes their opinions as to the best rifle nearly worthless. Different rifles are "all the rage" in different sections of country, and scarcely anything else is worth having. And this according to the opinion of the ablest shots and hunters.

All American "sporting" rifles now shoot accurately enough, and all about equally well. That is, if properly loaded and handled they will shoot as well as any rifle in the world in which the ball is seated in the shell and started below the grooves. The finest shooting can be done only by detaching the two and starting the ball in the grooves, either by pushing it in ahead of the shell or loading from the muzzle. One or the other of these modes is now followed by all long-range experts.

The question of twist, depth, and number of grooves, etc., you can quite safely leave to the rifle-maker. The slower the twist up to a certain point, however, the better for all high-velocity rifles. One turn in fifty inches is enough for rifles shooting heavy charges of powder and very short bullets.

For accuracy, range, and penetration .44 caliber is sufficient, and with an expansive ball properly made is amply killing for nearly all shots on the soft parts of an animal. For the solid parts a large round ball of soft lead is the more effective, and taken for an average of a hundred shots is the most effective form in which the same weight of lead can be cast. It is objected to large calibers that they tear and spoil the animal too much, But they bleed an animal so much more, and kill so much more quickly and certainly, that in the long-run there is not a tenth of the waste with them that there is with solid balls in the small-bores; and owing to the comparative lightness of the ball, it being generally round or very near the weight of the round ball, the recoil is not at all unpleasant. Popular opinion, however, favors the smaller bores with solid balls, in spite of the amount of game crippled and lost by them.

No rifle need be over thirty inches long, and even twenty-eight is enough for quite high velocities even with quite coarse powder. It should be as handy and as well fitted to you as a shot-gun. For the ill-balanced, clumsy, straight-Stocked, long-stocked, awkward things often seen on the market there is absolutely no excuse. Neither is a crescent-shaped scoop in the stock that requires adjustment to the shoulder anything but a nuisance, especially for running shooting. It is a stupid relic of the age that thought sixteen pounds of iron four feet long necessary to shoot a pea-bullet with accuracy.

A hunting-rifle of caliber as large as .55 need not weigh over ten pounds, and eight pounds is plenty for one of .44 caliber.

The only other point important enough to mention now is the trajectory of the rifle for a hundred and fifty yards or so. The trajectory is the path of the bullet through the air, and is always a curve, although for some distance no curve can be detected either by shooting at targets or at game.

The greater the initial velocity or the speed with which the bullet is driven from the gun, and the greater the bullet's power of retaining that speed, either by increase of caliber, elongation, or sharpening of the bullet's front, the greater the distance over which the bullet will be driven without making curve enough to overshoot or undershoot your mark.

When you have once had some experience of the marvelous tendency to overshoot game under most conditions of light and ground, of the extreme difficulty of calculating and allowing for distance, of the great danger of missing by raising sights, holding over game, taking "coarse bead" on the front sight, etc. etc., you will see that it is of the utmost importance to extend as far as possible this distance over which the path of the bullet appears to be level. And when you find that a hundred yards for the woods, a hundred and fifty yards for open hills, and two hundred yards for the plain (plain rolling enough to be worth hunting antelope on by stalking) are the distances within which five sixths of your opportunities to kill game will occur, you will be still more convinced that the higher the velocity the better the rifle for hunting all else of course being equal, as it may easily be, except very long-range power.

For high velocity slow twist is best; but two things are indispensable; viz., plenty of powder and a light load for it to drive.

Nearly all American sporting-rifles, as now manufactured, are low in velocity. They are chambered for too little powder, nearly all the makers furnish molds, loading-tools, etc., for too long a bullet, and the bullets in the factory ammunition are all too long. A long- bodied bullet is indispensable for a long and steady flight, and hence is essential for long-range accuracy. But making a ball three or four times the weight of the round ball of the same caliber acts precisely like doubling or tripling the charge of shot in a shot-gun. It cuts down immensely the speed with which it passes up the barrel, and decreases immensely the amount of powder that can be endured by the shoulder. It gains only in momentum or continuing power. And though by virtue of this it will make a thousand yards in about half the time that a round ball from the same gun could make it with any amount of powder, the round ball will, on the other hand, make seventy or eighty yards or more in half the time the other does, and therefore make much less of a curve. And if the weight of the round ball be increased one half by making a longer ball, and the charge of powder be doubled behind it, it may make a hundred and fifty yards in the same time the long-range ball makes a hundred, and thus add fifty or sixty yards to the point at which you will be able to hit your mark without in any way allowing for or thinking about its distance; in other words, in- crease what is unphilosophically but popularly called "the natural point blank" of the rifle.

This is what is now called the "express" system; although it is commonly confounded with the expansive principle, owing to the fact that the bullets for the "express rifle" are generally made expansive also. The "express" or high-speed system concentrates all the power of the gun on the first hundred and fifty or two hundred yards, a thing you will in time deem eminently wise if you take the trouble to measure your distances instead of guessing them, and practice target-shooting at a mark between seventy-five and a hundred and fifty yards, with the mark changed from twenty to forty yards in distance be-tween each shot. This high-speed idea is supposed by many to be an English notion. But it is in fact nearly as old as American rifle-shooting; although there were few of the old hunters who ever put powder enough behind the light sharp-pointed cones short, sugar-loaf-shaped balls that they used for the pur-pose.

For measuring the velocity of balls an instrument called the chronograph is used. But there is much reason to suspect its accuracy in registering high ve-locities. At all events, it is expensive and difficult to use. It is far easier, and better for your purpose, to measure it by the fall of the bullet below the mark at certain points. This gives you the mean velocity for the distance at which you shoot; a mean compounded of the ball's initial velocity and its sustaining power; its starting speed and bottom. Moreover, the velocity in feet per sec-ond is of no consequence to the mere hunter. The velocity compared with the velocity of other rifles is all he need consider. This method shows not only the comparative mean velocity in a way easily measured, but gives also a view of the bullet's path that no chronograph can ever give. The method I use is as follows:

Twisting a wire into a hoop, I fasten it on the end of a stake about shoulder-high. Two of these are set in the ground about fifteen yards apart, the first one about eight or ten yards from the firing-point. Over these thin paper is pinned. In line with them, but at a hundred yards, or a hundred and fifty yards, or whatever the distance for which you wish to measure the drop of the ball, is something to catch the balls; a smooth tree-trunk or old door, etc., will do. The rifle is then fired through the screens so as to strike the tree or other object.

As the fall of the bullet up to twenty-five yards is imperceptible to ordinary observation, and is a constant factor in all the experiments anyhow, the two holes made by the bullet through the two papers may be considered the line on which the bullet leaves the muzzle. The distances of the screens may of course be reduced to the nearest point at which the powder will not spoil the first hole, if greater accuracy be desired.

A heavy pencil-mark is then made on the side of each screen on a level with the bullet-hole. By the aid of a glass these are then "ranged in" by an assistant with a horizontal line on the tree. The distance from that line to the bullet-hole will give the fall of the bullet within at least an inch if care be used in making the lines.

Greater accuracy may be obtained by setting a surveyor's "transit" tele-scope-bearing instrument at the first hole, centering the two holes with the cross- hairs of the telescope, and having someone to "line in the point on the tree as in "centering" a corner post. This test may be made almost perfect.

By putting another screen a trifle over half way between the gun and the last target (say at fifty-five yards from the rifle for a hundred-yard shot), then stepping aside and looking down the line of the screens, you will see how much the bullet has to rise to strike a bull's-eye at the farther target. This may also be nearly obtained in inches by "lining" the hole in the first screen and the bullet-hole in the tree on the side of the half-way screen, and measuring from that line to the hole in the same screen. It will be between a third and a fourth of the fall at the tree.

Such experiments may be simplified or made still more accurate by a little care and ingenuity, and will give you an idea of the most important thing con-nected with the rifle an idea, too, that you will never get in any other way. The ignorance upon this point among even good practical hunters is positively appalling. The vast majority even of the best shots think a good rifle "shoots level" up to two hundred or three hundred yards; and he who should have the audacity to assert that a rifle that will make twenty successive bull's-eyes at a thousand yards may at a hundred and twenty yards drop its ball many inches below that of another rifle that probably could not hit the same bull's-eye at all at five hundred yards, would be considered a fool by fully three fourths of the best rifle-shots in the country.

Chapter Thirty-Two - The Sighting of Hunting-Rifles

The more I experiment with sights and shoot with other people's rifles the more I become convinced that bad sights are nearly as fruitful a source of misses as anything so far considered. Though more accurate shooting can be done with globe-sights, there is no question of the superiority of open-sights for all quick shooting or shooting in dim lights or in the woods. And they are accurate enough to two hundred yards at least.

The open sight usually put upon rifles by manufacturers can scarcely be considered "the pink of perfection." The very essence of a front sight is that it appear always the same, and be visible in every light. The huge piece of dull metal, shaped like a slice of watermelon, that adorns the muzzle-end of most factory rifles can hardly be seen at all in some lights. And when it can be seen it is often nearly as bad as if it could not. Stand out in the sun with a rifle having one of these, and holding it at arm's length, with your eye upon the front sight, turn completely around. You will probably see the center of brightness shift all over it from base to tip and from side to side. This center of brightness is what you will take for the true center in nearly every case where there is the slightest need of expedition in shooting. And upon running game you will be quite certain to always do so. You can see for yourself what the result of so doing must often be, especially when a fine shot is necessary.

No metal shows in so many lights as ivory or white agate does. And they hardly ever fail to show the true center at a glance. For running shooting on snow or flying shots against the sky, gold or brass or even iron is better, but for bare ground the whiter the sight the better. The liability of ivory or agate to break seems the only objection. This can be readily obviated by having an extra sight. But ivory can be so set that there is little or no danger. It should be screwed into a screw-hole in an iron block having a guard of iron on the muzzle-side. When filed away on the sides and top this guard and the ivory will be of the same width and height. The guard will be invisible, but will be quite sure to protect the ivory; will, at all events, preserve a part of it; can itself be used as a temporary sight if the ivory should go; and is a ready guide to the adjustment of another piece of ivory, or bone if you have no ivory or agate at hand. Ivory must be kept free of grease, though grease can soon be taken out of it by boiling in alcohol, alkali, etc., or by rubbing it well with ether.

The beginner with the rifle lays to his soul no unction so flattering as the idea that a shot a few inches above or below the mark is a good shot because it is what the world is pleased to term "a line-shot." In dueling, "a line-shot" means something. In shooting at game where there is seldom six inches to spare above or below the center, and much less if you intend to hit the vitals, and where the mark is from five to twenty times the distance of the mark in dueling, "a line-shot" also means something; to wit, a clear miss three times out of four. It is on the horizontal and not on the vertical line that "a line-shot" that is worth anything for game must generally be made. And this is just the hardest of all to make. Except in a cross-wind the veriest tyro can with ease hit above or below the mark at quite long distances. But to reach the horizontal line requires the very best of work. And it is on this line that all defective work in the rifle, all bad loading, all bad shooting, etc., shows itself three times out of four. And in the long-run, a horizontal line-shot a foot from the center on either side will miss less game than a line-shot six inches above or four inches below the center.

The top of the front sight should therefore be so flat and broad as to insure the best horizontal shooting without too much sacrifice of accuracy on the

179

upright line. But it can be made quite flat and broad upon the top without any such sacrifice of vertical accuracy as would be supposed necessary. If sharp it cannot be depended on for quick work or in every light; though when there is plenty of time the best of shooting can be done with a sight as sharp as a knife-blade. A front sight about as broad at the top as a common pin-head and perfectly flat will be accurate enough for all hunting purposes when your eye gets used to it. And even if a sacrifice must be made, it had much better be made on the vertical line. It will do no harm to have the top of the back edge slightly sloped off. With a metal sight this had better be done so that a little spot shines there like a star; all below it being kept dull in color, and the star portion being kept polished by a few rubs with a bit of wood as often as it gets tarnished.

The front sight is generally made too high. It need be just high enough to enable you to see when you catch too much of it with the eye. High sights are harder to catch with the eye and easier to catch in anything else than low ones. In falling snow they are better, but then even high ones are bad enough, and the rifle should be carried upside down, and occasionally wiped, with any sights. With low sights you cannot so well raise the trajectory by what is called a "coarse bead" taking a coarse view of front sight. But this in the long-run will be the greatest blessing that could happen you.

It is often convenient to have a quickly adjustable globe-sight on the rifle. The principle of Beach's combination-sight is a good one, but the open part of it is entirely too dull, besides the objection of varying play of light upon it. Cut it down one half and solder a little strip of. gold on it. Or, which is better yet, cut it off entirely and set a low ivory sight in front of it that can be seen over the ring when flat, and above which the globe can be seen when the ring is raised.

But here is one, in my humble opinion, better yet for one who needs a globe-sight at all; and with it the best of horizontal shooting can be done. I have never known any one else use it, but I found it very good.

Take a common long-barreled globe-sight and cut away with a file or drill all of the top half of the barrel or cylinder except just enough to protect the thread and ball making a perfect cage of it and admitting all the light possible. Then put a golden ball upon the thread and whiten all the inside of the cylinder with paint so as to cast as much light as possible on the underside of the ball. Shape this ball somewhat like a pin-head flattened a little on top. Or make it round if you choose. Adapt the size to your convenience. You can now use this as an open sight with the open back sight, or can use it with a peep-sight on the stock. It works well either way. If you wish it shaded you need only a little slide of bent tin to slip over the cylinder. By cutting out the top a little more you can insert two threads or arms with different-sized balls, or one of silver and the other of gold. These arms should be set at right angles and work on a pivot in the center. It is easy to set them so as to come exactly to the same place, one lying flat when the other is up. They can be easily changed with the finger or a stick. After they are set in, a strip of wire may be soldered over the top where it was cut away to admit them.

Beyond the importance of some flatness at the top of a plain open sight to insure good horizontal shooting, the fineness or coarseness of sights is very much a matter of what the eye is accustomed to. Except at long distances, one can with practice soon do excellent shooting with a tolerably coarse sight, and excellent quick shooting with a fine sight. But it must be remembered that much of your shooting must be done in a dim light.

Bold indeed must one be to say a word in derogation of the venerable and fashionable buckhorn sight. But, even at the risk of being considered too iconoclastic, I must mildly insinuate that very good shooting can be done without the aid of this long-revered idol.

One who has never tried it would be surprised to see how well he can shoot over the open barrel with only a small front sight. The eye takes the center of the barrel as naturally as a duck to water. The main use of a back sight is to cut off the amount of the front sight necessary to give the right horizontal range. Getting the vertical range is mere child's play compared with this. For doing this the high sides or horns of the buckhorn or back sight are of no use whatever. Their only use is to prevent reflection of light which would glimmer from the corners of a notch in a flat-topped bar of iron.

There is, however, one thing that these horns or sides do most fully accomplish. They cut off and partly destroy that clear and comprehensive view of everything ahead that is so important for running shots. They also actually delay one in "finding the sights," instead of aiding one as many suppose who have never tried anything else. The notch at the bottom, by pinching out the view of the front sight, prevents the eye from taking always the same exact amount of front sight, especially when the sunlight pours into the notch from in front or from behind. Almost the entire trouble that old-sighted persons have in shooting a rifle is with this notch, it being almost impossible for them to see the. exact bottom and shape of it so as to align the front sight with it. Or as they express it, they "can't get the front sight down into the notch." When one has good sight and plenty of time first-class shooting can be done with the buckhorn sight. Possibly for very fine target-work it is a trifle better than any other open back sight.

But for quick shooting, and especially for good horizontal-line shooting quickly cutting off the right amount of front sight I long ago discovered that a straight short bar, without horns, scoops, or notches of any kind, was far superior, especially for quickness. And on the vertical-line shooting there is no such difference as would be supposed. The eye finds the center of it so instinctively that you do not have to look for it at all. You merely raise the rifle and look for the proper amount of front sight, or "the right bead." Then the eye finds the center so exactly that except possibly for the very finest kind of target-shooting, you can detect no difference. I say possibly, for I have never tried it on anything finer than an inch bull's-eye at twenty yards that being about my outside limit with any rifle. But a dozen or more of my acquaintances have at the first trial with my rifle so sighted shot exactly the same as with their own. Many of my friends have adopted it; all of them are pleased with it; none desire any other. One friend made the best shooting with it at bullet-holes and rabbits running that he has ever made with anything. This may be used as well with the globe-sight above described as the buckhorn may be.

The back sight I use is a straight bar of hard black rubber about thirty-five hundredths of an inch wide, perfectly level on top. Iron or bone soaked with ink will do as well; but iron should be kept corroded with tincture of iodine and then blackened with ink. With such a sight and ivory on the ball in front you can swing your rifle around the horizon in the sun and see no change of light-center and not a glimmer from the bar. And you can shoot ten degrees closer to the sun's eye with them than with any other set of open sights. The very best of all is a piece of hard sole-leather, made still harder by boiling and hammering and drying in an oven. Soaked with ink, not a ray of light will this cast. It can be screwed in through a hole.

If, however, you prefer a notch, you need no horns around it. Cut a notch with a knife only a line or two deep in the center of the bar, keep well rusted with iodine and ink, and you have all the advantages of the buckhorn, with its disadvantages greatly modified. Iodine and ink are in fact indispensable for keeping any back sight of iron in proper order, and should be frequently applied; the iodine a day or two before the ink. But give the straight bar a fair trial and you will not want notches.

Elevating-sights upon a rifle are very prone to tempt one into using them where the level sight only should be used. For this reason many hunters will not have them upon a rifle at all. This, however, is unwise. The remedy is not to discard them, but learn to use them properly. Just so surely as .the game is beyond the natural point blank of your rifle, so surely must the rifle-ball rise in its flight to reach it. There are four ways of making it do this:

- Sighting rifle to "artificial point blank."
- Taking a fuller view of front sight, or, as it is called, "a coarse bead."
- Holding high on game.
- Elevating the back sight.

The great trouble with all these methods is that of all long-range shooting the calculation of distance. The artificial point-blank is no better than any elevated sight except in requiring no adjustment. Unless the game happens to be at the right distance it has no advantages. And inside of that distance it is as much a nuisance as level sights are beyond their proper distance.

Holding high on game is well enough tip to a certain point; but as soon as the game is so far off that you have to hold entirely above the body, then arises the same trouble that makes the "coarse bead" unreliable beyond the same point; to wit, it involves a double guess where a single guess is bad enough. It involves not only a guess at the distance, but a guess at the distance you are holding above the game, or a guess at the amount of front sight you are taking. The eye cannot every time accurately measure off the same amount of front sight even when you know just how much you want. And at a hundred and fifty or two hundred yards the eye, in measuring off a yard or so above a deer's back, will be extremely apt to be a foot or so out of the way.

A good elevating-sight, when tested and marked entirely avoids the second trouble. It involves only the estimate of distance. And this difficulty is no worse than in the other cases. But the sight should be thoroughly tried at a target and marked for different distances. The factory markings are not at all reliable.

The common elevation on the open back sight a small set of steps is of very little use beyond the second or third step. The best way to use it is to have the first step for the level sight or natural point blank of your rifle. Then file the second step so as to make an artificial point blank of a hundred yards. File the third step so as to raise the point blank to a hundred and fifty yards, and cut away the front edge of this step so that it can be pushed into place in a second with the thumb instead of requiring both the best adjustment for the woods. Carry the rifle with back sights set on the middle step. This is better than having it firmly fixed at the lowest point blank you wish to use. For all close shots where there is much danger of overshooting, as in bad light, against the sun, down hill, etc., slip out the elevator to the first step, provided you have time. Use the second step for all else up to a hundred and fifty yards; that is, what appears to be a hundred and fifty yards. Use the third step for all beyond that up to what you consider two hundred yards. This dis- count of fifty yards on your estimate of distance is intended only for cases where you have no time to make any careful estimate. But you had better discount twenty-five at least, even where you have time. Especially is this the case in the woods. This arrangement of open back sights is better than leaf-sights, etc.

Beyond two hundred yards open sights, even when very fine, begin to get unreliable. And coarse sights begin to be so at a hundred and fifty yards. For distances beyond two hundred yards there is nothing like an elevating peep-sight on the rifle-stock. This may be used with a globe-sight at the muzzle-end or with a plain open front sight, ranging the top of it with the center of the hole.

The elevating principle of Lyman's back sight is very good the best perhaps up to ordinary ranges for game. It also gives two holes, a fine and a coarse hole.

There is, however, no need of any such fine hole as is generally used in peep-sights. It is too hard to find the game through it, especially in the woods. The eye finds the center of a large hole just about as accurately as it does the center of a small one.

The common sliding elevation of the rear peep-sight as now placed upon many rifles can be much improved by the following plan; and taken for all distances is perhaps the best elevating-sight there is: Ream out the peep-hole to the size of a large pin-head and rust it with iodine. Find the lowest point at which you wish to use it; say a hundred and fifty yards if your open sights be coarse, two hundred if very fine. Put a drop of solder on the track there so that it will stop at that exact point when suddenly pushed down. Next find the two-hundred- or two- hundred-and-fifty-yard point, or fifty yards above sol-der, and cut a deep mark there that, if necessary, can be found with the thumb-nail while you are watching game. Put similar marks at the three-hundred-yard and three-hundred-and-fifty-yard point, etc. Then carry the slide on the lowest mark above the solder. To push it from there to the solder is no trouble whatever. You will rarely need to raise it above where it is. If you do, it can be quite easily done. It is best not to shift the sights for a slight vari-ance above or below the game; but when you see a ball strike above or below, hold a little lower or higher the next time. This will be better than at- tempt-ing to use twenty-five-yard intervals. The quickness of finding this sight with the eye can be increased by cutting away the upper part of the plate contain-ing the peep-hole, so that the upper half of the hole is like a half-ring.

A telescopic sight will do finer work than any sight that can be put on a ri-fle. But of course the same trouble of estimating distance remains. Up to three hundred yards globe and peep sights are accurate enough if you know your distance. A telescopic sight is troublesome and bungling; is in the way of open sights on the barrel; the open sight upon top of it is too troublesome to find for quick shooting; and all quick work through it is nearly impossible.

The back open sight is generally set farther back than it should be. Theoret-ically it will in this way do better shooting, any variation being more appar-ent. Practically it will do no such thing. Set six inches farther up the barrel, the difference can hardly be detected at the target. Whatever is lost by the differ-ence in appearance of variation is gained by the greater clearness of the out-lines of the back sight. This is important even to young eyes, and especially to aged ones. So set, a sight is also more quickly taken by the eye, its center is more easily held, and it will cut off the proper amount of front sight more dis-tinctly.

Having chosen the kind and shape of sights, the very important- question of how to adjust them still remains.

All rifles shoot for a short distance on a line practically level. That is, if the line of the sights be adjusted perfectly parallel with the axes of the bore, there will still be a distance at which the fall of the bullet will be almost inapprecia-ble. And even after the fall becomes appreciable there still remains a distance beyond that point where the fall may be disregarded in shooting at game. Both of these points are called indiscriminately and carelessly the "natural point-blank." This is a very unphilosophical term, but it is so common and expresses a practical truth so well that it may as well be retained. For practi-cal purposes it may best be defined as that distance at which the ball will strike the regulation bull's-eye for that distance without rising in its flight. This will cover nearly all game that is ever shot at. For instance, the bull's-eye for twenty-five yards is one inch, for fifty yards is two inches, for seventy-five yards is three inches, for a hundred yards is four inches, corresponding to a grouse's head at ten yards, a squirrel's head at twenty-five yards, a duck's or hare's body at a hundred yards, a turkey at a hundred and fifty yards, a deer or antelope at two hundred, an elk at two hundred and fifty, a buffalo at three hundred, etc., all on the same scale.

This "natural point-blank" is much less for all rifles than is commonly supposed. In many it is not fifty yards. It probably cannot be made to exceed a hundred and thirty yards in any rifle. Conceding that outside of the plains three fourths of the chances to kill game fall inside of a hundred and forty yards, the vast importance of this point-blank is at once apparent. Every rod that can be added to it is more than equal to a yard added to the killing range of a shot-gun. It is often said in answer to this that more deer are killed inside of seventy-five yards than beyond it. Admitted; but where are the most missed? Between seventy-five and a hundred and fifty yards. And why are the most of them missed there? By undershooting, and overshooting in attempting to is.

By so adjusting the sights as to make the ball rise in its flight and sink into the mark another point blank may be given to it. This is the point where the ball descends into and cuts the line of sights after rising above it. Thus when a Winchester rifle of '73 model is sighted to hit the bull's-eye at two hundred yards, the ball at ten or fifteen yards from the muzzle rises into and cuts the level line of sights, keeps above the line of sights, rising all the way to about a hundred and ten yards, then descends toward the line of sights, and touches it again at two hundred yards the bull's-eye. This is called the "artificial point-blank," and may be varied to any distance to which the rifle may shoot. It is contended by good authority, and on very strong grounds too, that this is the only point-blank, that no such thing as a natural point-blank exists, and that the distinction should be abolished as absurd. My answer is, that though according to strict philosophy there may be no natural point-blank, yet that practically there is; that the idea is firmly lodged in the heads of the great majority and never can be dislodged; and, above all, that there is no sounder philosophy than that which recognizes a useful, practical truth, although it may be in fact an error.

By the artificial point-blank all the practical advantages of the natural point-blank may not only be retained but much extended. Suppose a rifle to have a natural point-blank of seventy-five yards, the ball at that point being about an inch and a half below the center. Now if the ball had been made to just cross the line of sights at forty yards, it would be in the center of the mark at eighty yards and not over an inch below it at a hundred yards. And yet it would not have missed a squirrel's head anywhere along the line. In this way a rifle throwing a very swift large ball may be made to shoot to a hundred and thirty or a hundred and forty yards, so that one can shoot all along the line at small marks and yet notice neither rise nor fall so long as he shoots off-hand and with open sights. And a very swift and velocity-sustaining ball may be thus sent for a hundred and seventy yards without missing a turkey anywhere along the line.

But if the rise at the middle of the course be too great there is, as we have seen, a loss. And this may be so great as to overbalance the advantage. A rifle sighted to a point blank too far off, or having so slow a ball that it has to rise high to reach a short point-blank, will miss far more game inside of a hundred and fifty yards than it will catch beyond that point. Such is the case with many rifles as they come from the factory; and attempting to hold low enough with them is one of the most delusive things in the world.

Keeping, then, clearly in mind that the less rise there is to the ball the better, the adjustments of the sights for large game will depend entirely upon the kind of ground upon which you are to hunt. Remember, however, that, on account of the strong tendency to overshoot, an inch of rise above is in the long-run as bad as two inches of fall below or three inches of deviation to either side the mark. And remember the natural tendency to overestimate the distance at which most game is killed, and that the most advantageous point at which to shoot at game is much closer than is commonly supposed.

The following rises of bullets at the middle point will, I think, be fully enough, supposing you use a swift ball:

• For the woods, one inch.
• For the open hilly ground, two and a half inches.
• For the plains, four inches.

No rise of ball higher than the above should be made with the open sights if you are to do any shooting at running game. If you are to take only standing shots you may set them as much higher, being very careful to shoot low at the midway point, and also down hill, or in dim light, against the sun, etc.

Chapter Thirty-Three - The Loading, Care, and Management of Rifles

Although upon principle the rotation of a rifle- ball balances inequalities in it as rotation does in a spinning top, yet the fact is that the effect of inequalities is simply reduced and not annulled. Though defectively cast balls may appear to shoot quite well, yet they will not average such accurate work as well- made ones; and however true some of them may go, any one of them is liable to stray at the very time when you most depend upon it. Lead for casting balls should be melted in a large ladle; or a small pot is better. It should be stirred to a uniform density, kept clear of dross, kept at a uniform heat, and not allowed to get too hot. It should be dipped out with a clay pipe or iron spoon, which should also be kept at the same temperature by being kept immersed in the molten lead.

It used to be thought that the softest lead is the 'best. This is true enough for solid balls as far as killing effect is concerned. The softest lead is not only the heaviest, but will expand the most upon striking. For a muzzle-loader with round ball or short cylindrical or conical ball it is probably the best metal. But whether softness is necessary for accuracy in any rifle, however light the ball, may well be doubted. It is, however, in such cases accurate enough.

But where the ball is very long and heavy relatively to its diameter it starts so much more slowly that if soft it may be mashed out of shape before fairly under way. This is the case with the breech-loader, especially with a heavy charge of powder. This has already been fully considered. The best remedy for this is the admixture of tin with the lead. Five per cent of tin or ten per cent of common solder will improve the shooting of any ball from a breech-loader, whether long or short, round or cylindrical, and whether shot naked or patched. Double this quantity is sometimes necessary for very long balls. And even double that may be used. I once tried some balls that were about forty per cent tin, so hard I could hardly hammer them into the shell with the loading-tools. I shot these naked from a Maynard rifle, and they did the best work I have ever seen from a breech-loader. Five of them in succession I placed in a four-inch ring at two hundred yards, with globe- sights and rest of course. Several more fired at short distances cut into the same hole with almost the regularity of a muzzle-loader. The same is the case with round balls, which generally must be hardened to work well in a breech-loader. It is possible that a little tin in the ball might improve its accuracy even when fired from a muzzle-loader, though I have never tried it.

The molds should be kept hot during the casting. Wrap the handles well with buckskin and let the molds get as hot as they please. Pour in only enough for one bullet at a time, putting the dipper back into the pot to keep hot. Pour in enough to fully fill the entrance-hole, and jar the molds a bit so as to have the metal well settled. In shaking balls out of the molds have a mat of cloth or paper to drop them on, and do not let them strike each other hard, as when hot they are very easily indented.

Reject every defective ball. If the molds are new and make wrinkled balls, smoke them in a candle, burn grease in them, wipe thoroughly, resmoke and rewipe, etc. If you have many defective balls, keep them to melt over together with some more soft lead, as they may be too hard to load easily if remelted; and if put in the pot with the others they may affect the uniformity of the hardness of the rest. Where balls are to be patched they should be smoothed off and made even with a swedge. And even when to be shot naked this will improve them.

These matters look like needless niceties. Of course good shooting may be done with carelessly made balls. But to observe this care will not make fifteen minutes' difference in the whole time of casting, and may some time save you a deer or an antelope. All through your dealings with the rifle observe this rule: whenever care costs little or nothing, use it.

It used to be a maxim of the old hunters that "too much powder makes a ball fly wild." There is some truth in this if the ball be soft and the twist of the rifle swift, and plenty of truth in it if the ball be both soft and long. But if the ball be short or round and well hardened with tin and the twist slow, the amount of powder that may be used without affecting accuracy seems to be unlimited.

It may be said that a small rifle cannot burn a large charge. Literally that is true. However small an amount of powder be put in a gun, some of it will probably be thrown out unburned unless in a very long barrel. But the greater the charge the greater the amount actually burned, although the proportionate amount burned will of course be less; just as two thirds of six drams is actually more than three fourths of four drams, etc.

More powder can be used with effect behind round or short balls than behind very long ones. The effect of an increase of charge is noticeable at once in the straighter trajectory of the ball at short range, while the increase of recoil amounts to little. The increase of the charge of powder behind a long heavy ball is noticeable at once at the shoulder, but is hardly noticeable upon the ball's trajectory until it passes five hundred or six hundred yards, when extra force begins to show itself. The reason is that the increase of velocity has been too slight to materially straighten the curve of first two hundred yards or so. But this very slight velocity, uniting with the great weight of the long ball, has made a very material difference in momentum, upon which a long flight depends. It may, however, affect the trajectory by recoil, as we have seen under that head. As the killing effect of light balls depends materially upon velocity, one can hardly use too much powder behind them.

For shot-guns both coarse and fine-grained powders have their champions. There is, however, now no dispute as to the best for a rifle. Fine powder used to be thought the best, and in a short barrel with a round ball doubtless will give a higher velocity. But coarse powder is generally quick enough, and for all long bullets is far the best. But where the bullet is not very long and you wish excessive force, as in an express rifle, it is well to put half a charge of coarse powder in the shell first with half a charge of fine upon the top of it. This will give a steady start and a swift send-off. But fine powder being quicker than coarse is more liable to jam or "upset" a ball, unless used upon this compensating principle.

At short range, especially with round or short bullet, a trifling difference in the quantity of powder or in its dryness is not very material. But, where possible, care should be used even in this respect. And the longer the ball and the farther you wish to shoot the more essential becomes this care, and the more essential becomes the even setting of the powder in the shell; and take care not to break the grains by hard pounding, etc. More powder may be put in a shell, and it will be more evenly packed, by pouring it into the shell through a tube a yard or so in length.

The mouth of the shell should be kept clean with diluted vinegar and a rag. The balls, if shot naked, should be thoroughly greased with tallow, which in hot weather may be mixed with a little beeswax, but in winter should be used pure. Beeswax dirties a rifle fast and should be used only when necessary, as in hot weather. A wad or two of heavy leather beneath the ball will do no harm, and will be apt to improve the shooting by preventing the flashing of fire around the ball as it passes into the grooves.

But no rifle will shoot a long series of naked balls as well as one of patched ones. And if you get any rifle besides a repeater you should have it chambered and the shells fixed for shooting patched balls. I say "besides a repeater," because they are now all made for shooting naked balls. But I see no reason why such a fine rifle as the Winchester express should not be made to shoot patched balls, and see no reason why it could not.

Long balls are patched with bank-note paper, gold-beater's skin, bladder, or parchment. Fair patching for deep-seated balls may be made of good strong linen smeared until stiff with hot tallow. This makes good patching for a muzzle-loader. Parchment is the best, and under the head of dressing buckskin I will show how to make some very easily that will be far superior in toughness to any you can buy. The material is cut into strips that will roll once and a half times or twice or two and a half times around the ball, according to thickness of material. It is wet with a little gum-arabic water, then rolled around the ball so as to cover about two thirds of its base, and the whole should then be dropped into a hole in a block to dry in that shape. You will, however, do well to buy a cartridge already patched and examine it before following directions from any one.

To load round balls so as to shoot accurately in a breech-loader is no trifling matter and has puzzled many a one. To be shot naked they must be made very hard. They must fit very tight. Plenty of grease must be put around them and a heavy leather wad below them. Then they may work fairly well.

But for good work they also must be patched. They cannot, however, be patched and pushed into the shell as into the muzzle of a muzzle-loader. The shoulder of the rifle will strip off the patch half the time. The following plan I find the most certain, and have picked up scores of patches in front of the rifle without finding any sign of stripping, tearing, or burning. Putting on a thick leather wad wads are even more essential under a round ball than under the cylindrical, as the fire leaks around them more I cut a strip of strong parchment well greased and about three quarters of an inch wide and just long enough to go once around inside the shell. Into this I push the ball, and turning over the edges of the patch put half a split wad upon the top to keep out dirt, etc. If round balls loaded in this way are not as accurate (at short range, of course) as the long ones, the fault is in the shoulder of the rifle-chamber. It is either too sharp or too far from the end of the cartridge, or some- thing of the kind. Buckskin makes even better patching than parchment, but is harder to use with full shells. The best patching varies, however, with rifles, and must be ascertained by experiment. This even of the muzzle-loader, and even more so of the breech-loader.

Patched balls like naked ones should fit very tight in the shell. And in order to get them in straight and prevent swelling the shell so as to cause it to stick, it is better where the balls are deep-seated in the shell, as round ones generally are, to put the shell into a solid tube of metal such as is used as a "loader" to retain the shell when the ball is driven home. The more lightly the ball sits in the shell the nearer it comes to being in the grooves when receiving the first blow of the powder, and therefore the better it will shoot, all else being equal. In such case you may not be able to drive the ball in with the loader without damaging the patch, unless you use much care. But with the loader you can get it in tighter and generally much more true than by hand. If you use a double rifle, the balls must fit tight enough to prevent recoil throwing them in the next barrel out of the shell into the chamber.

The shoulders of some rifles, especially of those made several years ago, may need some beveling off or other fixing before they will shoot patched balls well, as the shoulder may strip or cut the patch. Care must also be taken in carrying patched balls; for if the patch runs outside of the shell, as it should do for all long bullets or very accurate shooting, it will get torn or frayed in carrying. It should be carried in a belt that will protect it perfectly. A leather belt is the surest for this purpose. But every few days the cartridges should be taken out and wiped free from the verdigris that accumulates on shells in a leather belt. For other shells canvas makes a better belt.

The cleaning of the rifle is a matter of much more importance than is generally supposed. Because a rifle may often shoot quite well when it is dirty many suppose that it either needs no cleaning or else cleans itself. All rifles need cleaning after every shot; that is, to do their best work. No rifle cleans itself except a muzzle-loader, and wiping will improve the shooting even of that. When shooting in damp air, cleaning is of less importance than in dry air, though its neglect may at any moment cause even the best breech-loader to throw a "wild" ball. But when shooting in dry air, especially on a hot day, the dirt burns so dry and hard that the bullet cannot push it out or slide over it without being affected by the roughness. A barrel containing such dirt is liable at any time to cut or even strip a patch, and is quite sure to wipe off lead from a naked ball. I have seen a Winchester of 1873 model shoot all over a two-foot candle-box at thirty yards after firing six or seven shots from it; and then after two or three good wipes shoot into a two-inch ring on the same box. The more powder you shoot, and the longer the barrel of the rifle, the greater the necessity of cleaning.

Of course no one can stop to clean when shooting at game. But when no more game is in sight there is generally no reason for not cleaning except laziness. The power of that I must myself admit. The more unnecessary work invention removes, the more we shirk what necessary work remains.

Cleaning in the field is so easy a matter that it is astonishing how we neglect it. A pocket wiper can be made and carried by every one. Every rifle should have a wiping-rod in the stock as does the Winchester.

Wet dirt can nearly always be taken out with a dry rag. Dry dirt will generally yield to it after the barrel has been breathed into a few minutes. When in haste you may pour water or any other convenient substitute.

Perfect cleaning may not be always convenient in the field, but there is no excuse for neglect of it, or for makeshifts of any kind when at home or in camp. The rifle should always be cleaned and oiled at night if it has been used during the day. Cleaning has been so thoroughly tested at the target that it is quite useless for any " practical man" to jump up and tell us how much game, etc., he kills with a dirty rifle, etc. We know all that. Of course it can be neglected as well as a dozen other points may be. The only question is, is such neglect profitable when all you gain by it is such a trifling bit of personal comfort?

Some say, "never pour water in a fine gun." Water hurts a gun just as it does a razor when it is left on the metal. But a razor may be wet every day for a hundred years without injury from rust. So may a gun. There is absolutely nothing that takes hold of powder-dirt like water. Half the substitutes for it, such as kerosene, benzine, alcohol, etc., are heartless hoaxes and make thrice the labor that water does. If new strong cloth be used for wiping there will be no danger from water. It is a common idea that any old rag will do to clean a gun with. On the contrary, to clean a gun well requires good, strong, new, and rough cloth. Nothing lighter than heavy unbleached muslin can be relied on to bring all the dirt, lead, and dampness from a rifle.

For cleaning, a strong rod of the best hickory should be used, notched and jagged instead of having a miserable eye or hook at the end, so that a heavy wad of cloth may be used without jamming. And this wad of cloth should occasionally be made so tight that the rod has to be driven against something solid to force it through. Only in this way can you be sure that your rifle is not leaded. The cloth thus driven through will either bring out the lead or show that it has passed lead.

For greasing, almost any animal or vegetable oil is good. Rattlesnake-oil has more body than almost any other oil and is often easy to make. An excellent oil is made by cooking the marrow of a deer's legs. Vaseline and cosmoline are also good.

But for a rust preventive scarcely anything excels mercurial ointment. Too much grease, however, may overshoot the mark. Enough is enough, and a tight and well-greased rag or bit of buckskin forced through the barrel once or twice is best.

Should your rifle happen to get rusty inside it should be attended to at once. This had better be intrusted to a reliable gunsmith. But if none is at hand you had better do it yourself than leave it so. Very fine emery is safe enough for any one to use who is careful, but the rag should be well oiled and run back and forth through the barrel several times before the emery is applied to it. Apply it as evenly as possible, make the stroke long and steady, use plenty of oil, and keep up the polishing no longer than is necessary. Emery may, however, be as hard to get as a gunsmith. In such case use fine wood-ashes and plenty of muscle, and in either case have the barrel firmly lashed or fastened to something solid.

But no amount of care with a rifle will obviate the necessity of practice with it in order to do good shooting. And this practice should be in the field, at natural marks, at varying distances, and in varying play of light and shade. It should be up hill and down hill, across valleys, etc. etc. Beyond the ordinary and obvious reasons for this I will mention an- other which affects me very much and must affect every one somewhat; viz., ocular aberration, or the impossibility of always measuring off with the eye the same exact amount of front sight necessary for good shooting on the horizontal line. The difference on the front sight of the thickness of two sheets of paper may cause a miss at one hundred yards. Who without much practice can tell the edge of six sheets of paper pressed together at the edge and held four feet from his eye from eight sheets held the same way? It would be hard enough even if both were seen side by side. Get a good carpenter to make you a foot-rule from memory, or ask a good draughtsman to mark you out by his eye a dozen or so separate one-eighth parts of an inch. Then get him to measure them and you will see one great cause of bad shooting.

All through the subject of rifles I have for brevity omitted much that is generally known, such as how to load a muzzle-loader, etc., and much that can be left to the reader's common-sense, such as which way to move a rifle-sight to make it shoot high or low, or to right or left, etc.

Chapter Thirty-Four - Moccasins, Buckskin, Etc. Advice Conclusion

There is a large amount of useful lore about wood-craft, camping, fitting out, etc. etc. etc., which must necessarily be omitted from such a work as this, especially as it can be found elsewhere. I therefore confine myself entirely to such few points as are either not considered in other works that I have seen or else are so generally treated as to be of little use.

White clothes are of little use for hunting wild deer except upon open ground with snow, and even then the face and rifle should be concealed as much as possible. In timber your motion across tree-trunks is caught by the deer's eye so quickly that you can relax no caution even with the whitest outfit you can get. Gray or brown, according to the color of your general background, is better for general use.

Clothes should not be stiff or harsh so as to make a noise against brush, and the coat should have no skirts or tail. Jackets made by cutting off the lower six inches of woolen shirts, slitting up the front and adding two or three buttons, are very good things to wear. Two or three may be put on for cold weather and fastened at the bottom with the cartridge-belt. An extra one may be tucked into the belt behind. A linen jacket over two or three of these will shed rain about as long as anything and stop considerable wind.

For durability buckskin is as important as it is to the hero of a sporting romance. It is also very good for dry cold weather. For warm or wet weather it is a nuisance. Still it is soft against brush, and pants will be much better if faced in front with it to half way above the knee and two thirds the way around on each side. For this purpose it should always be well smoked so as to dry soft when wet.

The simpler and lighter your dress the better. An immense butcher-knife, hatchet, pistol, watch, whisky-flask, etc. etc. etc., may, like the fifth wheel of a wagon, come handy once in a year or two. But it hardly pays to pack a fifth wheel around with one. Everything unnecessary, all leggings, fancy clothes, and "toggery" of every sort, are nuisances. The most valuable knowledge in the world is to know what we can dispense with. And nowhere is this more valuable than in getting up a still-hunting outfit.

Every kind of sole-leather add to your litany. Go not astray on "deer-stalker's shoes," "English walking- shoes," or "hunting-boots" of any kind. If you cannot wear moccasins, get a pair of shoes made with soft heels and soles; the latter projecting at the edge so that a new piece of soft leather may be added in a few moments with an awl and buckskin thong when the first is worn through. India-rubber overshoes are very good worn loose without boots, but are uncomfortable on the feet.

Everyone who hunts much should get his feet accustomed to moccasins. When the foot is once toughened to them, which, with care in beginning gradually, will occur in two weeks and often less, nothing can equal them for quiet and rapid traveling. On some kinds of ground it is almost impossible to approach wild deer without them. One can walk farther in them with less fatigue, with less slipping on rocks, hill-sides, dry grass, etc., and less danger of spraining an ankle, tripping, or falling, than with anything else that can be worn. In dry cold snow, when worn with two or three pairs of woolen socks or a doubled piece of heavy woolen blanket wrapped outside of one pair, they are absolutely unapproachable for ease and comfort. And even in wet snow or wet grass, mud, etc., they are as good as anything that can be worn without making too much noise, except india-rubber shoes. They will hold you on any slope where anything but spiked shoes can hold you, and are far better than those for running along rocks, logs, etc. The uppers, if of good material, will last as long as those of a good pair of boots. New soles can be speedily cut out of old boot-legs, and put on with an awl and buckskin thong.

The best of all moccasins are those of buckskin. As buying cannot always be depended upon except buying poor ones one who expects to hunt much should learn to make his own moccasins. This is a very trifling matter for anyone of any ingenuity; and with a little practice such a one can soon make them as shapely as any he can buy.

The easiest pattern to make is that of the Sioux Indians. A piece of buckskin the exact length of the foot and about seven and a half inches wide (for a No. 7 foot) is first cut out. This should be cut from the rump or along the back of the hide. To insure even cutting it should be laid on a board, the piece marked out with a square and lead-pencil, perfectly square cornered, and then cut with a sharp knife so that there is no pulling it out of shape. It is then folded once lengthwise, and about a quarter of an inch of the lower corner of one end rounded off, so as to keep the toe from being too sharp-pointed. The two ends are then sewed up. But when you get within four fifths of an inch of the end of the heel press it down upon a board and cut off the lower part, so that when sewed up it will look like a narrow inverted. You may, however, sew it straight down, as it is mainly a matter of "looks." The thing now looks a little like a birch canoe with a pretty straight bow. This bow is then gathered to a tongue rounded to an oval end in front and fastened across the center of the canoe. The whole thing must be sewed inside out, and every seam should be sewed with a strip of heavy buckskin in it to protect the stitches. A buckskin needle a cutting needle should be used with heavy waxed linen thread, and the seams run over twice for durability. But an awl and shoemaker's "waxed end," or a buckskin thong with the end waxed and twisted, is better yet. A person of any ingenuity cannot fail to make at the first trial a pair that will answer all demands but those of beauty. Tops three or four inches high should then be added, and both buttoned to a button in the center of the tongue, and one buttoned to the other on one side of the ankle at the top. For snow these tops should be of cloth, as they wet too quickly if of buckskin. If the pantaloons be tied tightly around these at the ankle one may walk all day in dry cold snow and have his feet perfectly dry and warm. For keeping out dead grass and other tickling things a shield of leather may be placed inside under the tongue and reaching half way down the sides and half way to the tongue. This with heavy buckskin facing on your pantaloons hanging loose and low will also be about as good a guard against snake-bites as you can conveniently have. An inner sole of sheep-skin with the wool half sheared off may be necessary at first if the feet are tender.

The most important part of every recipe for making buckskin is never given, and the rest is so generally stated as to be of little use. The important part is that the undertaking should always be sublet whenever possible. It is tedious, tiresome, and disagreeable, the best way it can be done. Still there may be times in every hunter's life when he may have to make it himself. And every one should know how to do it. The operation requires no skill and may, moreover, be done by any common hand under your supervision.

There is no tanning process about it. Leather is a chemical compound. Buckskin is simply the raw fiber broken up, loosened, and retained from stiffening again when wet.

The hair, the fine little outer skin in which it is embedded, called "the grain," and the fleshy and membranous parts adhering to the inside must first be removed. To do this is no trifling matter unless one knows just how, and then it is simple enough though it takes work. The, hide is first soaked in water from two to five days, according to temperature of water. In warm water a dry hide will soften in two days, and soon after that will begin to spoil. In cold water it may, and often must, be left longer. A hide will be soft enough when first stripped from the deer, but will be better if left a day or two in water. If stripped off from the neck downward a hide will be more easy to clean on the inside.

A graining-log and knife are now necessary. A log of hard wood eight or nine feet long and six or eight inches thick, having about two or three feet of smooth hard surface on one side of one end, is fastened in the ground (under a root or something) so that the smooth end is about waist-high. Two auger-holes may be bored in it near this end and legs inserted. The hide thrown over that and held fast by pressing it with the waist against the end of the log, is in condition to clean.

The knife must have a scraping edge and not a cutting edge. A rib of a horse or cow, back of a draw-knife, etc., may be used. But the best is the back of the blade of a common table-knife. Drive the blade lengthwise and half its depth into a piece of stick about eighteen inches long so as to leave two good handles on the stick. With a few minutes' trial you will get the proper stroke with this.

A hide will generally "grain" better the way the hair runs. But the "grain" will stick in spots, and sometimes you must run over it in different directions. Each side should be run over twice, so as to insure good cleaning. Clean them alternately.

When cleaned, a hide may be softened at once. But if in no haste, let it dry and resoak it for a day. Then pull, haul, and stretch it in every part until it all becomes white. Continue this until it is dry, rubbing out between the knuckles all places that show signs of stiffening. Should it be too hard to work soft the first time, resoak it and rub dry again. Sometimes this must be repeated two or three times. Stiff spots can, however, be moistened separately afterward by laying a damp cloth on them and rubbing them dry separately. The stretching of the fiber on a large hide is often no trifling matter. Pressing and sawing over the edge of a sharpened board a little over waist-high, turning the hide around each time, is about as effective a way as any. Two men standing in the sun and turning it around constantly can soon pull a common-sized hide soft. Stretching firmly in a strong frame and dancing on it until dry will stretch and loosen the toughest hide.

A hide may be rubbed soft much quicker if brains be rubbed into it. When the fiber is loosened up so that the hide looks white, rub the brains of a deer or other animal into it. Or the brains may be dissolved in water and the hide soaked in it. Mashing in with the hand is, however, the quicker way. If one application is not enough, rub in more. Grease answers this purpose some-what. But it is much inferior to brains and requires warm water and soap, with considerable work also to wash it out. Some may be left in, but the most of it must come out unless you wish an "oil-tanned" hide, which you do not, however, for any purpose but strings.

The oftener a hide is wet and rubbed soft the better it is for clothes etc. But where toughness is the main point, as for strings, etc., it should be softened no more than is necessary. Some hides are very obstinate, and cannot be worked soft the first time except by a person very strong in the hands, and in patience.

Without smoking, buckskin cannot be depended upon to dry soft when wet. Nothing will take its place. Smoked to lemon-color or light buff will generally do. To get an even color a smoke-house and slow smoking is best. It may, however, be done in one day by setting a tight barrel or big box over a deep

195

hole in the ground and forcing the smoke. Or it may be wrapped around poles over a hole so as to make a wigwam of it.

I have tried sulphuric acid, lye, and the whole list of agents contained in all the recipes, and find them all useless nuisances. Some, such as the acid and lye, will soon ruin a hide if used too strong or too long. There is absolutely no chemical agent that will enable you to dispense with stretching and rubbing the hide hard and rapidly while it is drying. By chemical agents you may make leather. But buck-skin can be made only by mechanical means. Apply the work and the other things are needless. Without the work they are unavailing. Excellent parchment for patching may be made from a fawn-skin by soaking it well with grease in the heat of the sun or fire, washing out about a third of it in blood-warm water, pulling the skin till white, then stretching it on a board tight and allowing it to dry hard. Dress it down with sand-paper and a knife-edge.

It is but a few years since I would as soon have been seen hunting with kid gloves, a "biled shirt," and "plug" hat as with anything to eat about me. Most hunters, I think, have the same stupid pride about being "tough." But no man, no matter who he may be, can, in hunting with the rifle, afford to despise the advantage of being well fed. He may not feel weak or faint, he may flatter himself that he is not hungry. But want of food will be apt to affect his shooting nevertheless; especially if he has a hill to climb, a run to make, or a very fine shot to make. Venison, cut in strips half an inch thick, soaked a day in strong brine, and dried in the camp-fire smoke or in the chimney-corner at home, makes a very portable and substantial lunch, conduces more to that desirable solidity of muscle and nerve essential to good shooting than anything else you can carry except beef, and, to say the least, is quite as palatable as doughnuts and similar "baby-feed," and takes up far less room.

You may find your first half-dozen deer all standing broadside in plain open sight and close by; may hit every one at the first shot with a dirty rifle carelessly loaded, and shoot every one dead in its tracks. I have myself seen deer so plenty and tame that a novice could do this. But beware how you conclude from such success that I have been unnecessarily particular in the advice I have given, or that deer- hunting is a thing to which you were specially born. Many of the most important principles of stalking deer and antelope are obtainable only by a considerable amount of careful observation. You might hunt a week by the side of a careless and bad hunter and a week by the side of a careful and good one, and yet notice no difference in their work if judged by its success. The trouble is that neither one week nor two weeks will suffice to test any important point in hunting of this kind. Follow sound principle whether you see its immediate results or not. Especially should it be followed where it costs nothing, such as raising your head slowly over ridges and taking your gun from your shoulder, etc.

In no other branch of field-sports is there such an array of exceptions to nearly every rule. Sometimes these are so numerous as to require long observation to determine which is the rule and which the exception. Often the exceptions are as important as the rule itself. In such case I have given them. But there are many others which have been necessarily omitted for want of space. On the whole, you cannot be too careful how you draw conclusions from a few instances. Sound principle often requires the entire disregard of a rule. Five times out of six it is useless to follow up a deer once started. Yet if deer are extremely scarce or you wish to go on the course the deer has gone, you had better follow him by all means. So when a single deer plunges into a very brushy hill- side the chances are very strong that you will see him no more. But it will cost you nothing to stand two or three minutes and watch for his appearance at some open place. And once in five or six times you may see him again and get a good shot.

Other things must be decided solely upon commonsense. A man with hob-nailed boots, bright-colored clothes, and big flop-hat gets as much game as one who wears moccasins, clothes of neutral color, and a small cap. Judging solely by visible results the one outfit is as good as the other. Yet your com-mon-sense alone is enough to tell you that the latter outfit must be the best, and that the want of difference in results must be due to other causes.

In scarcely any branch of life is one more apt to draw wrong conclusions from hasty observation than in hunting deer and antelope and shooting with the rifle. Passing over the whole host of absurd and contradictory theories held by good hunters and good shots, who either do not follow them in prac-tice, or, if they do, succeed in spite of them by virtue of their other qualifica-tions, I will mention a remarkable case of two gross errors resulting in suc-cess.

A friend of mine had a rifle which he fully believed had a natural point blank of two hundred yards. He supposed the ball would drop about two feet in the next hundred yards, or have a total drop of two feet for three hundred yards. These ideas he had gotten as most hunters get their notions from his imagination and careless observation; never having tried his rifle. He saw a deer at three hundred yards as he supposed, sighted about two feet above its back, and down came the deer shot through the heart. He had never shot many deer, and of course was highly delighted with such a shot. He looked the ground over and felt satisfied he had not done himself justice. So he took the trouble to do what few ever do on long shots: he paced the distance. Rash man! such a thing is even worse than weighing a trout. By the shortest strides that would satisfy his conscience it was only a hundred and eighty yards. The ball had fallen about three feet, about its natural drop for that distance. Had he been right in his estimate of distance it would have fallen about sixteen feet.

It is rare that you can thus utilize errors, making them counteract each oth-er. But you can make a far better use of them. That is, study them. Study them:

1. To see whether they really be errors or not.
2. To learn how to avoid them.

In no way will you learn as much as by doing this. If there be anything that makes this book of any value, if there be any soundness of principle in it, any thoroughness and carefulness of analysis, any clear ex- position of mistakes that will be likely to entrap the beginner, anything new or unwritten about before, it is due solely to two facts:

1. That I have stumbled over nearly every error that it is possible for one to encounter.
2. That I have studied those errors in a way that not one in a thousand has either the humility of soul or the patience to do.

The End

CPSIA information can be obtained
at www.ICGtesting.com
Printed in the USA
BVHW090147151219
566703BV00015BA/504/P